MONTY RAW!

'raw'
Pronunciation: 'ro'
Function: *adjective*
Inflected Form(s): **raw·er/raw·est/**
Definitions: Brutally or grossly frank: *a 'raw' portrayal of human passions.*
Unnaturally or painfully exposed, open to wounding.
Not having undergone processes of preparing, finishing or refining.
Unfair treatment from others; *received 'raw' treatment; a 'raw' deal.*
A natural ability or great skill: *he had a 'raw' talent; a thing of 'raw' beauty.*
Disagreeably harsh or chilly: *a 'raw' wind.*
A sore or irritated place, painful because of being rubbed or damaged.
To upset someone: *The newspaper article touched a 'raw' nerve.*

MONTY RAW!

The definitive biography of Colin Montgomerie

Dale Concannon

To Laura Girl – my inspiration, encouragement and pitch-and-putt partner

First published in Great Britain in 2007 by
Virgin Books Ltd
Thames Wharf Studios
Rainville Road
London
W6 9HA

The paper used in this book is a natural, recyclable product made from wood grown in sustainable forests. The manufacturing process conforms to the regulations of the country of origin.

Typeset by TW Typesetting, Plymouth, Devon

Printed and bound in Great Britain by
Mackays of Chatham PLC

Picture credits
All images: Matthew Harris/TGPL, except
page 7 bottom right: Chris Cole/TGPL and
page 8 top: Dave Pinegar/TGPL.
© World copyright images of www.golfpicturelibrary.com

CONTENTS

'[Golf] is a contest, a duel or a melee, calling for courage, skill, strategy and self-control. It is a test of temper, a trail of honour, a revealer of character. It affords the chance to play the man and act the gentleman.'

David Robertson Forgan, 1898

'Golf is twenty-percent mechanics and technique. The other eighty-percent is philosophy, humour, tragedy, romance, melodrama, companionship, camaraderie, cussedness and conversation.'

Grantland Rice:
American Golfer Magazine, 1920

'The least thing upset him on the Links. He missed short putts because of the uproar of the butterflies in the adjoining meadow.'

P G Wodehouse:
The Clicking of Cuthbert, 1922

'Good golfing temperament falls somewhere between taking it with a grin or shrug and throwing a fit.'

Sam Snead, 1959

ACKNOWLEDGEMENTS

All books are collaborative affairs and this is no different. When the idea was first mooted about writing a biography of Colin Montgomerie, Virgin Books and their innovative Sports Book Editor, Ed Faulkner, reacted with enthusiasm and encouragement. It is down to them this book has been published and I cannot praise them highly enough, despite the impossible deadlines. Regarding sources, I have to thank my media colleagues, most notably John Huggan, Peter Higgs, Paul Forsyth, Jock Howard, Peter Masters, Paul Trow, Alan Frazer, Mark Reason, Lorne Rubenstein, Connell Barrett, Alasdair Reid and David Feherty (still the only man to appear on the cover of two bestselling golf books in his underwear!). Thanks also to Peter McEvoy, a hero of mine since our early Warwickshire days, for kind permission to use information from his excellent autobiography: *For Love or Money: Inside the Professional Game Through the Eyes of a Leading Amateur Golfer* (HarperSport, 2006). As for the 'pro' side of the game, thanks to the innumerable Ryder Cup and European Tour professionals, caddies and administrators who helped with information. Thanks also to the hard-working staff at the European Tour, most especially the King of the Stats, Steve Doughty. The great photos that illuminate this book came from Matthew Harris at golfpicturelibrary.com. Cheers Matt, great work. Last but not least, a huge thank-you to those I cannot name, especially the lady. You read the manuscript, helped with advice and were of immeasurable help. You know who you are.

PREFACE: TWO HALVES OF THE FULL MONTY

VALDERRAMA, SPAIN, SEPTEMBER 1997

S tanding on the eighteenth tee Colin Montgomerie could only guess at what the next few minutes held for him. It was late Sunday afternoon and the singles matches had proved a real blow for European hopes. One after another his team had fallen to defeat against their American opponents. Painstakingly building up a five-point advantage at one stage, that precious lead had all but disappeared as the day played out to its dramatic conclusion. Now the destination of the 32nd Ryder Cup would be decided by the last game still out on the course – Montgomerie versus the combative American Scott Hoch.

With the evening light fading fast and the sky unseasonably heavy with rain clouds, members of both teams gathered nervously behind the final green. With Europe needing just a half-point to retain the trophy the match had been a brutal affair. Europe's most experienced players in José Maria Olazábal and Nick Faldo had both lost. Bernhard Langer had beaten Brad Faxon barely minutes before and now Montgomerie and Hoch were the only two players left out on the course.

Neither man had been able to carve out a winning position. Hoch had birdied the par-five seventeenth to draw level and would have the honour. Eyeing the tee shot nervously, the American pulled his drive in the left rough. Stepping up to the tee, the closing hole at Valderrama presented a unique challenge for Montgomerie. A downhill par-four stretching over 440 yards through a twisted forest of cork trees, the fairway was barely visible from the tee. Having built a hugely successful career on a piercing left-to-right fade, he knew better than anyone that the ideal shot on this occasion was a high right-to-left draw. Even with the tee boxes pushed forward a few yards it had proved a difficult hole for him all week. With the pressure at its zenith, the closing drive would prove not only a test of skill but also one of character.

The record books show that Montgomerie hit the three-wood shot of his life and split the fairway. (Former PGA Champion Steve Elkington once commented how 'Monty is the only guy who could drive it up a gnat's ass every hole'.) Left with a nine-iron approach, the Scot found the green in regulation. It was advantage Europe as Hoch was forced to play around a tree from the heavy rough. Scrambling onto the green in three strokes, he was left with a lengthy putt just to make par. Knowing that two putts would give his team the precious half point they required, the European number-one calmly stroked his own birdie attempt to within a few inches of the hole to effectively win the Ryder Cup. Knowing that, Europe's captain Seve Ballesteros conceded Hoch his putt by picking up his ball before running over to Montgomerie and hugging him like a long-lost son.

The celebration that followed was well deserved. Never having achieved the major-winning feats of players like Faldo, Langer and Olazábal, Colin Montgomerie's performance drew plaudits from all corners of the golfing world. Returning home to England even the normally critical British golf media were unstinting in their praise. Yet Monty harboured a unique regret. Proud of his unbeaten record in Ryder Cup singles, he felt slighted at Seve's arbitrary decision to run onto the green and 'give' Scott Hoch his lengthy putt for a par. Instead of a winning point for the Scot, the record books now show a halved match. Nobody really cared. Europe had won and everyone wanted to celebrate, but for the hugely competitive Scot a win was a win, no matter what the circumstances – and a half is not a win!

Amazingly, it would stick in his craw for years: 'These singles matches take a hell of a long time,' he complained almost a decade later, 'and when you've got someone to the point where they need a fifteen-foot putt to get a half and someone goes and give them the putt, well . . .'

In the midst of an historic Ryder Cup victory for Europe, what other professional would have expressed the view that they were somehow denied a meaningless win? Yet how many of us can truly understand the pressure Montgomerie was under that day? As the match moved inexorably to its tense conclusion the media had mentally written their headlines long before the game had ended. Win and he would be declared a national hero. Lose and he would have been vilified like no other British golfer before or since.

For 'Monty' it seems there is never any middle ground, then or now.

1. EARLY DAYS

Peter McEvoy was as dominant a player on the British amateur scene in the 1970s and 80s as Colin Montgomerie was as a European Tour professional in the 90s. Also brought up on the west coast of Scotland, their paths crossed at the Eisenhower Trophy in 1984 when they were both selected to represent Great Britain in the prestigious world team event.

Playing alongside Garth McGimpsey and future Ryder Cup professional David Gilford, they had flown out to Hong Kong via Bombay and arrived wide-eyed at the wondrous sights and sounds that greeted them. That first night, they headed to a restaurant and amid the exotic food on offer they began to talk. Discussing everything from golf to the luxurious hotel they were staying in, attention turned to Monty. Picking at his food, the young Scot was noticeably quiet.

'You're not saying much, Colin,' said team captain Charlie Green, who had organised the evening meal in an attempt to forge a little team bonding. Barely looking up from his dinner plate, the round-faced young Scot answered tersely, 'I'm concentrating on my food.'

Competitive young men who have a talent for any sport can be cruel sometimes and so it proved that night. 'How recently was your last victory?' asked another member of the team, turning the spotlight on the embarrassed Montgomerie.

'It doesn't matter,' replied Colin.

'Was it this year?' said another, bringing sniggers of amusement from everyone else in on the joke.

'I can't remember,' responded Monty, still focused on his dinner plate.

'You must remember!' they seemed to say in unison as the conversation took on a sharper edge. 'You haven't won one, have you? Not anything important.'

As Peter McEvoy admitted in his critically acclaimed 2006 biography, *For Love or Money: Inside the Professional Game Through the Eyes of a Leading Amateur Golfer*, the questioning was both 'brutal and a little unnecessary', concluding that 'we nailed him to the wall with the cruelty of schoolchildren'.

Then as now, Montgomerie was an enigma to those who did not know him. Born in Glasgow, he represented Scotland but spoke with an odd mix of public-school English and a twanging Yorkshire brogue than tended to rub his fellow competitors up the wrong way. He had a shy, almost prickly edge about him that shouted, 'Leave me alone!' and encounters like the one in Hong Kong were not uncommon. He also had a consistent record of top-ten finishes in amateur events from 1983 onwards but had not actually won anything of real note. (He would later win the Scottish Stroke Play in 1985 and the Scottish Amateur in 1987 but still nothing with 'British' in the title.)

Put simply, Montgomerie was in the Eisenhower team because he had finished runner-up to José Maria Olazábal in the (British) Amateur Championship at Formby earlier that year, together with a number of other consistent finishes. Before that, few people outside Troon had ever heard his name! In stark contrast, McEvoy had a record that would shame the devil including winning the Amateur twice in 1977 and 1978. The unavoidable conclusion was that Monty was a talented enough golfer but nothing exceptional.

'I'm not suggesting that he did not get into the team on merit, he did,' wrote future Walker Cup winning captain

McEvoy, 'It's just that he had achieved it through consistency rather than relentless winning like, say, Nick Faldo did. As with almost all players, this amateur trend followed him into the pro game.'

Two years later at the 1986 Eisenhower Trophy, McEvoy witnessed first-hand another side of Montgomerie's complex personality. Played in Caracas, Venezuela, he described it as an 'unpleasant trip' with an 'unhappy team'. In the sauna-like conditions of South America, Montgomerie ploughed his own successful furrow with four solid rounds while McEvoy, McGimpsey and rookie David Curry could barely swing the club in the oppressive heat. The marked differences also extended to social interaction off the golf course: 'Monty was not naturally one of the boys and tended to do his own thing,' recalled Peter, adding that he was 'out of step with the rest of us'.

While his attitude has obviously changed in relation to team golf, most notably the Ryder Cup, Colin Stuart Montgomerie MBE, OBE still finds himself occasionally 'out of step' with the world around him – whether it is with the media, American golf fans or even his fellow players. With his tough, uncompromising attitude to the profession of golf, he has shown a particular aptitude for confrontation and controversy. Even today, many of his friends and close associates are from a non-golfing background. Like his amateur days, he finds the day-to-day social interaction of tournament players unappealing and foreign. Yet he remains one of the most accomplished golfers of his generation. Not in terms of major victories like giants of the game like Nick Faldo or Seve Ballesteros, more the impact he has made on European golf in general and the Ryder Cup in particular.

While his place in the pantheon of British golf may not be as assured as, say, Henry Cotton, Harry Vardon or even Tony Jacklin, Montgomerie's contribution cannot be underestimated. When people ask today, 'What have you actually won?' he can point to eight Order of Merit titles and over thirty tournament victories worldwide. But still the question hangs in the air like a heavy sea mist at St Andrews; without the one major championship that would validate his entire career it is hard to judge whether his youthful promise has been truly fulfilled or not. After all, no player in the history of the sport has been a five-time major runner-up without winning one, and that brings a certain pressure of its own. Today, Montgomerie describes the prospect of winning a major in the autumn years of his career more a reason for 'relief rather than celebration', and who could disagree.

Like his trip to Hong Kong as a young amateur, it has been a fascinating and often wondrous journey. And as in Venezuela, he has endured inspirational highs and tormented lows in his relationships with those around him. Either way, it all began back in Scotland more than four long decades ago.

Colin Montgomerie was born in Glasgow on 23 June 1963. The small town of Troon on the west coast of Scotland was his childhood home for the next four years, then he moved with his family to Ilkley in Yorkshire after his father James was offered an executive post at Fox's Biscuit Company. It would be here in the heart of England's White Rose Country that 'Monty II' – his older brother Douglas was always called 'Monty' by the family – would develop a passion for the game of golf.

With both parents joining Ilkley Golf Club, Colin had his first series of 'proper' lessons with club professional Bill Ferguson at the tender age of six. Booked by his mother Betty, the youngster must have found it quite daunting as he was dropped off outside the pro shop on Nesfield Road each Saturday morning. A no-nonsense character with a bone-dry sense of humour, Ferguson was an accomplished player in his own right and had a growing reputation for teaching juniors. Developing a bond that would last many years, Monty would later caddie for 'Mr Ferguson' on his regular captain and pro challenge matches at the weekend. Earning a little pocket money, the real value was in the many tips and pointers he would pick up along the way: tips and pointers he would take into his golfing life – first as a top Scottish amateur and beyond that into adulthood as a hugely successful tournament professional.

Not that golf played a vitally important part in his life up to the age of eleven. Preferring team sports like cricket and hockey, Monty played the game because that is what his family did. Visiting Troon for the summer holidays, Colin would join Douglas and his mother on the Chiltern and Portland courses while his father would be out playing at Royal Troon across the road. Like all juniors under the age of sixteen, Colin was effectively barred from playing the championship links until he was older. Indeed, by the time he did step onto Troon proper, he would be an accomplished golfer playing off low single figures.

After passing his eleven-plus exam, Monty moved from being a day pupil at Ghyll Royd Preparatory School in Ilkley to join his brother at Strathallan near Perth, one of Scotland's leading independent boarding schools, boasting a formidable reputation for academic and sporting excellence. Even then, golf came a distant second to other sports like cricket, hockey and rugby. Restricted to a handful of moth-eaten flagsticks randomly placed around the edge of the school playing field to simulate a short course, it was hardly Gleneagles.

Leaving Strathallan aged seventeen, Colin headed back home with no real idea of what he wanted to do for a job. His less-than-average exam results reflected his uncommitted attitude to schoolwork and, while the prospect of joining his father at Fox's Biscuits was suggested, nothing really excited his teenage imagination. For an upper-middle-class family who had spent a small fortune educating their youngest son at a private school, this was not particularly welcome news. A career in golf was mooted but his handicap of six was by no means exceptional. It was then a deal was struck. No doubt encouraged by the odd sub-par round, Monty persuaded his father to subsidise two years of amateur golf in the hope of fanning the embers of potential into a raging fire of realisation. James Montgomerie finally agreed, with one proviso – that his son took it more seriously than his schoolwork!

Then came the problem of which country Colin should represent should he reach his ambition of achieving international honours. Brought up in England and playing the majority of his golf at Ilkley, an English golf club, Montgomerie made the surprise decision to represent his country of birth – Scotland. (Competition south of the border in England was considered a lot stronger at the time, which may have influenced his decision to aim for Scottish honours.) Targeting an appearance in the Youth team within two years, his game benefited greatly from the extra hours of practice. With his handicap down to three within months, he now faced the prospect of regularly commuting from Yorkshire to play in Scottish tournaments if he was to catch the eye of the selectors.

The problems of transport and costly accommodation saw him take up a temporary job with his father's company as a trainee salesman/representative over the winter months. It was not a match made in heaven! In between crashing the odd car in the typically icy conditions found in North Yorkshire, Monty found enough time to hit balls at the local driving range. His reward was a third-place finish behind Stephen Keppler in the British Youths Championship in the summer of 1982 and a debut for the Scottish Youth team the following August. It had been two years well spent, but now with even more financial support from his parents, it was time to step out of his comfort zone and head to the United States in search of a golf scholarship.

In September 1983, he made a brief but memorable journey to the New Mexico Military Institute at Roswell. Arranged through one of his father's American business contacts, he had barely unpacked before he decided the strict army lifestyle was too much like Strathallan. Grabbing his suitcase and pulling his golf clubs over his shoulder, Montgomerie headed down the nearest drainpipe and towards the nearest airport. A few hours later, the twenty-year old was pacing the corridors of Houston Airport in Texas wondering what he was doing on the other side of the world without a bed for the night! Once again, his father came to the rescue. Arranging hotel accommodation, he pulled out his contact book and, within a week, an interview was arranged with the director of golf at Houston Baptist University, David Mannen. Playing off three handicap was not that impressive for a Huskies golf team that already boasted more scratch golfers than you could shake a sand iron at, but Mannen saw something in the young Scot that he liked. Admitted as an out-of-state student on a trial basis, studying business management and law, once again it was down to Dad to fund the not-inexpensive tuition fees over the next four years.

After a problem-laden start to his new life in America, Colin began four happy years in Houston making friends and travelling around in a beaten Mazda GLC with a twenty-buck number plate spelling out 'Monty'. Occasionally picking up a few dollars as a car valet at the local Country Club, it was a time of new experiences for the burly Scot. Along with taking a course in touch-typing (for a future job in the media, perhaps?) he even found time for romance with a beautiful Texan girl called Catherine. 'I started to fancy her in one of my university classes in Houston,' admitted Monty years later.

They say if you want to get better, play against better players, and that is exactly what Colin Montgomerie did at Baptist University. Competing against some of the finest young golfers in America, both at Houston and in inter-collegiate matches against other American universities, Montgomerie got to know future professionals like University of Texas golfer Brandel Chamblee and University of Phoenix's Billy Mayfair. Add to that future US PGA Champions Davis Love III and Steve Elkington, and Ryder Cup professional Scott Verplank, and the level of competition was pretty stiff.

Returning at periodic intervals to compete on the fledgling amateur circuit in England and Scotland, Montgomerie brought back a technically stronger golf game and a far more competitive attitude. Success was immediate and lasting. He was Scottish Youth champion in 1983, won the Scottish Stroke Play Championship in 1985 and the Scottish Amateur Championship at Nairn two years later in 1987. In between, he cemented his growing reputation by getting to the final of the (British) Amateur Championship at Formby in 1984 when he lost to future Ryder Cup colleague José Maria Olazábal by 4 and 2. Achieving Walker Cup honours at Pine Valley in 1985, he had already left Baptist University with a BA in Business Management and Recreation by the time he made his second appearance at Sunningdale two years later.

Returning to Scotland's west coast, where his father was now secretary of Royal Troon, Colin Montgomerie had been on the losing team both times, and this was someone who did not like losing at anything. Discussing his future with his beloved parents, what he could not have imagined was the next time he would play against a representative USA team it would be in the Ryder Cup as a professional.

2. LIFE IN THE PROFESSIONAL RANKS

Turning professional was a surprisingly difficult decision for Colin Montgomerie. At the age of 24, the Scot was no spring chicken in golfing terms and, with a degree from Houston Baptist University behind him, he had other career options. One of those options was to join Mark McCormack's IMG (International Management Group) as a client manager. The premier sports management company in the world, it was an attractive proposition for someone like Colin, whose curriculum vitae included Walker Cup selection. His parents had paid for an expensive education and his subsequent foray into amateur golf. At least this way he could earn a good living and perhaps even pay them back. He would spend time around many of his sporting heroes; he might even be asked to play golf with them.

Invited by two IMG executives to travel the forty-odd miles down the coast from Troon and play a few holes of golf with them at Turnberry, Montgomerie is fond of telling people how he joined them for nine holes. Then, after playing them in seven-under par, they turned to him and said, 'Well, Monty, how about you forget working for us – we will come and work for you!' He then talks about a 'Road to Damascus' moment that inspired him to take up his clubs and travel forth into the world of professional golf. Whether it happened exactly that way is unimportant. What is significant was the way he justified his decision to turn professional. Throughout his entire career, Montgomerie has been plagued with niggling doubts about his ability to compete at the very highest level. Unlike Seve Ballesteros, who believed in *destino*, or Nick Faldo, who never doubted that all his hard work would pay off with major championship glory one day, Monty needed constant positive reinforcement that he was as good as people said.

At the 1987 Scottish Amateur for example, the local TV station were interviewing Paul Girvan, a talented Walker Cup player from Prestwick, about his chances of winning. 'There's only one winner of this tournament,' he announced firmly, 'and that's Colin Montgomerie!' Inspired by his comments, Monty breezed through his matches and won. Seventeen years later, European Ryder Cup captain Bernhard Langer quietly asked his team to 'big-up' Monty in the build-up to the 2004 match at Oakland Hills because he knew how well the Scot played when he thought the Americans were frightened of playing him! It was the same story two years earlier under Sam Torrance. For someone troubled by occasional bouts of self-doubt, positive reinforcement has always been the key to his success.

That was certainly the case after his first tournament as a professional in August 1987. Indeed, it proved such a trial that he actually considered giving up any thoughts of playing golf for a living and returning to the amateur game for good! In contrast to the first-class travel arrangements he would enjoy a decade on, Montgomerie made his own way to the Alpine Resort of Crans-sur-Sierre for the Swiss Open – later renamed the European Masters. Flying from Glasgow to Geneva via London, he arrived on Tuesday lunchtime minus his golf clubs and suitcase. Hopeful that he would be reunited with the tools of his new trade long before the opening round, he turned what should have been a straightforward journey to Crans Montana in a rented Peugeot 205 into a four-hour nightmare. Long before the days of satellite navigation, he got lost several times before rolling into the sleepy Swiss hamlet well after dark. Finding his hotel, he awoke the next morning to find the nightly rate at the Rhodania was akin to the national debt of a third-world country. Not that he was exactly pleading poverty. While most of his fellow rookies were sleeping three to a room in some Swiss version of a dosshouse, Monty spent the week at the upmarket residence overlooking the third tee of the golf course. Handing out business cards printed with 'Colin S. Montgomerie, B.A., European Tour Golf Professional', no wonder his fellow players looked at the new young pro and thought, what do we have here, then?

Returning to Geneva Airport the next morning, he collected his luggage but left himself no time for a practice round. Playing with Andrew Murray and a Swiss amateur, the result was a confidence-sapping 77 in the first round. Followed by a 70 the following day, he missed the halfway cut by eight clear strokes. It was not a good start financially or otherwise: 'I thought, what is this all about?' he admitted later.

Driving back to Geneva for the second time, Monty got on a plane and came home having spent almost a thousand pounds in the process. 'I decided this was not for me,' he lamented. 'I was going to ask for my amateur status back.'

With total earnings of just £2,051 for 164th position on the end-of-season money list, it did not take a mathematics genius to work out that Montgomerie could not afford to play a full season unless he pulled his competitive socks up. After an impressive amateur career more was expected of him. No doubt wondering if he had made the biggest mistake of his life, Colin was encouraged by his father to persevere over the winter. It proved good advice. Returning the following year physically stronger, Montgomerie rocketed 112 places up the Order of Merit to finish 52nd with £60,095 in official prize money: good enough to win him the Henry Cotton 'Rookie of the Year' award for 1988. His target for 1989 was simple: to win his first professional title and break into the top 50 in the European Order of Merit for the first time.

After a stuttering start to the season, when he blew a golden chance to win the Catalan Open in Pals, he hooked up with his old coach Bill Ferguson at Ilkley and managed to turn things around. Having missed five consecutive cuts and failed to qualify for the Open at his home club of Royal Troon, Montgomerie hit back in spectacular style by demolishing a strong field to win the Portuguese Open at Quinta do Lago by a massive eleven strokes, helping him to a final position of 25th in the Order of Merit. People were finally beginning to take notice of Colin Stuart Montgomerie.

His family could not have been more happy, especially his mother Betty. While his father James had provided the financial backing that made his son's dream of success a reality, she had provided the constant anchor of support that he had needed since childhood. While James had played golf for most of his life, Betty had taken up the game when her sons were still in short trousers. As boys Colin and Douglas had spent countless hours with their mother chipping and putting their way around the children's course near Troon while their father was playing golf on the championship links. They had a shared bond that had stretched into adulthood, so when Douglas broke the terrible news to his brother early in 1990 that she was terminally ill with lung cancer, it was a cruel and devastating blow.

Travelling back and forth to Troon, Montgomerie was regularly updated on her progress but the impact on his season was considerable. He instinctively felt time was short and rather than being weighed down with dark thoughts of losing his mother, Colin focused hard on adding to his tournament victory in Portugal the season before. Recording second place finishes in Italy and France, his consistent play throughout the 1990 season contributed to a fourteenth place in the end-of-season Order of Merit.

There was better news for the family that summer when Colin married Eimear Wilson, an attractive Ayrshire girl he first met after winning the Scottish Youths Championship at Nairn in 1987, at Troon Old Parish Church on June 27. Six months later, the couple headed north from their new home in Walton-on-Thames to spend Christmas with his parents. It would be the last holiday they would spend together as a complete family; on 10 January 1991, Betty Montgomerie passed away at the tragically young age of 53. Her death, even though it had been expected for some months, was devastating for the tight-knit Montgomerie family. Life took on an unreal feel for all of them, most especially James, her husband of thirty years.

For Colin, Eimear and Douglas, the next few weeks were spent supporting 'Dad' and helping bring a semblance of normality before everyone headed back to their own lives. Taking comfort from her incredibly brave fight against the illness that finally overwhelmed her, Colin and his family would never forget her inspirational example over those last few terrible weeks and days. Many of his life values he got from her, and the wise counsel Betty Montgomerie would dispense would continue to drive him. Now it was time to say goodbye and move forward. Within three years he and Eimear would have a family of their own and his ambition was to make his children as proud of him as his mother Betty had been of him and Douglas.

As ambitions go, it was not a bad one.

Following his first European Tour victory in Portugal in 1988, it would be almost two years before he added another trophy to his cabinet at Monty Towers. The Scandinavian Masters at Drottingholm in August 1991 was a landmark victory in many ways. After the death of his mother in January 1991, his career had stalled. He was still making money, but tournament wins eluded him and his game had not moved on the way he envisioned. Missing five cuts in ten starts in the second quarter of the year, he found some form at the prestigious PGA Championship at Wentworth in May. Tied with Seve Ballesteros, even that ended in disappointment after the Spanish maestro nailed a five-iron approach to a few feet on the par-four first play-off hole for a winning birdie. Over almost before it began, it would not be the last play-off Montgomerie would lose in his career.

With four top-ten finishes between Wentworth and his win in Sweden, his all-round consistency saw him rise up the rankings from fourteenth at the end of 1990 to fourth in 1991. Bringing automatic selection for the European Ryder Cup team to face the USA at Kiawah Island, South Carolina, it made Montgomerie one of an elite group of players to represent his country at both Walker Cup and Ryder Cup level.

Played since 1927, the biennial match between Europe and the United States had grown from humble beginnings into one of the most eagerly anticipated occasions on the sporting calendar. How different from fourteen years earlier, when the match looked to have little future as a contest between Great Britain and Ireland against mighty America. Now, with the advent of Europe's golden generation of Ballesteros, Faldo, Langer and Woosnam, the match had evolved into a truly great contest. Unbeaten since 1985, Europe now had the upper hand and it was widely predicted that this match could provide the first 'away' victory on US soil in the event's long history. All four greats were present at Kiawah Island and now Colin Montgomerie had the opportunity to write his name into the history of the Ryder Cup alongside theirs.

The match itself was always going to be tough, but few realised just how tough! Played in the aftermath of 'Operation Desert Storm' in the Gulf, the 1991 contest came to be known as the 'War on the Shore' for its unprecedented intensity and battle-zone mentality. Held on the newly constructed Ocean Course, temperatures remained at boiling point throughout the week and by the time the opening foursome (alternate shot) matches began on Friday, there was little love lost between the two teams. It was hardly the ideal Ryder Cup to make your competitive debut, and Monty's opening game proved a real baptism of fire. Partnering his fellow rookie, David Gilford, against the veteran pairing of Hale Irwin and Lanny Wadkins, it surprised nobody when they were beaten 4 and 2. It was like lambs to the slaughter, and European captain Bernard Gallacher admitted later that it was a mistake putting two such inexperienced players in together.

Forced to sit out the next two series of four-ball and foursomes, Gallacher paired Montgomerie with Bernhard

Langer in the afternoon four-balls. Vital as it was that Europe gained the upper hand if they were to have any chance of retaining the Ryder Cup, it proved an inspired choice as the Scottish/German partnership concluded a narrow 2 and 1 win over Corey Pavin and Steve Pate. For someone whose name would be so associated with the event, Monty had put his first Ryder Cup point on the board.

With the match score level going into the final day the singles began brightly for Europe. In the opening match Faldo got off to a fast start and won the first three holes against Ray Floyd. Playing in the match behind, David Feherty was also getting the better of Payne Stewart, winning the first two holes, while Ballesteros was up on Wayne Levi. In stark contrast, Montgomerie was having a torrid time against the 1989 Open Champion, Mark Calcavecchia. Five down after nine holes, the Scot looked down and out as the match headed for home. Still four down with four holes remaining, the strain and pressure finally got to his opponent. As the wind changed, both men found water on the short sixteenth but Monty won the hole courtesy of a missed three-foot putt by his opponent. Standing on the final tee, captain Tony Jacklin whispered in Monty's ear, 'If you can just keep the ball in play, you will win,' and that proved the case.

Mongomerie won the eighteenth with a par four and the defeated Calcavecchia left the green in floods of tears. The Scot had played the final four holes in double-bogey, par, double-bogey and par to win every hole! Even today, the 1989 Open Champion must wonder how he turned a certain win into a halved point for his side. (The buzz around Montgomerie's remarkable fightback even affected his fellow players, including David Feherty. Though the Irishman was four up with four to play, his opponent Payne Stewart pulled back two holes, leaving Feherty 'frightened silly' that he would suffer the same result.)

Even with a victory for Feherty and a half for Montgomerie, the final result came down to a six-foot putt by Bernhard Langer on the final green. If the German holed it to beat Hale Irwin, it would tie the entire match and Europe would retain the trophy. If not, it would give the Americans a narrow one-point victory. The record books show the putt was missed and moments later, Montgomerie looked on as Langer and Ballesteros hugged each other, sobbing tears of disappointment. 'Up to that point, I had no real idea what the Ryder Cup really meant,' recalled Monty. 'I knew it was a big event but when you see it reducing men the stature of Seve and Bernhard to tears, you cannot help be caught up in it.'

Little did Montgomerie realise how much his career and the Ryder Cup would become inextricably linked over the next fifteen years. Before long, he would become the senior player and it would be him shedding tears on the final green of a Ryder Cup.

3. HIGH AS A KITE AFTER PEBBLE BEACH LETDOWN

The following season was spent locking horns with two giants of European golf, Nick Faldo and Bernhard Langer. His first full season with his new caddie, Alistair McLean, 1992 was best summed up as 'close but no cigar' for the young Scottish professional. Ending the season a creditable third behind his two famous rivals, the final few holes of the Bells Scottish Open at Gleneagles summed up his year. Wearing a blue Pringle jumper with the white cross of St Andrews emblazoned across the chest, he looked like a target and that is how it proved! Shooting 65 in the final round he looked certain to win. That is before he ran into a whirlwind in the shape of Peter O'Malley. With single putts at the last five holes on the King's course, the Australian caught and passed the patriotic Scot with a record-breaking finish including two eagles and three birdies!

Challenging for number-one spot in Europe inevitably brought more invitations to play in America, including the US Open at Pebble Beach in June. Played in some of the most brutal conditions anyone could remember, wind, cold and rain contributed to making this the toughest test possible. Fortunately, Monty was up for the challenge and by the final round on Sunday was in superb shape. Playing ahead of the leading groups, his score of 70 had given Montgomerie the clubhouse lead on level par. Not unlike his youthful days at Royal Troon, he now spent the final hour anxiously killing time in the clubhouse watching the action unfold on television. 'I holed a very good putt on the final hole, a five-footer left-to-right, and I must admit, I felt I holed that putt to win,' Montgomerie said afterwards. Then none other than Jack Nicklaus congratulated the Scot live on air on winning his first US Open.

Never one for idle praise or rash predictions, it was an understandable remark for the winner of eighteen major championships to make. As he spoke, Tom Kite was up to his ankles in deep rough just off the seventh green. With the weather worsening by the minute, a three-stroke lead looked no guarantee of even finishing in the top ten, never mind winning the championship. Was it really any wonder that the Golden Bear felt confident enough to predict the first Scottish US Open Champion since Tommy Armour won at Oakmont in 1927. 'I did not disagree with him,' Monty admitted later.

Then came the miracle that turned the championship in favour of the bespectacled American. Grabbing his 60-degree wedge from the bag, Kite pitched the ball out of the grass and, like Tom Watson's chip on the penultimate hole in 1982, it slam-dunked straight into the hole for a birdie! Inspired by his huge slice of luck, Kite battled through brutal winds on the back nine to card an even-par 72 (three under par for the championship) to beat Montgomerie by three strokes. Adding salt to the wound, his fellow American Jeff Sluman then pushed the Scot back into third place with another 71 of his own for a 287 total. A bitter pill to swallow, Montgomerie could only reflect on the 77 he had the day before in similar conditions. Returning home, at least knew that experience in the majors never came cheaply.

Montgomerie came out the following year determined to take the small but hugely significant step up to number one. Assisted by Nick Faldo's decision to play more events on the PGA Tour in the United States in 1993, he powered up the official money list after two second-place finishes in the

Johnnie Walker Classic in March and the PGA at Wentworth in May. After a mid-season stall that saw him finish 33rd in the US Open at Baltusrol and miss the cut at the Open Championship at Sandwich, he bounced back to win the Heineken Dutch Open at Noordwijkse at the end of July.

European Tour rivalries were put on hold in September for the Ryder Cup battle with the USA at the Belfry. After the controversial 'War on the Shore' at Kiawah Island in 1991, it was hoped that good sense would prevail as rumours of feuds between individual players surfaced in the media. Everyone agreed that something had gone wrong with the biennial match, including one journalist who commented, 'American professionals sporting army fatigues, unruly crowds influencing the play and accusations of gamesmanship have no place in the Ryder Cup. What next we ask? Arm wrestling to decide who has the honour on each tee?'

Greeted by a two-hour delay caused by autumn mist, Montgomerie renewed his successful partnership with Nick Faldo by demolishing Ray Floyd and Fred Couples by 4 and 3. Out last in the afternoon against Couples and Paul Azinger, the game was suspended with one hole to play because of bad light. A Faldo birdie on seventeen had pulled the match back to level, and after some discussion on the final tee, it was agreed to resume at eight o'clock the following morning. Walking up the final fairway in the dark, Azinger said, 'It's gonna be a long night waiting to play one hole.'

Early next morning, the four players were ferried back to the eighteenth to conclude their match. In overcast and cold conditions, crowds already lined the fairways hoping that Europe could win the hole and take a valuable two-point advantage into the second day. A poor drive by Montgomerie and Couples left Azinger and Faldo to fight out a tense half and it was honours even.

With barely enough time to prepare for the morning foursomes, let alone breakfast, Monty and Faldo barely broke sweat in beating Lanny Wadkins and Corey Pavin 3 and 2 in the first match out on Day Two. Thrown in against John Cook and Chip Beck in the afternoon, the out-of-form

American pair looked to have drawn the short straw. Cook even remarked on the practice ground, 'Nothing like skipping the frying pan and going straight into the fire, huh?'

Over ten hours after Faldo and Montgomerie played that extra hole in the morning mist, Cook and Beck had a real surprise in store for the unbeaten partnership. With the Americans one up on the eighteenth tee, Monty failed once again to make a contribution, leaving his partner with yet another nerve-jangling eight-foot birdie to win the hole and halve the match. Sadly Faldo missed, leaving John Cook two putts from an even shorter distance for a two-hole win. Stretching out his hand to concede it was a bitter pill to swallow for both men. (Before the match had even started, Monty sensed something was wrong after Faldo changed from white shoes to a blue pair! Even today, the superstitious Scot only uses white tees after finding a water hazard with a red one!)

With Europe trailing by a single point going into the final-day singles, the mood of the American camp had turned full circle on the back of beating the golden boys of the European team – Montgomerie and Faldo. This was reflected in the singles as they took it right down to the wire. Matched against Lee Janzen in the third match out, Monty contributed a vital win on the eighteenth green by one hole. Unfortunately, it would not be enough as the Tom Watson-inspired USA team came through to win 15–13.

The controversy leading up to the match was all but forgotten as Watson, the US captain, dignified the closing ceremony by reading out a short speech made by former United States President Theodore Roosevelt. Summing up everything Watson felt about the Ryder Cup and the nature of competition, these words could have been written for Colin Montgomerie.

It is not the critic who counts, the one who points out how the strong man stumbled or how the doer of deeds might have done them better. The credit belongs to the man who is actually in the arena whose face is marred with sweat and blood. Who strives valiantly, who errs and comes short again and again; who knows the great enthusiasms, the great devotions and spends himself in a worthy cause and who, if he fails, at least fails while bearing greatly so that his place shall never be with those cold and timid who know neither victory or defeat.

Two more top-ten finishes after the Ryder Cup put him in a strong position for the end-of-season Volvo Masters at Valderrama in October. Over £100,000 behind Faldo in the money list, Montgomerie powered to three rounds of 69, 70 and 67 to lead the tournament going into the final day. With his rival struggling all week with a heavy cold, Monty knew victory would seal top spot in the Order of Merit, but he had yet to win at Valderrama. Not his most successful hunting ground, he had lost a play-off to former Masters and Open Champion Sandy Lyle exactly twelve months earlier, which had effectively handed the number-one spot to Faldo. Determined not to make the same mistake again, he battled to a superb round of 68 to beat Ulsterman Darren Clarke by a single shot.

Presented with the Volvo Masters trophy by Jaime Ortiz Patiño, owner of Valderrama, he stepped up moments later to accept the Harry Vardon trophy for winning his first Order of Merit from European Tour executive director Ken Schofield. 'I came into the last tournament in fifth place trailing people like Seve Ballesteros, Nick Faldo, Ian Woosnam and Bernhard Langer,' recalled Montgomerie. 'Those guys were my heroes and beating them meant a lot.'

Setting a new prize-money record of just under £800,000 for the season, Montgomerie used the substantial bonus paid by Volvo for winning both titles to buy a new family home in Oxshott in Surrey. Now established among the game's elite, Montgomerie was afraid of nobody – a position he had confirmed in the Ryder Cup that September at the Belfry. As European number one, his earning potential was now virtually unlimited as invitations to play in lucrative close-season tournaments began to flood in.

Now all he needed was that first elusive major.

4. HOT UNDER THE COLLAR AT OAKMONT

Financially secure, Montgomerie could now challenge for the prize he really wanted – his first major championship. But which one?

Golf, like tennis, boasts four premier tournaments in the season – the US Masters in April, the US Open in June, the (British) Open Championship in July and the US Professional Golfers Association Championship in August. In terms of importance, they often rank according to the nationality of the player involved. For most Americans, winning their 'home' Open is seen as the pinnacle of achievement. The same applies to British and European professionals when it comes to the oldest major of all, the Open Championship. The youngest in terms of longevity is the Masters, played since 1934. It is also the only major played at the same venue each season – the sublimely attractive Augusta National in Georgia. The brainchild of golfing legend Robert T Jones Jr, it remains many people's choice as the premier event of the golfing calendar, with the PGA Championship ranked the least important of the four in prestige and the quality of the venues it is played on.

The bruising experience of the US Open at Pebble Beach in 1992 had made Montgomerie even more determined to erase that disappointment with a major success of his own. Blessed with a languid, rhythmical swing that launches the ball with piercing accuracy, he had long felt that either the US Open or PGA Championship offered his best chance of victory. Unlike the wide-open fairways of Augusta National that put the premium on long hitting and a razor-sharp short game, or the Open Championship, which often emphasised ball flight in windy conditions, those two majors favoured accuracy over brute power. With narrow fairways, deep menacing rough and lightning-fast greens, both rewarded accuracy off the tee and distance control with the approach shots – the bedrock of the Montgomerie golf game.

With the 1994 US Open scheduled for the legendary Oakmont Country Club in Pennsylvania, Montgomerie travelled to America in confident mood, looking to become the first British player since Tony Jacklin in 1970 to capture the prestigious title. After a slow start to the year including a missed cut in the Masters in mid-April, his season suddenly clicked into gear with a second-place finish at the Cannes Open two weeks later, followed by a narrow one-stroke win in the Peugeot-sponsored Spanish Open at the Club de Campo, Malaga, two weeks after that. Even the normally sceptical British golf media were talking up Monty's chances of victory.

Like the steel town of Pittsburgh, which it bordered, Oakmont had a tough reputation. When hot-iron magnate Henry Fownes first opened his 'inland links' golf course in 1905, there were almost as many bunkers as there were days in the year! Even when he reduced them in number some years later after facing a potential revolt from the members, he introduced a thick-ribbed bunker rake to roughen up the surfaces like those found throughout Scotland. Aptly named the 'Devil's Backscratcher', it was still in use well into the 1960s. Three decades later, the difficulty of the layout could still not be underestimated. Boasting narrow fairways bordered by hardwood trees, all eighteen greens include a layer of Allegheny River clay, rendering them neither receptive nor forgiving, like upturned porcelain plates. Sam Snead joked how he once marked his ball with a ten-cent coin only to watch it slide off the green! Ben Hogan, who won there in 1953, considered Oakmont among the hardest tests in golf, yet three players finished the week tied first and all under par – Montgomerie, Loren Robert and 24-year-old Ernie Els!

Played in boiler-house conditions all week, with humidity up to 92 per cent at times, the opening two rounds were a blast from the past as Jack Nicklaus, Tom Watson and Hale Irwin all took their turn at the top of the leader board. Add to that the emotional scenes that surrounded Arnold Palmer as he made his farewell US Open appearance at a course he had first played in 1941 as an amateur, and the tournament had 'classic' written all over it.

It certainly was for Montgomerie as, with scores of 71 and 65, he took a two-stroke halfway lead over Irwin and the Golden Bear. 'I didn't realise he is leader in Europe of fairways hit,' said Nicklaus in the broadcast booth, 'and that's a pretty impressive statistic and when you bring that over to the US Open you are going to play pretty well.'

Bringing back memories of that golden day in April 1986, when Nicklaus captured his eighteenth major title at the age of 46 in a dramatic final day at Augusta in the Masters, Oakmont proved a step too far as he fell away with weekend rounds of 77 and 76. Fortunately for British and European hopes, Monty kept up the pace with rounds of 73 and 70, leaving him as clubhouse leader. Both Els and Roberts then squandered golden opportunities to win after bogeying the last hole. Locked in a three-way tie with South African Ernie Els and the little-known Californian Loren Roberts, the Scot was now only an eighteen-hole play-off away from his break-through major championship. 'It is a real bonus to make the play-off tomorrow,' said Montgomerie on Sunday. 'I never thought five under par was going to be good enough.'

With the needle on the clubhouse thermometer touching 94 degrees, Montgomerie's major dream quickly turned into a nightmare. The day began badly for the flustered-looking Scot in his floppy Panama hat even before a shot had been struck in the play-off. Dressed in dark blue from head to toe, even though the forecast was for searing heat, Monty stood red-faced on the first tee with a white towel around his neck as Els and Roberts looked ice cool in light-coloured clothing. (He later admitted to running out of his sponsor's shirts and being forced to purchase one from the local pro-shop because it was the only one without a logo!)

At the par-four first, Montgomerie made a disastrous double-bogey six after mishitting two poorly executed chip shots. Fortunately both his opponents made bogey, but instead of taking his medicine and moving on to the next hole, his increasingly bad temper contributed to another double-bogey at the second hole. Constantly mopping the sweat away from his eyes, the play-off was becoming a comedy of errors. Even when the South African ran up a triple-bogey on the same hole, Montgomerie was unable to take advantage.

A lengthy birdie putt at the third helped repair some of the damage for Els, but Monty was in free fall. A confidence-sapping four over par after three holes played, Montgomerie sent his birdie effort at the fourth ten feet past after being half that distance away in two shots! Missing the return, you could visibly see his shoulders slump as he played to the turn in a glassy-eyed haze. The only ray of hope came on the long ninth when he had an opportunity for a score-saving eagle three. Three putts later, his crushing disappointment was obvious. His manager John Simpson looked on in horror as the Scot stumbled to an error-strewn 42 for the first nine. He must have known this would not be his client's day.

Reducing the deficit to just two strokes after a par on the 458-yard tenth, Montgomerie played so-called 'military golf' at the eleventh, finding the right rough off the tee, left rough with his second, over the green with his third and finishing off with three putts. Adding up to yet another double-bogey, it was the final nail in the Scottish professional's coffin. Eight over par for the round, Monty was now five strokes behind with seven holes left to play. Barring a miracle, the contest was now between Els and Roberts. Even a birdie two on the short thirteenth hole was greeted with barely sympathetic applause as the other two protagonists battled it out for the title, with Monty reduced to a mere onlooker. 'The pins were very difficult and the greens a lot slower than yesterday,' said the Scot. 'I was just not getting the pace until it was too late.'

By the time the threesome reached the sixteenth hole, Roberts, chasing only the second tournament win of his career, was one ahead but gave it back after a three-putt green. Holing a ten-foot putt on the treacherous eighteenth green to take the play-off between himself and Els to yet more holes, 38-year-old Roberts found a greenside bunker on the second extra hole – the 378-yard eleventh. By the time Els holed out for par, Montgomerie was in the locker room receiving treatment for heat exhaustion. Monty had finished strongly but it was never good enough to catch the flaxen-haired South African, who had finished in the top ten in five of his last six majors. 'I played the last seven holes in one-under,' explained Monty, 'but I never felt I was going to win.'

Describing it as 'a learning process' Montgomerie went on, 'I'm obviously very disappointed, especially knowing what would have been good enough to win today . . . This is by far the most difficult course I've ever played, but I came here saying this was my best chance to win a major and I gave it my best.'

Determined to remain upbeat, Montgomerie explained that he was now looking forward to the Open at Turnberry the following month. It had been a mature performance on an extremely testing course and what he had started in Oakmont he could surely finish in his homeland of Scotland. Once again, though, he was not quite up to the task despite a superb 65 on Saturday that had his growing army of fans purring with delight. Recording his best ever finish in the Open, he ended the week in eighth place. Looking to retain his number-one spot in Europe, it proved a good springboard for the second half of the year, despite finishing outside the top thirty at the US PGA at Southern Hills in August.

Bouncing back in style, his Order of Merit ambitions received a huge boost after Monty relegated former Ryder Cup professional Barry Lane into second place in the English Open at the Forest of Arden two weeks later. Making it two in a row at the German Open the following week, he pushed home favourite Bernhard Langer into second both at Hubbelrath and in the race to top the 1994 money list. By the time the Tour arrived at Valderrama in October, he now had a stranglehold on the Order of Merit after three consecutive top-four finishes in August and September at the European Open, the British Masters and the Lancôme Trophy. With Langer, Ballesteros and a young José Maria Olazábal occupying the top three places respectively, his fourth-place finish in Spain set the seal on the year.

Montgomerie should have been delighted but he was more annoyed at missing out on a chance to win the tournament. As he stood in the middle of the final fairway needing a birdie to tie with clubhouse leader Bernhard Langer, his playing partner Seve Ballesteros was under a cork tree and called over a rules official, looking for an unlikely free drop. The long delay disrupted Monty's concentration and he ended the round with a bogey. Having won his second consecutive European Order of Merit, the incident should have been relegated to a minor footnote in his career except for one thing – it would be mirrored in a similar incident almost twelve years later at Winged Foot in America. In 1994 it cost him the Volvo Masters – the second time it would cost him the United States Open Championship!

5. THAT RIVIERA TOUCH

While Montgomerie's form in Europe remained top class in 1995, with fifteen top-ten finishes including two wins in the German Open and Lancôme Trophy, his performance in the majors was patchy.

A creditable seventeenth place in the Masters at Augusta National in April was followed by poor middle rounds of 74 and 75 in the US Open at Shinnecock Hills in June, when two scores of level par or better would have given him his major championship breakthrough. Finishing a frustrating week in 28th position, eight strokes behind the eventual winner Corey Pavin on level par, 280, it was a similar story at the Open at St Andrews in July where two bad-tempered rounds in the mid-70s resulted in a missed cut. That left only the 77th US PGA Championship in August at the Riviera Country Club in California to make an impact – and what an impact he would make.

There may be longer golf courses on the major rota than the 6,956-yard Riviera, but few could match it for old-world style and luxury. Designed by George C Thomas Jr and opened in 1926, the welcoming layout became a popular haunt for many of the world's best-known film stars in Hollywood's golden era of the 1930s and 40s. Located in the swish Los Angeles suburb of Pacific Palisades, only a block away from Sunset

Boulevard, it is not difficult to see why it was such a favourite with screen legends like Clark Gable, Katharine Hepburn and both Douglas Fairbanks Jr and Sr (Humphrey Bogart even had a tree named after him on the par-four twelfth).

The course is built on a gently rolling hillside, and spreading eucalyptus trees come into play on almost every hole. Hosting both the US Open in 1948 and the PGA Championship in 1983, the course was affectionately known as 'Hogan's Alley' after Ben Hogan won the Los Angeles Open here three times and finished second once back in the 1940s and 50s. The original course cost $243,827.63 to build and, just under seven decades later, the winner in the 1995 PGA Championship would return home with a cheque for almost double that amount – Monty naturally hoped it would have his name on it.

At the start of the week, the signs were not good. Switching from Wilson clubs to Callaway, the transition proved more difficult than Montgomerie imagined. Fortunately, all that was quickly forgotten after he carded three remarkable rounds of 68, 67 and 67 against par of 71. Amazingly, he still found himself five strokes behind tournament leader Ernie Els, and even two shots behind American Jeff Maggert in second place! 'Why is simple,' explained Montgomerie after the third round. 'I've had fifty birdie chances this week and I'm only eleven under.'

Ahead in 'greens hit' for the week, the putts just had not dropped for Monty. The greens were certainly spiked-up and uneven in places but, as Els had proved, it was the same for everyone. With the South African hot favourite to win his second American major in two years, Montgomerie needed a miracle to pull him back into contention. That miracle began to look possible as Els lost his advantage over the chasing pack by dropping shots early in the final round. On a day of low scoring – Brad Faxon reached the turn in a record-breaking 28 strokes en route to a superb 63 – Monty was surprisingly dismissive of his chances against the man who had already beaten him in a play-off for the US Open the previous June. 'This is Ernie's championship to win or lose,' he had said the previous evening.

Slowly, things began to turn in his favour. Reaching the turn in 32 (three under par), including birdies at the opening two holes, the Scot was now only one behind joint leaders Els and Australian Steve Elkington at fourteen under. He then birdied the eleventh but after making bogey at the thirteenth his chance appeared to have gone. Elkington, who admitted to an allergy to grass early in his career, was out in 31 and looking the strongest of the leading contenders, especially after starting back with three straight birdies to open up a two-shot advantage. Playing in the group ahead of Montgomerie, the 'Elk' could only manage even par over the remaining six holes but it looked like being enough. Riviera boasts a tough finishing stretch of three holes and Monty needed a miracle just to tie. The short sixteenth hole required an accurate iron hit into a small green surrounded by bunkers. The par-five seventeenth was the longest hole on the golf course, playing mostly uphill, while the eighteenth hole was a world-class par-four with a blind tee shot to a sloping left-to-right fairway.

Knowing the ball must find the fairway to have any chance of reaching the green brought pressure of its own, but the Scot was up to the task. Holing from six feet on sixteen and making a chip-and-putt birdie on seventeen, Monty came to the final hole still needing to make a 22-foot birdie putt to force a play-off. The pressure had never been greater as he drew back the bronze coloured Ping Pal putter in one of the biggest natural amphitheatres in golf. The straightest putt on the green, when it finally rattled into the hole, you could hear the roar back in Glasgow!

Returning a superb 65, Montgomerie tied with his Commonwealth colleague on a 17-under-par total of 267, equalling the lowest aggregate in the history of major championship golf. It was certainly too hot for Ernie Els, who scored 72 to be joint third with Jeff Maggert, whose 69 put him into the US Ryder Cup team (their scores of fifteen under would have been enough to win any PGA Championship since it evolved into a stroke-play event in 1958).

Thirty minutes later Monty was standing alongside Elkington on the eighteenth tee. Allotted 'tails' in the coin toss, 'heads' came up and he would go second. Red-faced but composed, at least he proved those critics wrong who said he could not handle the pressure after his US Open screw-up at Oakmont in 1994. The only question now was, how would someone who had never won a play-off in his entire professional career cope with sudden death against the sweet-swinging Australian? 'My play-off record went through my mind on the buggy ride back to the eighteenth tee,' said Monty afterwards. 'But I thought the law of averages have got to come into effect and I thought it was my turn today.'

Unfortunately, the law of averages did not work in his favour at the Riviera. Hot on the heels of his final round of 64, Elkington put his second shot in exactly the spot where Montgomerie had holed from earlier! Monty in response hit a superb, arrow-like approach to within eighteen feet but it came up half-a-club short. Left with a twisting left-to-righter, the Scot was nearer than his old college rival but had the far harder putt. After 73 holes, it all came down to a matter of inches. With his wife and baby sitting by the back of the green, Elkington sank a birdie bomb that sealed the tournament. Shell-shocked Montgomerie was never going to match it as his own effort slipped narrowly by on the low side of the hole.

'I was very unlucky,' recalled the Scot some years later. 'Steve Elkington holed a shot from the back of the green. I was left with a putt to halve it and I missed. And I just stood there, thinking, "Hang on, what happened there? I've just lost a real opportunity to win my first major."'

Suffering his fifth play-off defeat out of five, all Montgomerie could do was mouth, 'Well done, well done,' to his opponent as they walked off the green. 'I did nothing wrong,' he said philosophically afterwards. 'I birdied the last three holes and when he made his putt I tried to gather my thoughts. I've played enough golf to expect the unexpected, but it wasn't to be . . . I don't feel I lost – he won.'

Defeat for Montgomerie meant a career-crowning triumph for Elkington, whose record in the seasons' four majors was second to none. Fifth in the Masters in April and sixth in the

Open Championship at St Andrews, he expected the Scot to hole his birdie putt at the last but was delighted when he failed. 'I was semi-prepared for Colin holing the putt on the last,' he admitted. 'Golfers are thick-skinned. It's not easy to regroup, but you do it.'

6. OAK HILL AND BEYOND

After the disappointment of losing out to Australian Steve Elkington in the US PGA play-off at Riviera in August, the Ryder Cup at Oak Hill in September provided the perfect opportunity for Monty to 'regroup' himself. Leading from the front in only his third Ryder Cup, he played a vital part in restricting the United States to a two-point lead going into the singles despite bringing little form into the match. Resuming his successful partnership with Nick Faldo, any magic they had two years earlier at the Belfry had disappeared as both players struggled with their game. Beaten twice on the opening day, the pressure on them was summed up by an incident in their morning foursome match against the hugely competitive pairing of Tom Lehman and Corey Pavin. As early as the second hole, Faldo berated Lehman for tapping in a par putt after it had already been conceded. 'When I say it is good,' barked Faldo, 'it *is* good!'

Lehman got the message but was not going to be intimidated by his major-winning opponent. 'I told him to speak clearly,' he said afterwards. 'He claims he said a couple of times that my putt was good. I wasn't going to put up with any crap, especially after he stretches his arm out as if to say, "Put the ball in your pocket, you idiot!" I was hot.'

Winning the match on the final green, the American pair knew just how important beating Faldo and Montgomerie had been. 'It was a statement that Europe's best team could be beaten,' said a delighted Lehman. Perhaps he was right. Though they lost in the afternoon to Fred Couples and Davis Love III, captain Bernard Gallacher persisted with the Faldo/Montgomerie pairing in the morning foursomes on the second day. Trailing 5–3 after day one, he sent them out first against former Wake Forest University pals Curtis Strange and Jay Haas. Europe could not afford many more defeats and needed top players like Monty and Nick to perform at their best if Europe were going to win back the trophy. Nicknamed 'Snooty and the Blowfish' by some American golf writers after their ill-tempered display the day before, they rewarded Gallacher with a 4 and 2 victory.

With that contribution to a 3–1 foursomes result, Europe was back in the Ryder Cup. Then came the bombshell that Gallacher was splitting them up in the afternoon, putting Monty out with Sam Torrance and Faldo with Langer. Whatever strategy the captain planned, it did not work as Montgomerie and Torrance slipped to a 4 and 2 defeat against Brad Faxon and Fred Couples, and Faldo and Langer lost to Loren Roberts and Corey Pavin.

The final day's singles would now settle the destiny of the Ryder Cup. With the USA holding a two-point lead, the Scot was sent out in a pivotal match against former Masters Champion Ben Crenshaw. Dominating the middle order, Monty beat Crenshaw by 3 and 1, followed by wins for Howard Clark, Mark James, David Gilford, Faldo, Torrance and, most significantly, Philip Walton. Winning by a single point, 14–13, it was Montgomerie's first Ryder Cup triumph and would not be the last.

Returning to Europe, it was time for Montgomerie to get his own season back on track and he did so in admirable style with victories in Germany and France. What he did not expect was his Scottish Dunhill Cup and Ryder Cup partner, Sam Torrance, shadowing him all the way to the finish line in the race for the Order of Merit. Second in both tournaments, Sam captured the British Masters at Collingtree Park a week later to race ahead of Montgomerie by the narrowest of margins. He was still ahead by £3,000 as Montgomerie teed it up in a dramatic season finale at the Volvo Masters at Valderrama. For a long time on Sunday afternoon, that small amount of money looked like making the difference between winning and losing as Torrance finished the final round with a 68. Monty had to play faultless golf en route to finishing second to German Alex Cejka – and, crucially, one place ahead of Torrance – enough to make it a three-peat of money-list titles.

'Like I told Colin,' lamented Torrance afterwards. 'I really cannot believe that I haven't won the Order of Merit! At least I didn't lose it – he won it and that's all that matters in the end.'

Elated at winning the 1995 European Order of Merit, even losing to his old rival Ernie Els in the final of the World Match Play at Wentworth in October failed to put a dent in Montgomerie's season. There were so many positives. For three consecutive years he had finished number one in Europe and had played well enough to get into two major championship play-offs. Surely it was only a matter of time until he won one?

In pure golfing terms, 1996 was probably Monty's best season so far. The year began in positive style after Montgomerie shed over thirty pounds in weight during the winter through a strenuous three-month fitness programme. There was also the arrival of a second child to celebrate after Eimear gave birth to another daughter, Venetia, on 22 January, joining Olivia, born three years earlier.

The new streamlined Montgomerie made his first appearance at the Dubai Desert Classic in February. It soon became obvious that he had lost none of his competitive edge. Coming to the 72nd hole needing a birdie to win, his second shot on this dogleg par-five had to be played over water to a narrow peninsula. Hitting a magnificent drive off the fairway to within a few feet, the subsequent birdie was enough to register his first victory of the season. It would also later win him the Canon 'Shot of the Year' Award.

In March, Montgomerie let slip a golden opportunity to win his first PGA Tour event at the Tournament Players Championship at Sawgrass, Florida, described by many players as 'the fifth major'. The Scot had birdied the tough par-four fourteenth to lead by one deep into the final round. Not long after, American Fred Couples went for the green at the par-five sixteenth knowing he needed a strong finish. Hitting a two-iron from 220 yards out, the ball ricocheted off the wooden sleepers that bordered the lake to the right of the green and bounced high in the air before coming to rest to within thirty feet of the flag! Holing out for an eagle, it was a decisive moment as he closed with a superb round of 64. Forced to play aggressively, Montgomerie bogeyed two of the final three holes and finished runner-up on fourteen under par – four strokes behind Couples. 'You didn't have to tell me who holed it or what it was for. It was loud enough,' said the Scot, who was walking to the sixteenth tee when he heard the crowd erupt after Couples sank his dramatic eagle putt.

Back in Europe, an intriguing yearlong battle was developing with Ian Woosnam, after Montgomerie finished runner-up in both the Deutsche Bank Open and Alamo English Open in June before winning the Irish Open at Druids Glen in July. While his performances in the majors were dire – missing the cut in both the Open and US PGA – Woosnam was setting a red-hot pace in the battle to be number one in Europe. The Welshman, who already had three wins in 1996, took full advantage of his rival's enforced absence from the Volvo German Open at the end of August by winning to narrow the gap before the final run-in to the end-of-season Volvo Masters at Valderrama.

The reason for Montgomerie's absence from Germany was the sudden illness of his father James. With his brother Douglas away on honeymoon, Colin cancelled his trip to Stuttgart after his father James complained of severe chest pains. Just under six years after he lost his mother Betty, Colin was taking no chances and raced up from Surrey to Troon to be with him. Three weeks later James was under the knife having what ultimately proved to be a successful heart bypass operation. The obvious relief Colin felt was mirrored in his play over the closing few weeks of the season. Starting with the British Masters at Collingtree in Northampton, where he finished tied for ninth, he won the Canon European Masters, was second in the Lancôme Trophy, tied fourth at the Loch Lomond Invitational, 24th in the European Open in Ireland and fourth in the Linde German Masters – all in consecutive weeks. By the time the tour reached Spain, the race was already over.

The key to this exceptional run of form was the Canon European Masters in Switzerland. With Woosnam surprisingly absent, Monty needed a top-two finish there to leapfrog the Welshman back to the top of the standings. After two rounds he trailed his fellow Scot Sam Torrance by six shots. His entire season turned around after pulling himself into contention with a magnificent ten-under-par score of 61 in the third round. Even in the rarefied atmosphere of the Swiss Alpine region, where the ball can fly up to 20 per cent further than normal, it was a remarkable score, especially when you consider the pressure he was under. The round began with a solid birdie at the 536-yard par-five first hole. Followed by two pars, the fireworks started with a birdie at the next, heralding a run of eight birdies over the next eleven holes. Even a bogey at the 208-yard par-three eleventh failed to dent his attempt at becoming the first professional to break the magical 60-shot barrier in a European Tour event. Ten birdies over the first fourteen holes had put him right on target. A comparatively easy stretch of finishing holes had journalists scrambling from the comfort of the media centre looking to witness a piece of golfing history first-hand. With the eminently reachable 520-yard par-five fifteenth looking to yield a certain birdie, possibly an eagle, the fabled 59 looked a real possibility, but it was not to be. The birdie trail simply dried up and it was a relatively disappointed Montgomerie who was left to describe his 61 to the awaiting reporters: 'I needed two more birdies but then the wind started to get up,' he said. 'It got quite severe and difficult. At eighteen, my second with a sand wedge was blown right over the back and I feel unfortunate not to have birdied at least one of the last four.'

It was one of the finest single rounds ever played in Europe, and the Scot followed it up with an equally exceptional 63 on Sunday to win the tournament, creating a new European Tour scoring record for the final 36 holes. Monty said afterwards, 'I've never played better in my life. If I'd finished yesterday like I did today, I'd have shot fifty-eight, never mind fifty-nine . . . Winning for a third time this year to go back to the top of the rankings was always my goal and it's got me up for finishing number one again.'

The only European golfer in history to break the $3m barrier in official prize money, his win in Switzerland took him ahead of Woosnam and the gap would never be closed. Describing how his almost flawless driving had taken the pressure off the rest of his golf game, it surprised nobody when Montgomerie named his third round at Crans-sur-Sierre as the 'Round of his Life' some years later. Ranking it alongside his 65 in the final round of the US PGA Championship the previous year, he also saw himself 'capable' of shooting 59 in the future.

Having won his fourth consecutive Order of Merit, Monty was undisputed King of the Hill in Europe. Voted Johnnie Walker 'Golfer of the Year' for 1996, the season had an emotional climax for the big Scot. Playing in the end-of-season Million Dollar Challenge in Sun City, Colin beat Ernie Els with a seven-foot birdie at the third extra hole. Watched by his father James, all he could say afterwards was, 'Dad had never seen me win before.'

What it meant to both of them can only be imagined.

7. MASTERFUL MONTY BECOMES TIGER BAIT

E ven before the Masters got under way at Augusta National everyone had heard of the new golfing wunderkind Tiger Woods. Making his debut at Augusta National in 1997, Colin Montgomerie got a close-up view after being paired with the 21-year-old American star in the third round.

Making history at almost every turn, the significance of Woods' appearance in this sleepy backwater of Georgia could not be overestimated. For decades, the only black faces seen around the colonial-style clubhouse at Augusta National were caddies, bus boys, green sweepers, waiters and, in later years, security officers working for the Pinkerton Agency that were hired to police the event. Even during Masters week, they were expected to enter the property through a side entrance well away from any of the paying 'patrons'.

An autocratic organisation, the club boasts just 300 members at any given time. Privately owned, membership is strictly by invitation only and there is definitely no application process. Run by the members for the members, Augusta National treats the Masters tournament each April in much the same manner. A throwback to the original Annual Invitation Tournament established back in 1935, the goal is simple – to maintain the highest 'Southern' ideals of its founder, Robert Tyre Jones Jr. Jones was the legendary winner of the 1930 Grand Slam of majors – the American and British Open and Amateur Championships – and his original idea was to build a course that would host the US Open. Rebuffed by the US Golf Association, 'Bobby' decided to host his own event, which eventually evolved into the Masters and gave us the fourth event in a modern Grand Slam of majors.

Even today, Augusta National is all about tradition. Organisation and preparation are flawless but this particular brand of organisation comes at a cost. On the subject of race or women members (or lack of them) they are increasingly sensitive about what they see as strictly private golf club matters. Though happy to open their doors to the world each April, the gates at the end of Magnolia Drive remain firmly locked at any other time. This polite but distant attitude is reflected in the way the Masters is organised each year. From the moment players, fans and press alike enter the gates they are subject to an extensive array of rules, guidelines and suggestions. Players, for example, are only allowed to play one ball in practice, when two or three is the norm. As 'invitees' they are also expected to be clean-shaven and smartly dressed, with audible 'cursing' a complete non-starter. With no on-course advertising, overhead air-ship blimps or tented pavilions extolling the virtues of one club manufacturer over another, logos on shirts and bags must also be kept to a minimum. Not that long ago, competitors were expected to use one of Augusta National's own black caddies but, under growing pressure from the players and PGA Tour, the members made a rare concession and allowed 'outside' bagmen to attend. As for announcing what the prize fund was to be each year, that was considered one step too far!

The world's golf media are also under no illusion when it comes to the first major of the year. Accreditation is granted year on year and can be revoked without explanation at any time, as CBS anchorman Jack Whitaker found to his cost some years ago when he referred to the gallery around the final green as a 'mob'. Likewise, the brilliant Gary McCord was 'respectfully' asked not to return after he described the greens at Augusta as so slick they must have been 'bikini-waxed'. He followed it up with a flip comment about needing a body bag to describe the degree of difficulty involved in overshooting the seventeenth green, and it was a case of 'don't call us, we'll call you . . .' Hardly the crime of the century, but fame and popularity are no protection against the green jackets if they do not want to invite you to their party!

As for the many thousands of Masters devotees that roll into this nondescript Georgia truckstop each April, they are subject to more guidelines than anyone. Harking back to the 'good ole days' when the South was populated by Rhett Butler lookalikes, restrained, almost reverent, behaviour is the order of the day. That means no cameras, no noisy or excessive cheering, no picnics or all-day beer sessions, and no asking players for their autographs anywhere on the course or practice ground. Running or walking in haste is also taboo and should you feel the need to rush around this hallowed property, there is always the burly figure of a Pinkerton security operative to subtly show you the nearest exit. From there, it is goodbye and 'have a nice day' anywhere else but here.

There is still nothing quite like Augusta National and the Masters in springtime. Still considered the traditional start to the golf season, the event has an Edwardian garden party atmosphere. Like an old school reunion, the great and the good of golf meet up each year under the spreading branches of the ancient oak next to the clubhouse. Offering a welcome respite from the oppressive sun, talk is of mint juleps, peach cobblers and the coming season as golfers set off down the nearby first and tenth tees.

Next to St Andrews, Augusta National is the best-known golf course on the planet. Also considered the most beautiful, the vibrant explosion of colours that greets its visitors each April cannot be overstated. An intoxicating mixture of cathedral pines, azure-blue lakes and blooming azaleas, each individual hole is named after a plant or tree in honour of the former Fruitlands Nursery that occupied this land for many years. Names like Yellow Jasmine, Carolina Cherry and

Firethorn all evoke a bygone age when issues like race and gender played no part in daily life in this anachronistic corner of the world.

Turning professional at the back end of 1996, Tiger Woods had turned the world of golf upon its head. Taught the game by his father Earl, a former Green Beret, Woods shot a 48 over nine holes at the Navy golf club in Cypress, California aged only three. Before his tenth birthday he was hitting golf balls on the Bob Hope television show and it came as no surprise when he amassed three consecutive US Amateur Championships before his 21st birthday. No player in the history of the game ever turned professional with more fanfare. On the back of a reputedly $55m sponsorship from Nike, he arrived at the Masters having already amassed over a million dollars in prize money and was virtually assured of a place in the US Ryder Cup team to face Europe in September at Valderrama. In a series of high-profile advertisements Woods had declared: 'Are *you* ready for me yet?' That was the question that must have vexed Augusta National in the run-up to the first major of the year.

The 1997 Masters was to be Tiger Woods' major debut as a pro, and the thorny issue of race was always going to be a contentious one. Criticised for its lack of Afro-American members, the tournament had become synonymous with race after Lee Elder became the first black professional to play in the Masters in 1975 – four decades after it began.

Tiger Woods' appearance was always going to be a groundbreaking event and so it proved. He partnered Paul Azinger and Montgomerie's Ryder Cup colleague Nick Faldo in the first two rounds, and the Englishman was left shaking his head in amazement after Woods came back from shooting four over par on his opening nine holes, only to return in six under on the back nine! As defending Masters Champion, Faldo bowed out at the halfway stage, but Woods just got stronger, shooting a superb 66 to go with his 70 on day one to lead the Masters after 36 holes. Meanwhile Monty had finally got to grips with Augusta National's slick greens and was in second place on four under after rounds of 72 and 67.

It had been a long time coming. Having played in the Masters since 1990, four of those as European number one, the Scot's best finish was seventeenth equal in 1995. Now he had a chance to face Woods head-on, but the signs were not good. Admitting that he was 'in awe' of the American sensation, it was an apprehensive and nervous Monty who stepped up to the plate on Saturday afternoon.

In the first round, Woods beat Faldo by five shots (70–75), and in the second round Azinger took his beating, 66–73. On Saturday it was Montgomerie's turn as he struggled around in 74 to Tiger's superb 65. With Ferguson unwilling to compromise his club duties at Ilkley to travel the world with Montgomerie, he decided to employ a new full-time coach in Dennis Pugh. Testing the water at the 1997 Masters, the two personalities perfectly complemented each other. Compared with his new employer, Pugh was a relaxed, easy-going individual with a ready smile and knockabout sense of humour. Boasting a sharp eye for detail, the Englishman had worked his way up the golfing ladder after turning professional in 1972 at the tender age of seventeen. A former tournament player himself, he had struggled to maintain his playing privileges on the fledgling European Tour throughout the late 1970s. In 1980, Pugh headed for America after being offered a more secure living with a Florida-based sports management company, which brought him into contact with top coaches like Phil Ritson and David Leadbetter, but he resisted a full-time career in teaching, preferring to play mini-tour events in 1982 and 1983. Returning to London shortly afterwards, Pugh took up a teaching post at Wanstead Golf Club and in the five years he spent there he built up a good reputation coaching the lesser lights of the European Tour. By 1989 he had given up his club duties to concentrate on teaching full-time and by the mid-1990s had coached in excess of 150 tournament professionals.

A regular fixture on the practice ground at European Tour events, it was only a matter of time before a top player took him on. Montgomerie offered him a twelve month contract, and the third round at Augusta National must have proved an uncomfortable introduction. With Pugh watching from behind the ropes Woods out-drove, out-putted and out-manoeuvred Monty so comprehensively that you wondered which player was making their major debut! Yet the Scot and his new coach could not have been more impressed; 'He stared the ball into the hole,' Montgomerie gushed at the post-round press conference. 'That went fathoms deeper than anything I had seen before.'

Montgomerie predicted that Woods would win on Sunday by more than nine shots, and he duly won by twelve. Strolling home with a three-under final-round 69, Tiger collected his first major championship along with a $486,000 cheque. After his final putt, he wrapped his arms around his father at the back of the green as he fought back the tears. Moments later he embraced his mother Tida. 'I accomplished my goal,' said an emotional Woods afterwards. As for becoming the first Afro-American to win the Masters, he would not be drawn on whether his example would break down hitherto impenetrable barriers. 'We'll see,' he said diplomatically. 'As time goes on, I think that young people who haven't normally pursued golf will.'

One professional who had definitely not accomplished his goal was Colin Montgomerie. Going into the final round in a tie for fifth place with Jeff Sluman at three under par – twelve shots behind Woods – he had high hopes of improving his woeful Masters record and perhaps grabbing the runner-up position from Italian Costantino Rocca.

Sadly, it was never going to happen. Affected by his drubbing from Woods the previous day, Montgomerie crashed out of contention with a nightmare 81. Finishing tied 30th, was it any wonder the *Augusta Chronicle* described him as 'a rumpled Scotsman who is a killer in Europe but can't get arrested in the United States'.

The comment was not only unfair but also inaccurate, as Montgomerie had finished runner-up in the Tournament Players Championship at Sawgrass just over twelve months earlier. 'It taught me that I *might* not win there,' the Scot admitted. 'I just have a love-hate relationship with the place.'

8. CONGRESSIONAL

M ontgomerie could be forgiven for having a 'love-hate relationship' with the second major of the year – the US Open, scheduled for the Congressional Country Club near Washington DC. The European number one arrived in Maryland hoping to make the same lightning-quick start he had at Augusta two months earlier. Finding some form since his disastrous weekend at the Masters, Monty had improved his chances of capturing a fifth record-breaking Order of Merit title by winning the Compaq European Grand Prix at Slaley Hall in early June. A superb 65 in the final round would be repeated in far more difficult circumstances one week later at the testing Blue Course at Congressional.

Opened in 1924, the par-72 course measures 7,250 yards from the back tees and is consistently rated among the top one hundred courses in America. Located in Bethesda, Maryland, not far from the White House and Senate Building in Washington DC, the tree-lined layout with its rolling fairways, strategically placed lakes and lightning-quick greens had previously played host to two major championships – the 1964 US Open, when a heat-exhausted Ken Venturi struggled around in a score of two under par to win, and the 1976 PGA Championship when Dave Stockton captured the title. The regular venue for the Kemper Open for much of the 1980s, Congressional boasted a select membership including at least five former US Presidents, among them Woodrow Wilson, Calvin Coolidge, Herbert Hoover and Dwight D Eisenhower.

At the start of the week, it was even hoped that current White House resident and keen golfer Bill Clinton would show up to watch the action. If he had, he would have found Colin Montgomerie in confident mood. Fresh from his five-stroke victory in Northumberland, he now led the second major of the year by a single stroke over Steve Stricker and Hal Sutton after a superb 65. It was an exceptional round and even his playing partners, Davis Love III and a fresh-faced Phil Mickelson, were stunned by the quality of his play. 'Both Davis and Phil were very complimentary about my ball-striking after that first round at Congressional,' recalled Montgomerie. 'And looking back that was as well as I've ever played. To shoot sixty-five round there was a good effort.'

It is fairly certain they did not say the same in the second round. It all went wrong for the Scot after a rain delay contributed to a birdie-free second round of 76. Hitting only five fairways out of fourteen, compared with thirteen the day before, Monty lost the plot completely in a bad-tempered display that did a huge amount to sour his relationship with American golf fans. Mumbling under his breath, he told one particularly noisy fan, 'Why don't you save that for the Ryder Cup?'

It got worse. 'Cut that out!' he shouted at another who had the nerve to call out 'You're the man!' after a Mickelson drive.

'Sorry, buddy,' said the fan apologetically.

'No, you're not,' responded an outraged Montgomerie, when he really should have kept his mouth tight shut. 'You're not sorry at all.'

'You're right,' said the man, walking away in disdain, 'I'm not!'

As usual, Montgomerie had his excuses ready as the British press pack made a beeline for him after the round, blaming his poor health, the steam-room weather and, most of all, the antagonistic behaviour of the home fans. Complaining at everything from noisy cameramen to inefficient marshalling, the atmosphere became so poisonous at one stage that he began to fear for his wife Eimear, who was following him from outside the ropes.

In direct contrast, Tom Lehman described how his 'concentration had definitely gone up a level' to cope with the distractions of US Open golf after his second-place finish the previous year. Perhaps the increasingly irritated Scot should have asked the new tournament leader for his advice, because the weekend would prove an emotional rollercoaster as events unfolded over the final two rounds. Four strokes behind going into the weekend, the excuses came thick and fast. Certainly the weather had been a factor over the first two rounds but it was the same for everyone. 'I haven't been well since I've been here and I don't feel well now,' he complained bitterly, 'and I tend to suffer more than most with the heat and humidity.'

Another rain delay on the Saturday saw the tournament leaders return early on Sunday morning at 7.00 a.m. to finish off the third round. Lehman had started the day with a two-stroke lead over Jeff Maggert and Ernie Els and three ahead of Montgomerie, but by the time all four players had reached the eleventh hole of the final round, they were tied at four under par. Two hours later, the 27-year-old Els walked off the final green still at that number with the broken hopes of his rivals strewn behind him.

As predicted, the tournament went right down to the wire. With Maggert falling back over the closing nine holes on Sunday and Lehman pulling his approach into the water on seventeen, the destiny of the championship was decided by a single stroke of brilliance by Els on the same hole. Described as 'the shot of the year', his five-iron approach from 212 yards to within a few paces of the pin on the dangerous peninsular green was the paper-thin margin of victory as his final-round 69 proved just enough. Montgomerie in comparison slipped from a share of the lead on the seventeenth as his own approach shot from 203 yards came up short in the right-hand rough. A poor chip left him a five-foot par putt that he later called 'probably the most important putt that I ever hit'.

Once again his concentration was disturbed. Glaring menacingly at those he felt responsible, the inevitable miss led to a bogey and a two-shot swing after Els holed out for his birdie. It was Montgomerie in a nutshell and, by the time his attempt at birdie from 25 feet came up short on the last, the tournament was over. Standing on the final green, Montgomerie could only look on as his nemesis holed out for his second US Open victory. Yet another opportunity wasted, he was unable to match the South African's superb four-under-par effort for 23 holes on Sunday, including recording three birdies in the five holes of his unfinished third round.

Coming up one stroke short in the final round at the Congressional had also proved a cruel replay of past disappointments. Struggling to keep pace with Els, he made seven consecutive pars on the back nine with some clutch putting but it had still not been enough. Afterwards none of the assembled media expected much in the way of an interview. His face was black with disbelief and their chances decreased considerably when Eimear appeared at the back of the eighteenth green to console her husband. When he spotted her he was simply overcome and began to sob loudly in her arms. It was a heart-wrenching display of emotion and as they walked away no one expected him to return to face the press. But return he did and, having pulled himself together, he walked up to a gathering of reporters by the scorer's position and said brusquely, 'I shall do this once. We can do it here or in the interview tent.'

Moments later, Monty was in the media centre fielding questions with humour and humility. Gracious in his praise of Els, he was asked how it felt to have recorded two seconds and a third in the US Open since 1992 and still not to have won any of the four major championships? 'If I knock on the door enough, as I seem to be doing, especially in this tournament, the door will open one day,' he said, facing the question head on. 'I've just got to be patient.'

What about the crying? 'Yes, I cried after the round,' he admitted candidly. 'Having come so close a few times, you do get quite emotional. I'm only human.'

It had been a watershed tournament in the career of Colin Montgomerie: he had now lost twice to Ernie Els, the first being the 1994 US Open play-off at boiling Oakmont. In between he had also lost the 1995 PGA Championship in a play-off to Steve Elkington. Add to that his third-place finish in the 1992 US Open at Pebble Beach after it seemed nobody would catch his clubhouse target, and a pattern was emerging. 'Funny things happen in majors,' Ernie had said at his own press conference. 'You've just got to hang in there.'

It was good advice but Monty was starting to have nagging doubts about his ability to win a major. Many years later he conceded that he wanted victory at Congressional perhaps 'a little bit too much and if you want something that badly, sometimes it doesn't quite come to you'.

Taking the positives out of his second-place finish in the US Open, Montgomerie's European season went from strength to strength. Winning the Irish Open at the end of June, there was the possibility he could move up to the number-one position in the world from his current place at number two. All he had to do was win at Loch Lomond and for Greg Norman to miss the cut on the PGA Tour in America. With the Australian in the form of his life, it was never going to happen and Monty knew it: 'He didn't miss the cut, I didn't win, and the gap widened,' said the realistic Scot. 'And then a Mr Woods entered the fray and stopped everything.'

A few weeks later in July, Montgomerie returned to his 'home' course at Royal Troon for the Open Championship. Hopes were understandably high for a Scottish victory and Monty was in a positive frame of mind, despite his recent US Open experience. 'Immediately after Congressional I was disappointed,' he admitted. 'You can't not be, but looking at the overview of the championship on the plane, I actually took a very positive view of the situation and that's why I have played well since.' For once, a typical bout of 'Monty-speak' was backed up by the facts. In the three weeks leading up to the Open Championship, Montgomerie had won the Irish Open and finished tied eleventh and tenth to put a firm stranglehold on the Order of Merit.

It was to be a similar story of disappointment in the Open, though. Beginning with a 76, any confidence he did have was quickly blown away in the high winds that swept mercilessly across the Ayrshire links during the opening round. While he would eventually recover to finish in the top thirty, it had been a tough four days in front of his home supporters. There was better news to come in the US PGA Championship at Winged Foot in Mamaroneck, New York. Finishing the week tied thirteenth – fifteen strokes behind winner Davis Love III – his four rounds of 74, 71, 67 and 72 gave him a boost of confidence moving into the last quarter of the year.

Back in Europe Montgomerie registered four top-five finishes in his remaining seven events, including two second-places in the British Masters and Linde German Masters in September. Bernhard Langer, who had recorded four victories over the year in the Italian Open, the Benson and Hedges International, the Czech Open and the Linde German Masters, really must have wondered what he had to do to get ahead in the Order of Merit! (The answer was miss fewer cuts – he had five to Montgomerie's zero.)

Putting their money-list rivalry aside for the week of the Ryder Cup, Langer and Monty would prove unbeatable as partners in the first match to visit mainland Europe. Unfortunately it was the hugely controversial run-up to the match in Spain that caused the Scottish professional most trouble as the tabloid newspapers investigated the incident dubbed 'Monty-gate' . . .

9. MONTYGATE!

The 'Montygate' affair took everyone by surprise, not least Montgomerie himself. In the weeks leading up to the Ryder Cup in Spain, he expressed the view that American team member Jeff Maggert was not that intimidating to play against, and his team-mate Brad Faxon was not ready to compete as he 'is going through a divorce and mentally I don't think he will be with it'.

The response was immediate. The normally placid Fred Funk responded angrily, telling *GolfWeek* magazine, 'He's the jerk of the world as far as I'm concerned – and you can write that down because when I see him I'm going to tell him to his face.'

'Taking shots at a guy's personal life is a little too much,' said the normally reserved Loren Roberts. 'You don't want to alienate guys. It's unfortunate.'

Bob Estes then added to the debate, saying, 'Who's Monty going to play practice rounds with? I always knew he was a crybaby. I respect his skills, but when he starts with the low blows ... that's poor ... I think when he comes to play over here he's going to get the cold shoulder from a lot of guys.'

Comment and counter-comment pinged back and forth across the Atlantic for days as Montgomerie sought to clarify his comments with little success. In the end an uneasy truce was declared and it was against this acrimonious background that both teams gathered in southern Spain for the Ryder Cup in September. (Faxon sensibly chose to stay out of the argument, but said after beating Montgomerie in the quarter-finals of the World Match Play Championships after the Ryder Cup in October: 'I hope Monty does not get cold-shouldered. I don't think he was being mean-spirited when he said the stuff he did.')

After all the media hype surrounding qualification for the Ryder Cup and Montgomerie's inflammatory comments, it must have been a relief to the European side to get the match under way at Valderrama in San Roque. Consistently rated the number-one course on the Continent, it was also the first time the Ryder Cup had been played outside of Great Britain and the United States.

Home to the Volvo Masters from 1988 onwards, the testing layout winds its way through a forest of ancient cork and was designed by Robert Trent Jones on the instructions of the golf-club owner and lifetime president, Jaime Ortiz Patiño. With the prevailing Levanter wind always a factor, the course had a reputation of never being in anything less than immaculate condition. A true risk-and-reward course, it was considered the ideal venue for the Ryder Cup and that is how it proved in 1997.

Highlighted by team captain Seve Ballesteros as one of his key players, Montgomerie began the week partnered by the experienced Bernhard Langer. Out last in the morning four-balls, it was certainly not the best start they could have wished for, losing 3 and 2 to the highly rated pairing of Tiger Woods and Mark O'Meara. The nerves must have been jangling as the two Europeans found themselves matched against the same American pair in the afternoon foursomes. Not for the last time that week, Monty came through in a clinch. Striking the ball superbly well, he and Langer avenged their earlier defeat with a 5 and 3 victory to make it honours even.

On the second day it was success all the way for Mont-gomerie. Leading the Europeans out in both the morning and afternoon matches, he recorded two wins from two – first with rookie Darren Clarke in the fourballs against Couples and Love III, then with Langer once more in the foursomes against Janzen and Furyk. Repaying the faith Ballesteros had put in him, the Scot showed what a cool nerve he had, winning both games on the final green.

As both teams appeared for the singles, the match was still finely balanced with Europe holding a slender two-point advantage. Traditionally stronger on the final day, the US made the expected comeback, taking four of the opening six matches. Montgomerie knew his game, going out in the third-last match against the tough American Scott Hoch, was pivotal – but even he could not predict how important it would ultimately prove. Neither player was able to assert himself in a tense battle. Then, after a superb birdie on the penultimate hole to draw level, it was somehow right that Montgomerie would be offered the chance for glory.

With Langer having defeated Brad Faxon minutes earlier, his was now the only game left on the course. Having been alone all day, Montgomerie was suddenly joined by most of the European team as he exited the seventeenth green. As experienced as he was, it made him uncomfortable to realise that he was now 'playing for them and not for me'. He was doing the job Seve had given him and just wanted to be left alone to complete it. After his tee shot split the eighteenth fairway, he felt a lot better. This was an opportunity for lasting glory and he would grab it with both hands as Hoch failed to find the green with his second. Moments later, Monty rolled his birdie putt to within a few inches and the halved point Europe needed to win the Ryder Cup was assured. The trophy effectively won, it was Seve Ballesteros who gifted the American his twenty-foot par putt for an undeserved half.

Leading Europe to a narrow 14½–13½ over Tom Kite's American team, Monty could now look forward to a Spanish double. With everything still in the balance for the Order of Merit a few weeks later in Spain, he had a huge slice of luck at the Volvo Masters at Montecastillo. With the tournament cut to three days because of unseasonably bad weather, his eighth place after three rounds put him seven places above Langer, his nearest challenger for the money list. With play ruled out on the Sunday, the German had no choice but to accept the result in good spirit. In the end, Montgomerie had come through under the most severe pressure imaginable and deserved the all the plaudits he received.

European number one since 1993, Colin Montgomerie had beaten the long-standing record of four Order of Merit titles held by Peter Oosterhuis. Yet there was a hint of disquiet in the Monty camp. Frustrated at not having captured one of the game's glittering prizes, the 34-year-old professional knew that time was not on his side to win that first major championship. Despite his failings, he was an intelligent and thoughtful character who recognised just how much winning one actually meant. Not in terms of financial security – he had that already – but the longer-term historic perspective. Having spent so many years chasing Peter Oosterhuis's seemingly unbeatable record, he had now improved on it, but at what cost?

Born within fifty miles of Prestwick Golf Club – home to the first Open Championship in 1860 – Montgomerie knew better than most that the only lasting testimony to a golfer's skill was having his name engraved on a major trophy. Money-driven Order of Merit titles will inevitably disappear as the game becomes more global but major champions will be remembered as long as golf is played. A perfect example was Oosterhuis himself: Winner of the European Order of Merit from 1971 to 1974, he was a hugely popular figure with British golf fans in the 1970s with over twenty victories worldwide. A former Walker Cup and Eisenhower Trophy golfer, 'Oosty', like Monty, also had an excellent record in the Ryder Cup along with two second-place finishes in the majors. Today, he is a respected on-air commentator for both CBS in America and Sky Sports in the United Kingdom, but ask any modern-day golf fan to point him out in a crowd, and they would struggle. A salutary lesson in what can happen to even the best-known professionals if that elusive major continues to elude them. Still, Monty had more immediate concerns as the

row caused by his comments about American players continued to rumble on well after the final ball had been struck
at the Volvo Masters.

Montgomerie had already written to US Ryder Cup captain
Tom Kite and every member of the US team, apologising for
any ill feeling that may have been caused by his comments in
the run-up to the match. His management company IMG then
issued a statement in the hope that it would draw a line under
the entire affair. Speaking at the World Match Play Championship at Wentworth in October, Monty addressed the
hushed ranks of the British media as he read it out:

In the light of some of the recent press coverage both in
Europe and the US regarding alleged comments of mine,
concerning members of the US Ryder Cup team, I would
like today to present to you what I believe to be a more
balanced view of the issues. When I was asked to
comment on the US Ryder Cup team my remarks did not
come out as I intended and I regret that this has occurred.
I especially regret the personal nature of remarks about
members of the team. I have written to each person on
the American team who was named in the press and to
captain Tom Kite. And I have made special efforts to
discuss this situation with Brad Faxon and I shall always
be grateful to him and shall respect his understanding,
which under such circumstances has been so professional.
As regards some of the reporting of my comments, my
words have at the very least been taken out of context
and twisted to suit the purposes of the writer. It goes
without saying that I have great respect for the performances and abilities of all the players in the US Ryder Cup
team and I am pleased to count many of them among my
friends. It has been particularly disappointing to me that
other parties not directly related to the situation have
taken it upon themselves to comment so aggressively on
uncorroborated and distorted reports. Nevertheless, I
would hope that this issue could now be considered at an
end.

It was typical 'Monty-speak'. Unable to resist a sideswipe at the British golf media, his comment about how 'my words have at the very least been taken out of context and twisted to suit the purposes of the writer' was typical of his inability to accept blame for anything. No tournament victories on the PGA Tour? That was down to the rowdy fans. No major championship? That had to be the fault of (a) the conditions, (b) his poor luck or (c) the crowds again.

Perm any two from three and take your pick. As for practising hard allied to a dedicated fitness regime – that was for other players, not Montgomerie (throughout his career, he actually relished the fact that he did not work as hard on the practice ground as other professionals). As for the apology, what else could he do? He had already dropped the bombshell that he was considering spending more time playing tournaments in the United States in 1998, and not even Monty was thick-skinned enough to think he could do that with the crowds *and* his fellow players against him!

'I've had better weekends, I must admit,' he said afterwards. 'I've put this together and hopefully this will finish it. I don't want to answer questions.'

Not that Montgomerie made many friends on this side of the Atlantic with his acerbic comments about the state of European greens. Hugely critical of the courses he was 'forced' to play in countries like Switzerland and Germany he said, 'Playing on bad greens like in Crans-sur-Sierre and in Munich means you have to work so hard to get a proper putting stroke going again ... The Americans meanwhile will come with near-perfect strokes because they usually putt on near-perfect greens.'

It was a subject he returned to after beating Phil Mickelson in a made-for-television challenge match at Cordillera golf resort in Colorado. Presented with a $100,000 cheque from former US President Gerald Ford (and a Rolex watch for Eimear), he complimented the owners on the fantastic condition of the three-year-old course, saying, 'It's a pity we do not have this type of course in Europe.'

Returning to the subject of playing full-time on the PGA Tour, he gave the impression that he was leaving the

European Tour for good. 'I have a big, big decision to make,' he told the media in September. 'If I were a bachelor I would be off to America tomorrow, but there are a lot of considerations. For instance, I have just sunk all my money into a new house. And taking the family to the States, especially with the children so young, would have its problems. Yet the temptation is growing stronger and yes, the kind of experiences players have had on the greens over the past few weeks will figure large when I finally decide.'

Another factor was the ever-expanding distances European Tour players were expected to travel in a year, including trips to the Middle East, Australia and South Africa – compared with much shorter trips across mainland America. Assured of a place on the lucrative PGA Tour, Montgomerie had until 6 October – the cut-off point for applications – to decide whether he wanted to take up US Tour membership or not.

Fearing that his decision might lead to an exodus of top European talent, the next month or so would prove a long wait for Ken Schofield, executive director of the European Tour, but at least the year ended on a high note for Monty. The first player to win five consecutive Order of Merit titles, the 34-year-old Scot was also presented with his third Golfer of the Year award. The very personification of consistency, Montgomerie made the halfway cut in all nineteen European Tour events he had entered, finishing an impressive 177 under par for the season.

10. THE COMFORT ZONE

T he 1998 European Tour season began with media speculation about where Montgomerie would play the majority
of his golf in the coming season. After his outburst the
previous September, it was generally accepted that he would
be heading over the Atlantic with his family in 1998. The
subject of much debate over the winter months, the possibility
of him competing full-time on the PGA Tour was the logical
progression for a player who had nothing left to prove in
Europe. As two-time major winner Tony Jacklin commented,
'How can he really expect to be competitive in the majors
without spending much of the season competing on the PGA
Tour in America?'

Even the official 'European Tour Media Guide' described
him in such glowing terms that he must have wondered what
more he could achieve. 'Montgomerie has quite clearly
reached that stage in his career on the European Tour when
he is not only the man to beat,' it opined, 'but stands also as
the player [by] whom all others judge themselves.'

But by November 1997 he had already made up his mind.
Winner of the individual prize at the World Cup of Golf at
Kiawah Island that month with brilliantly consistent rounds
of 68, 66, 66 and 66, he remained privately convinced that he

could compete for the majors just as successfully from Europe. 'Take a look at Faldo,' said Monty. 'He won his majors while still playing in Europe and so did Langer.'

While he intended to play more tournaments in America, especially around the majors, Montgomerie announced that he had a responsibility to support the European Tour as a full member. His final decision to stay in Europe – even with a 'considerably reduced schedule' – brought a collective sigh of relief from the European Tour and sponsors alike. 'There are two paramount factors in my decision,' announced Monty. 'The first, as it always has and always will be, is that my family comes before anything else and the schedule I am choosing will work for all of us. Secondly, the European Tour has been very good for me and I hope I have repaid it a little ... The game of golf is now truly global and I believe one's choice of home base does not affect one's ability to compete at the highest standard, which I look forward to doing in the coming years.'

It was a stronger, fitter-looking Montgomerie who began his 1998 campaign at the Dubai Desert Classic at the end of March. Exercising during a seven-week break at home, his confidence, along with his bank balance, was on a real high after winning the $1m Anderson Consulting World Championship of Golf in Arizona the first week in January. Playing at the Grayhawk Golf Club's Raptor Course in Scottsdale, he defeated Davis Love III by two holes in the 36-hole final to claim the biggest payday of his career since he won the 1996 Nedbank Million Dollar Challenge in South Africa. The culmination of a yearlong match-play tournament featuring 32 players, the qualification process was divided into four groups – United States, European, Japanese and International. Montgomerie qualified for the final after winning the European group back in May at the Oxfordshire. Defeating Ernie Els, winner of the International group, in the semifinal, the only downside was that it was not an officially sanctioned PGA Tour event. That would only happen the next year when it would be renamed the Anderson Consulting Match Play, featuring an elite 64-man field based on the Official World Golf Rankings. (For years to come, Monty's critics would hold his lack of an *official* tournament victory in the United States against him.)

The Scot had now won £4m in prize money over the past two seasons – more than any other professional – yet he would have given up every last cent for that first major championship. 'I'm hoping, not expecting, to change that this year,' said Montgomerie in Arizona. 'That will to win has never, ever diminished. I've always wanted to win and it's even stronger now because people are expecting it.'

Armed with a new set of irons (and the old ones just in case he did not like them), Montgomerie returned to the United States in March, where he recorded three top-ten finishes in succession. Angered by a magazine article that labelled him 'The Goon from Troon', he missed the cut at the Doral-Ryder Open – his first missed cut anywhere in the world for almost eighteen months! In mid-April, he finished a highly creditable tied eighth in the Masters at Augusta with Darren Clarke and the reigning US Masters Champion, Tiger Woods before returning home to await the birth of his third child, Cameron Stuart. After a short break, Montgomerie returned to action at Wentworth where he comprehensively saw off a top-class field to win the Volvo PGA Championship.

Following a trip to Paris to watch Scotland play Brazil in the soccer World Cup, Montgomerie headed to America for the US Open at Olympic Country Club in San Francisco. Looking to make a strong challenge, he was surprised by the hostile reception he received from some sections of the home crowd. Partnered by Jim Furyk and David Duval, he was consistently heckled throughout his second round. Monty said afterwards that he had not been distracted, but Duval disagreed as the Scot's 74 put tournament leader Payne Stewart effectively out of range: 'I've not known it as bad as that before,' said the American, 'and it's not an obstacle anyone else has except Colin. It certainly makes it more difficult.'

Reports of rowdiness in the crowd reached United States Golf Association executive director David Fay, who immediately raised security levels around Montgomerie. 'When it was reported on the radio to me,' he said. 'I immediately sent out added security, and it will be there again tomorrow.'

David Feherty once described how Colin Montgomerie attracted idiots on golf courses the way Arnold Palmer attracted pretty girls, but why now? The rumpus concerning his comments about Brad Faxon was over nine months ago, but the brooding resentment felt by American fans lingered on. Exploding in the final round of the US Open, shouts like 'get in the trap' were commonplace as matters threatened to boil over.

Not that Monty helped the situation. Catching a bunker off the eighth tee, someone in the crowd shouted out, 'You should put your driver away, you jerk!' Red-faced with anger, Montgomerie turned on his heel before shouting: 'You should be ejected!'

Things were no better up at the green. Putting out, Montgomerie stomped off towards the next tee when a shout of 'Go home, Monty!' echoed through the trees. Bristling with anger, the Scot demanded to know who had said it.

Silence.

Reacting to the crowd was a mistake and even with armed state troopers on hand the atmosphere was openly antagonistic as Montgomerie asked again, 'I want to know who said that?' Refusing all requests to move on, the spotlight settled on a large man with a cigar hanging from his mouth. 'Why did you say that?' shouted Monty after he finally admitted making the comment.

'Because of the Ryder Cup,' replied the fan.

'There was nothing wrong with the Ryder Cup except we won!' announced Montgomerie, before walking off to catcalls and slow hand claps.

'I have had happier weeks,' admitted Monty afterwards. 'And in spite of last year I certainly didn't anticipate any of what happened. My partner Tom Kite gave me great support and so did a USGA official. It is all to do with the Ryder Cup. Even though I had eleven strong men at my side at Valderrama, I seem to be regarded by some Americans as the cause of winning it.'

Finishing with a 77 for an eleven-over-par total of 221, Montgomerie ended the week fifteen strokes behind the new champion Payne Stewart. Refusing to speak to the media afterwards other than a cursory 'not today, thank you', he appeared out of sorts both on and off the golf course. Asked whether he would continue to compete in American PGA Tour events, Monty shrugged off the suggestion, saying that he was 'not soured by the incidents. I always like playing here and will continue to do so.'

Having witnessed first-hand the confrontation between Monty and the fans throughout the day, his playing partner Tom Kite tried to defuse the situation by saying, 'Colin is a nice man and a good player and I like playing with him . . . There were some unwarranted remarks out there but it happens all over the world, not just here.'

On the subject of unwarranted remarks, the situation had not been helped by a number of local journalists portraying Montgomerie as moody and petulant. One Saturday news-paper even published the headline GOLF'S BASKET CASE, with a photo of him next to it! The article was not much better as it argued the reason he did not have many fans in America was 'they have all been scared away, one by one'!

Whether it inflamed the crowd or not, one article published before the final round even ended with a wish that Mont-gomerie would lose by ten shots. Placing a question mark over the sale of alcohol at future USGA-run events, David Fay commented: 'Colin seems to be like a lightning rod for these guys.' Insisting that changes would have to be made, he continued, 'We don't want to see any player treated like that.'

Colin Montgomerie returned to more familiar territory in the 127th Open Championship in July. Sadly his lacklustre performance in the US Open at Olympic a month before was repeated at Royal Birkdale as he crashed out at the halfway stage. In May 1998, approaching 35 and with a wealth of top-flight championship golf behind him, Montgomerie had offered a small insight into the huge pressure he was under as *the-best-golfer-never-to-win-a-major*: 'Expectation is greater than ever before,' he admitted. 'From myself, my family, the media, the public and even the players. I have to perform, therefore I'm even more determined to do so than ever before.'

Sadly for Montgomerie, his family, the media, the public and the players, his performance in the third major of the year was hugely disappointing. In some ways, it mirrored the frustration many of his supporters felt. He was certainly good enough to win a major, so why did he fail so often to complete the job? Indeed, these were questions Colin must have been asking himself as the season rolled on.

Something had to change before the season turned into a complete flop. He sought advice from renowned short-game coach, Dave Pelz, hooking up shortly before the PGA Championship at Sahalee Country Club near Seattle. The statistics spoke for themselves. He was rated the 'worst putter' from the top-ten leading contenders in the world rankings, it was a decision that would eventually turn his season around. 'I've come off too many tournaments having played well and not got the results,' he said before the opening round. 'I've had enough of that and I possibly regret not seeing a specialist about my putting before.'

Another important change was his work ethic. Never one to linger long on the practice ground, Monty rarely hit more than 100 balls per session, far fewer in a pre-round warm-up. To the surprise of players and media alike, Montgomerie was a constant fixture on the practice putting green at Sahalee, where he eventually finished the week tied in 44th place. Returning to Europe, Montgomerie renewed his partnership with boyhood coach Bill Ferguson. The effect was immediate as he bounced back to complete his second European Tour victory of the year in the One-to-One British Masters at the Forest of Arden course. Having lagged behind Lee Westwood and Darren Clarke in the race for number-one spot in Europe, Monty was now coming up on the rails fast. 'It's not that I desperately want to win my sixth European Order of Merit,' said a typically diplomatic Monty. 'It's just that I don't want anybody else to win it!'

Montgomerie posted rounds of 65, 68, 66 and 67 for his third win of the season in Europe at the German Masters, Cologne. Like a thoroughbred racehorse taking the lead going down the final straight, his one-stroke victory took him ahead of both Clarke and Westwood in the race to be top of the money list. It had been a gutsy win over two rising stars of the European Tour and must have delighted his short-game guru Dave Pelz. 'I think in the last month, I've had the best putting statistics of my entire career,' said the Scot. 'I was averaging 26.5 putts per round during that spell, which was about three putts per round better than I had done earlier in the season.'

Clarke and Westwood kept the pressure on Montgomerie right down to the wire. With Monty taking the week off, Westwood captured the Belgacom Open the following week to draw £66,660 closer. Whether that result gave Monty cause for concern is unclear, despite his early-season comments that winning a sixth Order of Merit was 'a low priority'.

Montgomerie had long believed that he had to improve season on season to retain his number-one status, citing the consistently high standard of the players he could be relied on to reel off whom he had beaten en route to winning his five previous titles. In 1993, Montgomerie overtook Nick Faldo by winning at Valderrama. A year later he held off a strong challenge by Seve Ballesteros and Bernhard Langer. In 1995, it was a down-to-the-wire battle with fellow Scot Sam Torrance. In 1996, Ian Woosnam was forced to concede defeat with one event to go and the following year Langer came through to challenge his supremacy once more.

What was certain is that the end-of-season shoot-out at the Volvo Masters in Spain would decide who would finish top dog in Europe. The mathematics were certainly intriguing: to win the Order of Merit, Irishman Darren Clarke had to win with Montgomerie finishing no better than ninth and Westwood finishing no better than third. Westwood needed to win with Montgomerie well down the field. In the end, it came down to how high – or low – Monty would finish at Montecastillo. If he played well enough, there was simply nothing either of his rivals could do about it.

Set up for a dramatic showdown in the sun, the possibility of a major anticlimax loomed large. What if they all played poorly? The pre-tournament publicity promised much, but this time it actually delivered. With all three playing quite brilliantly the Volvo Masters proved a wonderful backdrop for all the final-round drama. Adding spice to an already red-hot competition, Clarke fired a blistering last round of 63 to post an unassailable 17-under-par total. Westwood, after superb rounds of 70, 68 and 67, faltered with a 75 to drop out of the race. It was now down to Colin to take full advantage, and he did.

Playing behind Clarke, Montgomerie knew what was needed. Trailing tournament leader Peter O'Malley by a single stroke going into the final day, a steady rather than spectacular round meant winning the event was probably beyond him. However, finishing in the top five and winning the Order of Merit for a record sixth time certainly was not. So, like the experienced competitor he is, he quietly cruised in with a score of 68 and captured third place. Monty was number one again and, perhaps most satisfyingly of all, he had shut the door firmly on two of his closest rivals to do it.

'It was nice to know I was on top for another year,' Monty reflected. 'I wouldn't change anything. I am very proud of the six Order of Merits. I would like to win a major, but I wouldn't like to win one and then have gone into oblivion as a few players have. This is a game of consistency and I've proved I've been at the top for six years. That means a lot.'

With Augusta, Olympic and Royal Birkdale now a distant memory, Monty had turned his season around completely. Honoured by the Queen with an MBE (Member of the British Empire medal) in November, his growing celebrity was acknowledged by a Christmas night appearance on the popular BBC satirical TV sports quiz *They Think It's All Over*. Taking a not-so-gentle ribbing from team captains Gary Lineker and David Gower, Monty took it all in good humour. The only time the mask slipped was after footage was shown of him missing a short putt, followed by another guest shouting how 'crap' he must be, not being able to hole it from that distance. The cold stare Monty gave him was priceless! The rest he took in his stride, even when someone joked, 'It was reported that Colin has recently been burglarised but all the thief got away with was twenty runners-up medals.' Completely untrue, of course, but it was the nature of the show to ridicule and cajole. Montgomerie in fact had won twenty titles up to that point but at least it showed he could laugh at himself, and in PR terms it was worth its weight in gold.

So what about that elusive first major? Older than both Tiger Woods and Ernie Els, he realised that for as long as his trophy cabinet remained empty of a green jacket or Open winner's medal, it would always be a case of 'Colin Montgomerie was a good player but . . .'

'I have let myself down mentally on some occasions but no one is perfect,' he admitted later. 'It takes some players a long time to come through. It took Mark O'Meara until he was forty-one. I'm only thirty-five and I'm as ambitious as I have ever been.'

He might bemoan his lack of luck in the majors, but it did not explain why he had missed the cut in five of his last seven appearances in the Open Championship. With Carnoustie due in 1999 to make its first appearance on the rota since 1975, he looked at its reintroduction as a positive sign. 'My record is poor and I've got to do something about it,' Monty said. 'Maybe I have to take the week before off and go and practise links golf . . . But Carnoustie is a course I like and I've played well there – I hold the course record – so possibly that's my best chance of not necessarily winning but hopefully doing well.'

Always able to talk a good fight, only time would tell if Monty could see out the last year of the old millennium with the major victory he craved.

European golf fans hardly saw Monty in the early part of 1999. Preferring to spend the first quarter of the year in the United States, the slimmer, fitter Scot was determined to break his competitive duck and win on American soil. The facts spoke for themselves: the Players' Championship in Florida in late March was his 42nd tournament on the PGA Tour and he had barely broken into the top ten in any of them. (His individual victory in the World Cup at Kiawah Island in 1997 and the World Match Play event in Arizona a year later were not deemed 'official' events and did not count. 'The first was primarily a team event,' said Monty defending his record, 'but the other was a really good win, beating Ernie Els in the semis and Davis Love in the final, but it has had no impact over here.')

So dominant in Europe, he was increasingly seen as a big fish in a small pond. Better known for his on-course bust-ups, not even his fellow professionals saw him as a credible threat when it came to winning in America. Indeed, the only people who expected him to win were his many fans watching on satellite television back home in Europe! 'I have proved myself in Europe and now I'd love to win over here,' he said prior to the Tournament Players Championship at Sawgrass. 'People expect me to win and it does grind a bit. I have been second a number of times but experience has shown that if you are one ahead, you have to be three ahead. There is no point just going for the fat of the green. You have to attack and attack and attack because there will be twenty other guys doing that and one of them will win.'

This reduced status was reflected in the treatment he received at the Bay Hill Invitational the week before, when he was drawn in the first group of the day. These early-morning slots are usually reserved for rookies, journeymen and veteran pros killing time before they reach fifty and a slot on the lucrative Champions Tour. No wonder Monty saw it as a snub and complained bitterly at his treatment. Here was the six-time European number one and Ryder Cup hero plying his trade on dew-swept greens and playing in front of fewer people than your average winter alliance!

It was not much better at the Players Championship, where even a second-place finish in 1996 could not guarantee him a plum spot among players like Woods and Els. It was time to return to Europe but, having been away for five weeks or more, he had some catching up to do. Perhaps he wanted to lull his competitive rivals into a false sense of security. If so, it certainly worked. By the end of April, he languished like a basking shark in the non-threatening waters of 34th place on the Order of Merit. While he boasted meagre earnings of £64,061, rivals like David Howell, winner in Dubai, had already placed a couple of fingers on the Order of Merit title with early-season earnings of £256,000! Howell, Ernie Els, Jarmo Sandelin and Miguel Angel Jimenez had all trespassed into the Scot's private fiefdom, with the great man nowhere to be seen. The year was almost a third over and where was the European number one?

Three weeks later they had their answer. Boldly predicting that he would win three tournaments in a row, he very nearly did! Victory in the Benson and Hedges at the Oxfordshire and the PGA Championship at Wentworth, plus a top-twenty finish in the Deutsche Bank, saw him rocket up the money list. He even won the World Match Play at Wentworth in convincing style. In fact, throughout the entire season he was unstoppable in everything but the majors. And, while never really threatening to win, his record in all four of them was excellent: at Augusta he played solidly for a share of eleventh; in the US Open at Pinehurst he overcame pre-championship rumours of crowd problems to finish tied fifteenth behind Payne Stewart; at Carnoustie he again came fifteenth; and at Medinah in the PGA he finished a highly creditable sixth behind Tiger Woods.

In the race for the European Order of Merit, further wins at the Standard Life tournament at Loch Lomond, the Scandinavian Masters and the BMW International put him in an almost unassailable position. Even with the massive amount of prize money on offer in the final two events of the season – the Volvo Masters and the new WGC American Express Championship in Spain – rivals Garcia, Westwood and Goosen were too far back to make a credible challenge. There would be no repeat of last year's drama, no close finish, no final-round heroics. Monty was crowned European number one for a record seventh time.

It had proved a remarkable year in terms of tournament-winning success, yet Monty still had his critics, not least of whom was six-time major winner Nick Faldo. Competing in the Canadian Open in mid-September, Faldo accused Monty of living in a 'comfort zone' on the European Tour.

'It's a bit like a Jumbo Ozaki scenario,' he commented. 'He's great in his own back yard, he's comfortable, happy. He knows he's only got to play half-decent and he's going to be there. Even if he plays badly, he's the sort of guy who turns around a good score the next day and gets himself into contention.'

With Montgomerie looking for his third win in a row at the British Masters at Woburn it was an unwelcome distraction – especially the implication that he was running scared of the greater competition on the PGA Tour. 'He goes out and wins a couple of hundred thousand each week and goes home,' continued Faldo. 'I'd be comfortable if I did that every week. He likes to earn his fat cheques and there is no harm in that – if you're motivated by that. A few are. Most of us go for ten claret jugs!'

Returning to the hoary issue of spending more time playing tournaments in America, Montgomerie had reconciled himself to that question many years before – he just did not tell anyone! At the end of 1991, he seriously considered entering the PGA Tour Qualifying School with a view to playing a full season in 1992. After finishing fourth in the European Order of Merit, the plan was temporarily shelved as he made a concerted challenge for the number-one spot in 1992 (when he finished third).

Then, after Olivia was born in 1993, any thoughts of moving lock, stock and golf clubs to the United States were quietly forgotten. Even when he was three-four-five-times European number one, Montgomerie paid polite lip service to the journalists and so-called golf experts who told him he should be battling with the best on the other side of the Atlantic. As far as Monty was concerned, he had done his time in the USA at Houston Baptist University back in the 1980s and never had any real intention of going back. King of the Hill in Europe since 1993, he had everything he wanted – money, success, respect and family.

'Am I in a comfort zone staying back here in Europe?' asked Monty in an interview with respected golf writer Paul Trow.

Well, I like to be comfortable but I don't play golf for money now. It's more the thrill of competing and having a chance to win. I have the utmost respect for Nick Faldo, we all do. He's obviously struggling with his game right now and I think he was caught out by the press in Canada. It was his first time in the pressroom for a number of weeks and people were asking him questions about the Ryder Cup and of course my name came up. I think what he said was blown up to be honest.

As if to confirm the point, defending Woburn champion Montgomerie preferred to concentrate on recording his sixth victory of the year in Europe. Taking a slim overnight lead into the final round, the 'row' finally caught up with him on the front nine where there was a six-shot swing in the first seven holes between him and the eventual winner Bob May. Blaming his putting, he returned a 71 to the American's 67. Insisting that he would not add to the debate that Faldo had begun, he must have taken comfort from May's post-tournament comments. 'I have backed Monty for every major in the last three years and soon it is going to pay off,' he said. 'It is incredible that when I finally get my first win it is over one of the best players in the world, if not the best. If he played more in the States he would get more points and could be the world number one.'

Having expressed his desire to captain Europe in the Ryder Cup one day, the candid comments made by Faldo were questionable at best. In his defence, they were intended to inspire Monty and other home players to push themselves to the limit – the way Faldo had done himself over the past three decades. Unfortunately, his words fell on deaf ears after being somewhat misrepresented by the golfing media. Plus there was a far greater controversy brewing just around the corner in the forthcoming Ryder Cup at Brookline – a controversy in which Colin Montgomerie would play his full part.

11. THE BATTLE OF BROOKLINE

Captain Mark James and his European team arrived in Boston aiming for an unprecedented third successive Ryder Cup victory over the US. Leaving Heathrow on Concorde they were in upbeat mood and anxious to prove that, despite having seven rookies on the team, they were confident of retaining the famous trophy.

As always, there had been a great deal of pre-match hype surrounding the biennial contest, but the Europeans had consistently refused to be drawn into the war of words, which ranged over television coverage, payment for players, ticket allocation and how the profits should be spent. Fully aware of the firestorm that awaited his players, James refused to be drawn into further controversy. Leaving Heathrow, his words echoed the feelings of his players: 'The Ryder Cup, as I discovered from personal experience, is not only about nationalistic pride and passion. More than anything, those wonderful matches between Europe and the United States have demonstrated that the game of golf is synonymous with integrity, fair play and goodwill. Both Ben Crenshaw and myself agree that the 1999 Ryder Cup at the Country Club will follow those exemplary traditions.'

Less than one week later, James must have regretted his words as the 33rd Ryder Cup ended in defeat and recrimination. With Nick Faldo and Bernhard Langer not being chosen as wild-card picks, Montgomerie was considered the senior man on the European side at the age of 36. It was a responsibility he accepted with relish. Partnering his fellow Scot Paul Lawrie in both foursomes and fourballs, they proved a wonderfully strong pairing, racking up two wins and a half under the severest pressure imaginable – both on and off the golf course.

On the Saturday, the behaviour of the partisan New England crowds was simply outrageous. Twice during the day, Montgomerie backed away from the ball after someone in the crowd distracted him. Heckled for the second time on the sixth green, he sank a straightforward six-foot putt to win the hole before dramatically thrusting his fist towards the bleachers in triumph. 'It started on the sixth hole on the first morning,' said Monty afterwards, 'and it annoyed me to the extent that I took Paul Lawrie aside for a chat on the seventh tee. Paul had never experienced anything like it. I was annoyed to the extent that I didn't want to lose. So I didn't. No one likes playing under those circumstances.'

There was worse to come. In the run-up to the competition, David Feherty, the brilliant golf analyst for CBS Television, was accused of labelling the thin-skinned Scot 'Mrs Doubtfire' after the Robin Williams character in the 1993 movie of the same name. The witty Irishman consistently denied it, crediting his fellow golf pundit John Hawksworth as the originator of the title. He did, however, accept full blame for thinking up the barbed comment that 'Montgomerie had a face like a bulldog licking piss from a nettle!'

Whoever it was, the rowdy minority picked up on the nickname and throughout the opening day there were persistent shouts of 'Hey – Mrs Doubtfire!' and 'Mrs Doubtfire – you forgot your dress!'

Partnered by Paul Lawrie throughout the week, Montgomerie managed to ignore most of the flack as the Scottish pair beat Duval and Mickelson in the opening match of the morning foursomes. A hard-earned half point against Love III and Leonard in the afternoon contributed to an impressive 6–2 lead for Europe after Day One. With the US team looking at a third consecutive Ryder Cup defeat, the alcohol-fuelled comments became increasingly personal the following day. 'You're a fucking bum, Monty,' were mixed with chants of 'Tuna! Tuna!' – the nickname of former New England Patriots coach Charles 'Bill' Parcells, who bore an uncanny resemblance to the Scot. Contemplating a shot from the thirteenth fairway in their morning foursome match against Hal Sutton and Jeff Maggert on Friday, some idiot shouted 'Shank it!' as Monty prepared to hit his approach into the thirteenth green. Forced to pull away from another stroke an equally loud shout went up, 'You're going down, Monty!'

Even a golf course marshal, reportedly there to maintain order, approached the European number one with the comment: 'We don't hate you, Monty – we just want you to lose!'

He got his wish as Montgomerie and Lawrie lost by one hole to Sutton and Maggert. Not exactly known for his placid nature, the combative Sutton played his part in whipping up the gallery by gesturing to the crowds on the thirteenth fairway. 'I don't want them to call out to Colin,' he said later. 'What I wanted them to do was get behind us.'

With an appeal going out on local television to 'get behind our boys in the Ryder Cup', Montgomerie backed off a number of shots throughout the day, including a putt on the eighth green in the afternoon after a camera flashed in the crowd. Holing out, the big Scot cast a menacing glance in the offending direction before stomping off the green to catcalls from the gallery. 'Their behaviour was just ridiculous,' Lawrie said later.

Defeating Steve Pate and Tiger Woods 2 and 1 in the final fourball on Saturday afternoon, the Europeans took a seemingly impregnable four-point lead going into the singles the following day. Unfortunately the record-breaking 10–6 lead was not quite impregnable enough. In a day of high drama, the series of twelve singles took on a nightmarish appearance as one European after another fell to their American opponents. Inspired by a pre-match speech by presidential candidate George W Bush (not to mention a video message from curvaceous *Baywatch* star Pamela Anderson), team USA arrived on the first tee with the 'Stars and Stripes' still playing in their ears. Taking every opportunity to whip up the large galleries that followed each match, the atmosphere was not only fervently nationalistic, but also totally hostile to anybody foreign.

Asked by James to play the anchor role, Montgomerie was matched against reigning US Open Champion Payne Stewart in game nine. Competitive but scrupulously fair, the American suggested to Monty that *he* should deal with hecklers in the crowd. The Scot agreed, but even Stewart found the excitable gallery far beyond his ability to control them. With stewards unable – or perhaps unwilling – to bring offenders to justice, the whole match was played in an atmosphere totally out of place on a golf course. Comments to Monty became increasingly personal as they focused on his weight, his lack of success in the majors and even his Scottish ancestry. James Montgomerie, who listened first-hand to the insults, was forced to walk in as it became intolerable. 'They've only targeted Colin because he's such a good golfer,' he said to reporters. 'It's upsetting to hear hurtful things said about your own family but Colin is ready for any barrackers.'

On a day that will live in golfing infamy, Michael Bonallack, secretary of the R&A, simply described it as 'a bear pit'. Finding reserves of strength, Montgomerie not only competed brilliantly but also conducted himself like a six-time European number one. 'I never want to have to go through it again,' he would say later.

By the time Justin Leonard holed a massive putt across the seventeenth green to effectively win the Ryder Cup, the result of Montgomerie's game against Payne Stewart was rendered irrelevant. Yet amid the controversial scenes, which saw American players stampede towards Leonard before his opponent José Maria Olazábal had chance to reply with a putt of his own, both players still had to play out the eighteenth. One-down coming to the final green, the flamboyant American had the advantage but, in typical style, offered his hand to Montgomerie and effectively conceded the match. Having spent much of their match pointing out hecklers to the marshals, Stewart made one last apology about the crowd's behaviour. Amid the chaos that surrounded both men, it was an emotional moment as they headed back to the clubhouse arm-in-arm. (Payne Stewart was killed in an aeroplane tragedy barely a month later and, for years to come, Montgomerie would carry a photograph of them both prior to the singles match in his business folder.)

Not surprisingly, apologies from the American camp were not long in arriving. In a press conference a few days later, captain Crenshaw expressed his regret at the poor standard of behaviour both on and off the golf course that week. 'Still,' the American offered in his defence, 'the Europeans got pretty heated up when they beat us last time out . . .'

Someone else who got 'heated up' after the Ryder Cup ended was Colin Montgomerie. After three days of abuse at the hands of the hugely partisan crowd, the Scot was fit to bust and David Feherty, the man he blamed for the 'Mrs Doubtfire' crack, provided the ideal target. Entering the European team room at the Four Seasons Hotel in Boston on Sunday evening, barely hours after the match had ended, the Scot spotted his nemesis casually chatting to other team members. It was like a red rag to a bull as he filled his plate with Caesar salad from the buffet. Visibly shaking with anger he shouted out to Feherty, 'You have no right to be here!' before hurling the salad in his direction. Seconds later he stormed out and refused to return. Blaming him for many of his difficulties at Brookline that week, it followed a vitriolic attack on Feherty by his wife Eimear just 24 hours before. Jabbing her finger at the bemused CBS man, she accused him publicly of 'ruining' Monty's week and said that her husband would never submit to an interview by the Irishman again!

Making his apologies to his close friend Mark James, Feherty left without fuss, aware that Montgomerie would not re-enter the room with him present. Once again, the Scot's temper had got the better of him and it was an embarrassing episode for all concerned. Yet Feherty remained a huge fan of the contribution Montgomerie had made, not only to the Ryder Cup but European golf in general. 'For me it was over in a second,' he recalled years later. 'Like any great competitor he was upset at losing and I understand that. The Boston fans had been riding him all week and I felt that Monty *should* be with his team. That is why I left.'

Joking that Montgomerie's attempt to crown him with a salad bowl was 'the only bad shot he made all week', Feherty had been among the first to welcome Montgomerie to the ranks of the European Tour after he turned professional. Meeting in the player's hotel shortly before the Dutch Open at Hilversumsche in 1988, he recalled Monty's delight at wearing denim jeans because his father James did not approve of his son wearing them back home in Troon! Coming from different backgrounds with diametrically opposed senses of humour, the relationship between the two men would have its ups and downs. Known for his ability to debunk the largest of golfing egos, Feherty had his own unique take on why Monty had such a poor relationship with American golf fans. 'He's soft, and there's always a few who are going to play on that,' he said. 'The "Mrs Doubtfire" thing was the moment of truth', Feherty commented in an interview with *Golf Digest* magazine in the US. That was when he should have done the publicity shot with the powdered wig on, the tweed dress, the string of pearls and stout pair of walking shoes. They would have loved him if he'd done that. The fact is the vast majority of the people out here *want* to love him because there's an unembraceable human frailty to him that other players don't show. His big mistake was being hurt by it all.'

Though he declined an invitation to appear on the front of a top-selling US golf magazine dressed in pearls and a tweed dress, a discernable change in American opinion towards Montgomerie did take place in the months that followed. Fans and players alike now looked at Monty with a new level of respect. In the United States he was everything American sports fans liked in a competitor – a gritty street fighter who was not afraid to tell it like it was. Perhaps for the first time, they began to appreciate 'Monty' the same way British golf fans had for the past decade or more.

An important point had been proved and there was nothing more for Montgomerie to say. At Brookline, the more they shouted and heckled, the harder he tried. Protective of rookie Paul Lawrie, he simply got on with the job of winning golf matches. Lawrie applauded his Ryder Cup partner's comments. 'Over the first two days I played four rounds with him and can tell you it wasn't pretty,' said the 1999 Open Champion. 'Eimear, his wife, was crying on a couple of occasions and his father had to leave the course on Sunday. So I can understand his feelings on the subject and appreciate how the slightest little thing will have him on edge. People say just put it out of your mind, but that's such a hard thing to do.'

Putting David Feherty out of his mind proved tougher still. Constantly bumping into each other at tournaments, it would be three years before a lasting truce was agreed. Not that Feherty had a problem, but he agreed to a face-to-face with Montgomerie at the 2002 Ryder Cup at the Belfry at the behest of European team captain Sam Torrance. With Tiger Woods a fascinated bystander, the two former Ryder Cup colleagues finally came together in the corridor outside yet another European team room. With a handshake they finally buried the hatchet and agreed to let bygones be bygones.

Describing his experience at the Ryder Cup in Boston as a 'huge learning curve', Montgomerie truly believed it would be a springboard to major success the following year. Focusing on the remaining three months of the year, he knew the tournaments to come presented some golden opportunities to further both his world ranking position and his bank balance. In October, Montgomerie went head-to-head against some of the best players available in the Cisco World Match Play Championship at Wentworth. Suffering from toothache all week, he beat American Notah Begay III in the quarterfinals, Padraig Harrington in the semis and Mark O'Meara in the final.

Achieving a long-held dream to win the Wentworth event, Monty was a remarkable 29 under par for his 99 holes played. While it was not an official Order of Merit event, this was still his sixth win in his last fourteen events in Europe, equalling a record set by both Seve Ballesteros and Nick Faldo. 'This is special,' said a surprisingly emotional Montgomerie afterwards. 'There is the word "world" in the title and to be champion of anything with the word "world" in it means a lot to me. Unfortunately, I can't see many other non-major winners on the roll of honour. I'd like to change that.'

Mark O'Meara thought that was more than possible. 'Colin is going to win a major and I see no reason why he couldn't do it within the next year,' said the former Masters and Open winner. Highlighting some of the reasons why Monty had *not* won a major championship, O'Meara offered a fascinating insight: 'When he is out there playing he can see a lot of things going on. He also hears a lot . . . I told Colin that I don't think there is one American player, or fan, who does not respect his ability to play the game. It is unfortunate there have been some situations, but I told him even Jack Nicklaus had people screaming at him when he started to take over from Arnold Palmer.'

Not wishing to embark on the same old discussion, this hugely complex individual had his own unique take on things. 'You can never say I will win one,' he said. 'There are only four. Tiger Woods will win one and I am sure Sergio Garcia will win another, so I'm down to two already. It's not easy. You have got to be there and be fortunate.'

Then came the bombshell news that Montgomerie was restricting his appearances in America to the three majors and three other top events from the start of next season! Not surprisingly, the questions came like a machine-gun from the incredulous British press hacks. 'How do you expect to win a major with little or no run-up to the majors themselves?' asked one. 'Did the crowd problems you have experienced over the past few seasons in the US influence your decision?' asked another.

Monty would not be drawn other than to confirm his decision. 'I am just not going to play quite so often, period,' he said. 'Not just in the States. I am going to take it easier at the start of the year. It's nothing to do with Brookline because I feel players and spectators alike respect me more after what happened there.'

Montgomerie had been the most dominant player in Europe for almost seven consecutive seasons, winner of six events and almost £1.5m in prize money in 1999. Was this really the time to throttle back on his efforts to win a major? With nothing more to prove in Europe, surely this was the time he should consider spending more time on the PGA Tour, not less! Perhaps Nick Faldo was right. Maybe Montgomerie *was* more interested in travelling around the globe making money than chasing major titles? By the time the truth finally emerged that he wanted to spend more time at home with his family in order to maintain his increasingly shaky marriage, his career had already taken a considerable downturn.

'Whether it happens or not, it won't hinder my career. I won't be a lesser player,' said Montgomerie about his inability to win a major. 'I might be in their [the media's] eyes but that doesn't matter. In my eyes, I've been successful even if I never win.'

12. EIMEAR

Ten weeks without 'touching a club' was how Colin Montgomerie described his preparation for the WGC Anderson Consulting Match Play tournament in February 2000. Spending time at home with his family in Surrey, the Scot found a few spare hours to record *Desert Island Discs* for BBC radio, where he selected Robbie Williams 'Angels' as a particular favourite. Always a little surprised at his own 'celebrity', Monty recalled watching a recording of the *BBC Sports Personality of the Year* on a flight back from the United States in 1999. Choking on his champagne and complimentary peanuts, he mistakenly heard his name announced in third place! 'I'd won six tournaments that year, four being shown on the BBC,' he recalled later. 'I don't know who won it or came second but when they said, "Third is Colin M–" I thought it was me, but it was [world rally driving champion] Colin McRae. I was ready to give up! If the award was *really* about personality I'd have won it by now.'

Not that it was all leisure and pleasure at Monty's mansion: in between practising at nearby Wisley golf club, he liaised with his manager Guy Kinnings over his growing golf-course design company, including a new project in the Zhuhai Golden Gulf District of mainland China. Add to that other courses in Korea, United Arab Emirates, Ireland and Lanzarote and his retirement years seemed well catered for as he headed off to California for the WGC World Match Play. One of four World Golf Championships events that debuted in 1999, the idea behind these lucrative events was to attract the top players in the world to compete against each other in events other than the four majors. Sanctioned and organised by the International Federation of PGA Tours, eligibility was limited to the top 64 available players from the Official World Golf Rankings.

Describing himself as 'fresh and ready to go', Montgomerie faced the 62nd seed Dennis Paulson in the opening round. Curiously the Californian-based pro listed among his special interests in the PGA Tour guide being a 'great dad'. Rusty or not, Monty disposed of the big-hitting American without too much effort, but then found his practice partner and Ryder Cup colleague Thomas Björn a much tougher proposition. No respecter of reputations, the Dane had witnessed first-hand how loose his opponent's game was and took full advantage.

'He was playing well but making a few mistakes that he does not normally make after he has played a few tournaments,' said Björn after winning at the fifth extra hole. 'Not so much with his game but in the mind.'

It was a revealing observation by someone who knew Monty well, as was an incident in the third round of the French Open nine weeks later. Montgomerie, New Zealand's Michael Campbell and England's Jonathan Lomas were tied for the lead at eleven under par, when lightning brought a temporary halt to play at the National golf club in Versailles. Under normal circumstances, a siren sounds and players stop immediately, but on this occasion there was confusion whether the siren had actually sounded or not.

Montgomerie, six under for the day, was held up on the seventeenth tee after playing partner Miguel Angel Martin refused to play on until officials had made a definitive ruling. Fearing a loss of momentum, the increasingly irate Scot insisted they go on, especially after his rival Campbell drove off on the hole behind. But the Spaniard refused and the incident became increasingly heated until John Paramour, the Tour's chief referee, made the decision to stop play a short time later. 'We have a lightning detection unit which we use and today it did not have the necessary readings for us to have stopped play,' he said. 'But the general idea is we play when it is safe and we stop when it's not.'

Eimear Montgomerie, who was following her husband, said, 'I don't see why they wait and there is so much indecision. In America they seem to stop straight away so people are safe.'

Miguel Angel Martin was unrepentant. 'I didn't see or hear any lightning,' he said, 'but it was crazy to play on.'

It was not just on the course that Montgomerie was getting wound up. His marriage was under increasing pressure as he struggled to capture his first major championship and retain his number-one status in Europe. At the US Open at Pebble Beach in June, the couple were barely on speaking terms as Eimear spent the week on the beautiful Monterey Peninsula looking like she would rather be anywhere else in the world than watching her husband play golf. Things came to a head at the Millennium Open at St Andrews in July 2000. The house they had rented for the week became a battleground in what had become a decidedly one-sided relationship, as far as Eimear was concerned. Under strain for some time, the cracks that had appeared in the relationship over the past few years had widened into a yawning chasm. Eimear had struggled hard to plug the gaps in her supposedly 'perfect marriage' to Colin over the past year or more. His black moods had become more frequent and she began to dread a missed cut or poor final round performance, and it was at the 'Home of Golf' that the dam would finally break.

When Colin Montgomerie defeated Alasdair Watt in the final of the Scottish Amateur Championship at Nairn in 1987, Eimear Wilson was in the gallery with her father. Chatting to her for a short time after the presentation, the 24-year-old Scot was swept away by her fresh-faced beauty and natural, easy-going charm. Six years his junior, she was currently undertaking a law degree at Edinburgh University and, despite her family living down the road from Colin's parents, they had never actually met.

It was against the unromantic background of a visit to the local unemployment office in Ayr a few weeks later that romance was first kindled. Colin offered Eimear a lift in his father's car; they got talking and not long afterwards began dating. Everyone agreed it was a good match. Eimear approached life calmly and with focus while Colin could be brash and moody in equal measure. She was calm and always ready with support and a kind word, while the insecure Monty would fly off the handle over a bad putt. But somehow it worked and it surprised nobody when they finally got married three years after they first met, at Troon Old Parish Church on 27 June 1990.

From the start, the fresh-faced Ayrshire girl devoted herself to his golfing career. After the passing of Colin's mother in January 1991, it was Eimear who provided the strength and support her husband so desperately needed. In the years that followed, she made a home for their three children, Olivia, Venetia and Cameron, while he set about establishing himself as one of the top players in the world.

In many ways, Eimear had been the inspiration for much of what her husband had achieved over the past decade. She may not have told him how to putt or how to win a golf tournament but she made it all possible. His best friend, his biggest fan, his sounding board, Eimear was his muse and his inspiration, and the problems really started for Colin when he forgot what a vital role she really did play in his life.

Winner of seven successive European Order of Merit titles from 1993 onwards, Montgomerie's obsessive desire to continue his run had become a source of friction between the couple. Still without the major he craved, by the time the couple arrived in St Andrews a week before the 2000 Open Championship it had become a real problem. Unable to communicate without it turning into an argument or awkward period of silence, Monty found it impossible to hide his disappointment after a poor round or a bad finish to a tournament. At the PGA Championship at Wentworth in May, he demanded that Eimear leave the course midway through the third round, describing her presence as an unwanted 'distraction'. The relationship could have ended right there and then had she not decided to bite her tongue for the sake of her children.

Increasingly concerned at the effect his black moods were having on their family, Eimear's patience was wearing very thin. 'We had a lot of rows,' she admitted later. 'Colin wasn't at home very much and when he was, it wasn't happy ... I was the one who encouraged Colin to the hilt in his career, but it got to the stage when that career was all-consuming.'

Time and time again over the past twelve months, Montgomerie would return to their marital home in Surrey barely able to conceal his disappointment. It was the same at St Andrews, where his desire to win his first major clouded the day-to-day niceties like communicating with his wife. Barely on speaking terms, she had wanted to schedule dinner with friends while he wanted nothing more than to concentrate on the championship in hand. It turned into a ferocious argument. Not untypically among tournament golf professionals, where divorce rates far exceed the national average, Monty was focused on golf and little else. After all, he was the breadwinner of the family, the provider of a luxurious lifestyle for his wife and family, so why should he feel guilty about concentrating on his own needs?

Eimear felt ignored and that was the spark behind her announcement that she wanted out of the relationship. Golf had taken over her life and her children's lives. In her mind, she was little more than a sounding board for *his* ambitions, *his* frustrations and *his* complaints. She had simply been pushed too far that Sunday evening. 'It's not that I expected him to be Mr Happy if things had gone wrong,' recalled Eimear, 'but I couldn't have his temper in the house. A perfect game of golf has never been played, but he was hypercritical. It made me nervous and was very bad for the children.'

Montgomerie's attitude to his wife was dismissive at best. When he ignored her simple request to discuss anything but the upcoming Open Championship, she finally snapped. No longer willing to tolerate her husband's erratic behaviour and single-minded focus on *his* career, it was her suggestion they end their marriage. The breakdown had a sad inevitability about it. To the outside world, Colin and Eimear had the ideal golfing marriage. He was hugely successful while she provided the seemingly ideal *Hello* magazine home life that power couples like the Montgomeries had – and other couples aspired to. Earlier that week, he was presented with an honorary Doctor of Law degree by St Andrews University – something Eimear had spent four years earning at Edinburgh University. Smiling alongside Seve Ballesteros, who also received the award, Monty seemed the epitome of the successful sportsman, but the cracks in his marriage had become fissures.

Montgomerie's initial reaction to Eimear's demand was unrestrained fury. Outraged at her inconsiderate attitude during the most important week of his year, he felt totally betrayed by her actions. This was the Open at St Andrews and everybody, from Guy Kinnings to the tea girl in the IMG offices in London, knew how confident he felt about winning. Ranked number three in the world, this had been a vintage season with victory in the PGA at Wentworth in May along with a raft of top-ten finishes in Europe. Even the media agreed this was his best ever opportunity to break his major duck, and now his wife had ruined it for him!

Unwilling to consider her point of view, Montgomerie stormed out of the rented accommodation in Market Street and into the St Andrews night. Revealing his remarkable ability to play first-rate golf when he is upset about something or someone, he performed admirably for the opening three rounds at St Andrews. Then the mask slipped as he suddenly burst into tears at the twelfth hole on Sunday as the reality of his situation hit him. With caddie Alistair McLean shielding him from intrusive snappers, he had spotted the ever-loyal Eimear in the crowd, and it became a supreme effort just to finish without attracting any unwelcome headlines. Quite what his playing partner Vijay Singh made of it all was anyone's guess.

Returning home to Oxshott in relative silence the couple attempted to reconcile their differences over the coming weeks. Portrayed as childhood sweethearts, the Montgomeries were often held up as the 'perfect' golfing couple: smart, successful, with three beautiful children. The world would soon discover that much of it was an illusion.

Not that the 'conveyor belt' of tournaments stopped during this difficult time for Colin Montgomerie – and neither did his antipathy towards American crowds. Shortly before the final major of the year – the PGA Championship at Valhalla in August – Peter Kessler of the *Golf Channel* grilled him on everything from David Feherty's comments to the death of Payne Stewart. Discussing at length his problems with US golf fans, he only became agitated when Kessler innocently asked what advice his wife had given him before leaving England? Clearing his throat, he simply said how she asked him to 'focus' and not to think about her and the children 'too much'.

Discussing the abuse he had suffered during the US Open at Pebble Beach in June, he said, 'I had just made an eight on the eighth hole and coming up the eleventh this guy yells, "Any more snowmen recently, Colin?" I looked in the direction it came from and the guy said it again! It's just mindless stuff.'

No one plays the victim quite like Montgomerie and it surprised nobody when he ended the week in a disappointing tie for 39th at Valhalla, following a tie for 46th at Pebble Beach, 26th at St Andrews and 19th at Augusta National. The millennium majors had proved a complete washout. Admitting that it would be 'very, very difficult' for him to win in America because of all the heckling he received, Montgomerie ended the interview by saying, 'Yes, I would love to walk around as if I didn't care. But I do – and it shows . . .'

With problems persisting in his home life, Montgomerie was penalised two strokes at the BMW International for missing his opening-round tee-off time at the end of August. At the Dunhill Cup in October, he announced that he was going to cut back his European Tour schedule in 2001, preferring to concentrate on the majors and spend more time with his family: 'I have made the decision to cut down my involvement on the European Tour next season,' he told the media. 'It will represent the start of a new phase in the lives of myself and my family – one in which I'll be very much more relaxed and will devote more of my time to them. My days of rushing from one European tournament to another without ever having time, to use the old Walter Hagen comment, "to stop and smell the flowers along the way" are over.'

Despite winning twice earlier in the season, his marital problems and subsequent loss of form proved too much in his chase for an eighth consecutive Order of Merit. Unable to finish better than sixth behind the new European number one, Lee Westwood, Monty's record-breaking run of seven successive titles had come to an abrupt end. Noticeably thinner at the Cisco World Match Play at Wentworth in October, Montgomerie was questioned about his twenty-pound weight loss since the Open. Looking tense and drawn, he would not be drawn into a wider conversation, saying only that he had lost it '. . . by keeping my mouth shut and not eating after 7.00 p.m.'

It was not the only thing Colin Montgomerie lost in the autumn of 2000. Unable to cope with her husband's mood swings and protracted silences, Eimear asked him to vacate their Surrey mansion in late October.

'My life certainly doesn't revolve around the Order of Merit any longer,' said a distracted Montgomerie after the final ranking tournament at Valderrama a week later. 'There are other, far more important things to consider.'

Returning from Spain after the WGC American Express Championship after two weeks away, Montgomerie moved into the Hilton Hotel in Chelsea Harbour. Like many newly separated spouses, those first weeks away from his family proved an incredibly difficult time. The fact that his marriage breakdown had now become public knowledge also made matters worse for the thin-skinned Monty. Apart from a made-for-television Skins Challenge in California in late November, where he picked up $415,000 first prize in beating Vijay Singh, Fred Couples and Sergio Garcia, Monty found time weighed increasingly heavily on him.

His closest relationship was disintegrating before his eyes and he seemed unable to stop it. He once described Eimear as 'the most influential person' in his life after his father, and now she was no longer there. Was it any wonder that Monty informed those closest to him that he might be unable to carry on as a tournament professional if his relationship with his wife ended for good?

Spending much of his day at the IMG offices in Chiswick or wandering aimlessly round stores like Harrods, it was a desperately unhappy period of his life. 'I just wanted to be around people and went walking,' he admitted on the BBC's *Breakfast with Frost* some time later. 'It was quite, quite therapeutic, in many ways.'

With the separation looking more permanent than he first envisaged, Montgomerie took out a lease on a three-bedroom Thameside apartment in Battersea – some thirty miles from their family home in Surrey. Providing a home where his children Venetia, Olivia and Cameron could visit him, it was the time *away* from his family that caused him most distress. Unable to sleep, he spent night after night walking the cold streets of London's theatreland until the wee small hours. Devastated that matters had gone so far, Montgomerie looked to his closest confidants, Dr Hugh Mantle OBE and Guy Kinnings, for help and advice. Both long-standing friends – Colin had worked with Mantle on the mental side of the game since 1993 – they confirmed that his desire to win more and more European Order of Merits *had* impacted on his home life. And while winning a major championship was a worthwhile ambition, it should not be at the cost of his marriage to Eimear.

Coming to his senses, Montgomerie desperately wanted to repair the damage his drive and desire had caused. 'My ambition was almost *too* strong,' Montgomerie admitted later. He suggested that Eimear take the children on a planned break to Barbados over the Christmas period, and she reluctantly accepted. Perhaps it was the time away from each other, the children missing their father or the massive change in attitude from Colin himself that brought them together again as a family. Inviting Colin to join them, the reconciliation process began under the sun of the West Indian island. Returning to England three months after they first split up, they reconciled their differences and Colin moved back in.

'It's great to be ambitious in life,' Montgomerie told David Frost on *Breakfast with Frost* eleven months later in November 2002, 'and it's super to want and, you know, to increase one's standard of living and everything that goes with that. But at the same time, to bring one's work home – as I was doing – and not understanding really, was causing problems, and I didn't see it. But, yes, I had to achieve, and the more I achieved the more I had to achieve, and it was a sort of conveyor belt that didn't want to stop and it got me into all sorts of problems.'

In an interview with Lewine Mair of the *Daily Telegraph* in January 2001, Montgomerie admitted that losing his Order of Merit title to Lee Westwood in October had probably saved his marriage. Describing how he and Eimear had been 'papering over the cracks' for years, the Scottish professional agreed that he had become obsessed with winning a major. Most significantly, having been to the brink of the marital abyss before pulling back from the edge, they both admitted to learning a 'painful but vital lesson'.

Provoking a storm of press interest, they openly admitted that vital changes had now been made – not least of which was Colin Montgomerie's attitude both on and off the golf course. Whether this highly competitive animal would be able to change his winner-take-all mentality for good was a different question entirely . . .

13. MONTY LOSES HIS RHYTHM AT ROYAL LYTHAM

After the emotional upheaval of the previous year, it was hoped that a period of stability would prove a turning point in Colin Montgomerie's career. That looked to have been the case as the 2001 season got under way with a narrow victory in the Australian Masters in Melbourne in February. Even a change to a heavier putter the night before the final round did not upset his game plan as he put together four consistent rounds of 72, 67, 70 and 69 for a ten-under-par total to beat Australian Nathan Green by a single stroke.

Benefiting from a two-month break from golf, followed by a trip to Texas in late January, where he hooked up with his old Houston Baptist University coach Paul Marchand, Monty looked relaxed and happy as he paraded the trophy.

'Colin's mind has not been focused on golf for about six months,' admitted manager Guy Kinnings, 'but he and Eimear are in good shape now. His priorities have changed as a result of what happened but that does not mean that his ambition has changed.'

The smiling Scot admitted that his win down under had proved a real turning point. 'I feel like I'm starting out in a new career,' he told journalists on his return to the more familiar hunting grounds at the Desert Classic in Dubai. His plan now was to become less 'obsessive' about his game and his elusive quest for that first major. Although he added, almost as an afterthought, that 'the competitive edge is still as sharp as it has ever been.'

At the Volvo PGA at Wentworth in May he struck an even more positive note. Describing how he was as 'keen as ever' to compete at the top level, he surprised everyone by saying, 'I do feel I have my best golf yet to play.'

Members of the media shook their collective heads, especially after he finished outside the top fifteen. It was typical Monty-speak, they muttered as he talked up his chances of a glory-filled comeback the year after Lee Westwood had taken away his European number-one spot. Far better players like Faldo, Lyle and now Ballesteros had all come and gone and here was someone who had never actually won a major, telling the jaundiced hacks how he was going to dominate European golf for the next six years! 'Come on, Monty,' you could almost hear them say. 'Pull the other one!'

In the run-up to the US Open in June, it was no better. Pre-tournament favourite in the British Masters at Woburn at the end of May, he finished down the field in 27th position. At least it was an improvement on the 52nd place he occupied at the second major of the season at Southern Hills in Tulsa. Thankfully, July saw an emphatic return to form in the Murphy's Irish Open at Fota Island. His first Tour victory since the French Open just over twelve months earlier, his five-stroke victory launched Montgomerie into sixth position on the Ryder Cup points list, to the delight of European captain Sam Torrance. 'I never had any doubt about him,' said his fellow Scot. 'His poor form has not been a problem for me. Monty is my rock, the strong man of my team. When I first started to play in the Ryder Cup, Peter Oosterhuis was the rock. Then it was Seve Ballesteros and Nick Faldo. Now it is Monty. The baton has passed to him.'

As early as the first round Montgomerie talked about having found something in his swing that had made him feel upbeat about his game – something he had not felt for some time. With the Open Championship at Royal Lytham just weeks away, things had finally turned around and his confidence was sky-high. 'This was one of the most important victories of my career, if not *the* most important,' said Monty after his wire-to-wire win. 'I have had an awful good look at myself in the past eight months. I am a better person now. I feel I can go forward. I think I have wanted success too much. But I've turned it around now. I am a whole lot calmer on and off the course.'

With Eimear walking among the Irish crowd on Sunday, they had come a long way in the last ten months. It was their well-publicised rift that had caused him to lose form and now everything appeared rosy in the Montgomerie garden. Now, all he needed to do was carry that form into the Open Championship at Royal Lytham two weeks later and his combined dream of marital harmony and major success could finally be fulfilled.

Royal Lytham and St Anne's Golf Club on England's northwest coast is hardly what you would imagine a true links course to be. One of the most unusual venues on the British Open rota, it is situated at least a mile from the sea. Dating back to 1897, the eighteen-hole layout occupies a narrow plot of land enclosed by red-brick Victorian houses on three sides and the main east coast railway line on the other. Yet a true links course it surely is; a fast-running course built on sandy soil with fiendish bunkering, it is considered among the toughest Open tests, especially when the prevailing wind blows in from the Irish Sea. It has also seen more than its fair share of competitive drama over the years. Host to ten Open Championships and two Ryder Cups, including the final match before Europe joined Great Britain and Ireland in 1977, its clubhouse walls are decked with the memorabilia of the past. From the mashie-iron Bobby Jones used to extricate himself from the 'sandy waste' to the left of the seventeenth hole en route to winning the Open in 1926 to Seve Ballesteros's signed scorecard from his Lytham double in 1988, the golfing ghosts of the past haunt this place.

As an amateur, Montgomerie had played Royal Lytham on a number of occasions. The course, with its narrow fairways and tightly bunkered greens, suited his style of play and a magnificent opening round of 65 illustrated the extra confidence he felt. Six under par, it was his lowest-ever score in the Open. Riding an emotional groundswell of support throughout the day, he was cheered on to every tee and applauded on to every green. Indeed, the Lancashire gallery were so loud at times that you might have thought that Monty had already been presented with the silver claret jug and was heading south down the motorway in his Lexus with a huge smile on his face.

The change in Montgomerie's on-course attitude was also remarkable. There was none of the impromptu marshalling of cameramen that marked out a typical Monty round. No finger-pointing at errant officials and no withering remarks aimed at two people having a quiet chat three holes away! If only it could be like this all the time for the 38-year-old Scot.

A solid 70 in the second round on Friday gave him a one-stroke lead over Swedish professional Pierre Fulke at the halfway stage. Striking the ball beautifully from tee to green, Monty admitted that he could not play much better given the rarefied circumstances. 'I've played an awful lot worse than this and won tournaments,' he said. 'I feel quite comfortable at this stage.'

Hard on the heels of his Irish Open triumph, some newspapers even claimed that his improved form could be attributed to his recent weight gain and Montgomerie agreed. 'I think we all have a sort of fighting weight,' he said. 'I lost a lot of weight towards the end of last year and have put half of that on again and it must help with the timing, yes, sure.'

Tiger Woods had a different take on things. Asked how Monty would be feeling as tournament leader his comments cut straight to the heart of the matter. 'I've won major Championships and I've won the Open,' said the American. 'That in itself relieves a lot of tension, a lot of pressure, because you know what it takes. If you haven't won one, it becomes a little more difficult.'

A 'little' more difficult? Given Montgomerie's ability to turn a major-winning position into heartbreaking failure, this was the understatement of the century! Trying to become the first player in eighteen years to win back-to-back Open Championships, Woods knew exactly what was required and, despite the Scot's heroic effort over the opening two rounds, the American superstar was only four strokes behind the lead at three under par. (Not surprisingly, the first question Montgomerie asked journalists after missing a short putt on the eighteenth was: 'What is *he* – three under or four under?')

It was the first time Montgomerie had led a major at halfway since the US Open at Oakmont in 1994, and he acknowledged the enormous support he had received from the crowd. 'I think they're quite glad to see me leading at this stage,' he said before offering a word of caution: 'There is an awful long way to go . . . We've managed to cover just half of it.'

He was right. Even though none of the six players between Montgomerie and Woods had actually won a major, the threat was obvious, especially with players like David Duval and Phil Mickelson in the mix. In the end it was a familiar story of so-near-but-yet-so-far after Montgomerie fell into a tie for fifth place after a lacklustre third round of 73 (the same score as Tiger Woods, whose own bid for the title also fell away on the Saturday). Despite being only one shot behind the leading group, his challenge faded along with the crowds that had supported him so magnificently throughout the week. Unable to mount any final-round charge that might have frightened the leaders into mistakes, he finished with a disappointing one-over-par 72, four under for the week.

Six strokes behind the eventual winner, American David Duval, Montgomerie finished tied thirteenth with Alex Cejka of Germany. Another major had come and gone and he was left feeling dejected and downright dumbfounded by his ability to turn a winning position into a losing one. Looking for a reason, he blamed his problems on his putting. 'I missed a putt for a birdie on Friday evening and the writing was on the wall then,' he admitted. 'I never felt comfortable with the putter after that.'

Finishing in his worst-ever position of 25th, Tiger Woods generously suggested that Monty was 'too talented *not* to win a major'. But after this hugely disappointing display at Royal Lytham, where he dropped off the leader board faster than John Daly devours a hamburger, the American superstar was in a growing minority. To paraphrase a common media-centre saying about Monty, he is 'wonderful on Wednesday, thunderous on Thursday, furious on Friday, seething on Saturday and smug on Sunday'.

At least you have to win to be 'smug' on Sunday and Montgomerie added to his fans' frustration after bouncing back a few weeks later to capture the Scandinavian Masters in Malmo, Sweden. Compiling a narrow one-stroke victory over Lee Westwood and Ian Poulter, it was a typically efficient European Tour victory that only added to the disappointment of Royal Lytham.

There was more frustration to come at the final major of the year at Atlanta Athletic Club in Georgia. After barely making the cut in the PGA Championship, Montgomerie mistakenly signed for a par three on the short seventh hole in the final round when he had taken four strokes. Out of contention, he gave his score as 71 instead of 72 and had already left the course by the time the accountancy error had been discovered. He was instantly disqualified for this school-boy mistake and to make matters worse it was a fellow Scot, Andrew Oldcorn, marking his card!

A double whammy in terms of Ryder Cup qualification, Montgomerie would have moved up to twelfth place in the Ryder Cup table and gained an automatic entry into the lucrative World Championship event at Akron the following week. The second half of his season was falling apart and there was even more bad news around the corner as the terrible events in New York on 11 September unfolded before an incredulous world.

With the Ryder Cup scheduled just two weeks later, the game's governing bodies were forced to decide whether the match, scheduled for the Belfry on September 28–30, should be cancelled or not. The decision was fraught with difficulty and opinion was understandably split. Montgomerie, like other top players on both sides of the Atlantic, was asked his opinion but sensibly kept his own council. When the decision to postpone the match to the following year was announced, he offered his support and said that he would now concentrate on improving his position both in Europe and the world rankings.

It proved a far harder task than he imagined as Retief Goosen ended the year as European number one. Dominant between 1993 and 1999, Monty had now been shut out two years running, despite his upbeat message that his title was only 'on loan'.

'It's been difficult the last couple of years,' he told the *Scotsman on Sunday*. 'I've had to watch as people have gone past me. But I can succeed again. I'm certainly going to try.'

Whether Montgomerie truly believed that or not was another question entirely.

14. BE NICE TO MONTY

The New Year began in a storm of controversy and once again it involved an altercation with a spectator during an American tournament. The difference this time was that Monty was so upset about the incident that he threatened to quit playing in the United States entirely!

Beginning his 2002 campaign at the Accenture Match Play Championship at La Costa in California in February, the combustible Scot finally lost patience with some hecklers who hurled abuse at him during his first-round defeat by American professional Scott McCarron. With his post-Brookline promise to 'try even harder the more I get abused' nothing but a distant memory, Monty spent most of his match reacting to the gallery with icy glares and sarcastic asides. 'The only thing worse than losing is spending another day in your country,' he told one particularly abusive individual.

Not that there were many people watching in the first place! 'No disrespect to Scott,' said Monty afterwards, 'but a first-round match against him is about as low-key an occasion that you can get in America and I still got heckled ... Can you imagine what it would be like if I was one clear with two to play in a major championship? It is hard enough as it is to take on Tiger, Sergio and the rest, and I can't do it if I have always got one hand tied behind my back.'

Then he dropped his bombshell about quitting US golf for good. 'I'm on my last legs over here,' he said to a hushed gathering of pressmen. 'I'm thirty-nine in June, and I don't need this any more. I have commitments until the end of the season that I will fulfil, but that will be it. It's clear to me there will never be a level playing field when I play over here. What can I possibly hope to achieve over here if spectators don't allow me to compete on the same terms as everyone else?'

Bernie Lincicome, reporter for the *Rocky Mountain News*, expressed the alternative view when he wrote: 'We know a clod when we see one. We heckle because, well, he deserves it.'

Before walking away from the PGA Tour for good, Montgomerie, corporate-minded to the end, confirmed that he would fulfil this year's commitments to sponsors and tournament organisers but that was all. From now on it was no more Mr Nice Guy and definitely no more getting verbally pounded by some drunken lowlife who really should not be within a thousand miles of a golf tournament! Who could blame him – his mind was made up – thank you and goodbye! Then came an about-turn so sudden that even the most hardened politician might have blushed crimson.

By the time he returned to competitive action at the Dubai Desert Classic a week later Montgomerie was already backtracking on his comments. 'Over the past week,' said Monty, 'the assurances I've received from the US PGA Tour and tournament promoters, coupled with the support I've received via phone calls, letters and e-mails from genuine US golf fans, has convinced me I shouldn't let a small minority dictate where I should play my golf.'

In truth, the way had already been paved by his extremely able manager, Guy Kinnings, who expressed the belief that Colin would almost certainly return to the USA in future years *but with a reduced tournament schedule*. 'I would be surprised if he avoided majors,' he said, 'but he may cut down on the other events ... He's not the kind of guy to let a small minority determine when he plays.'

They were laudable comments and Monty's fellow professionals agreed. 'I have got to tell you Colin gets a bad rap over here,' said former US Open Champion Curtis Strange. 'I like Colin, and I always have. I get along with him very well. He's a wonderful player, and it's too bad some of our people don't give him the due that he deserves and treat him like a gentleman.'

He was right. Unlike baseball or soccer, where personal comments from the fans are a generally accepted part of the sport, golf was a different matter entirely. The past decade had seen a disturbing rise in loutish, often drunken, behaviour and no player had suffered more than Colin Montgomerie. His critics argued that his combative attitude – especially during tournaments in the United States – had contributed to the rise in boorish behaviour, but that would probably be unfair.

'Monty needs to stick his head down and get on with the job of it in America,' said Thomas Björn, offering a slightly different point of view. 'If he does that, then he can still win majors.'

Montgomerie kept up his defiant stance by confirming that he would not be returning to America to compete in the Bay Hill Invitational in Florida after missing the halfway cut in the Desert Classic in Dubai with a disastrous second-round 79. The possibility of a standoff between Monty and the PGA Tour loomed, but before anything could be read into his absence, he confirmed to the press that he would honour a commitment to play in the Tournament Players Championship at Sawgrass two weeks later in March. According to his management company IMG, the deciding factor for his inexplicable change of mind was his fans. 'I have so many supporters and friends over there,' said Montgomerie, 'that it would be a pity to let a tiny group sour the great experiences to be had competing on the US Tour.'

There was an alternative point of view. Had Montgomerie *not* reconsidered, the stubborn Scot would effectively rule himself out of three of the four major championships held each year. The effect on his world ranking would have been disastrous, not to mention the many lucrative sponsorship deals he would put in jeopardy if he did not appear in tournaments like the Masters, US Open and PGA Championship. Until now, no top-ranked player had ever threatened such action, simply because it would be professional suicide.

The decision to return to action on the PGA Tour was one Montgomerie would come to regret. Despite his well-publicised spats with American crowds he declined the offer of armed uniformed officers at the Tournament Players Championship similar to the type regularly assigned to Tiger Woods. Feeling it might attract the very sort of nut he was trying to avoid, Montgomerie insisted that he would rather concentrate on his golf than worry about what was going on outside the ropes. 'Everyone gets heckled to some extent, particularly towards the end of the afternoon,' he said, hinting at the easy access to alcohol. 'But I don't want an armed guard. I'm here to play golf and that's what I want to focus on.'

Revealing that he had received late entries into the next four events on the PGA Tour including the Houston Open and the BellSouth Classic, he hoped that familiarity with American audiences might breed a mutual respect. 'The response from fans, players and the PGA Tour after what happened at La Costa has been tremendous,' he said. 'Everyone seems happy to see me over here.'

Making an effort during the practice rounds to sign autographs and interact with people, his PR efforts seemed to be paying off until he arrived at the notorious island-green par-three seventeenth in the first round. Hitting his ball onto the green, he made his way past the huge crowds that gather on this hole like those who hung around the guillotine during the French Revolution. Suddenly a heckler called out, 'Doubtfire! Mrs Doubtfire!' as Monty walked past.

The next hole was no better as someone shouted out from the bleachers: 'Montgomerie, you've got no majors. You're a loser. Go back to your own country.'

Two security officials who were following Montgomerie approached a middle-aged man but took no action. It seemed that Monty was fair game as long as nobody tried to shoot him, and all this barely a month after he had threatened to quit playing in the USA!

Making the cut at two over par, a rain delay at the end of the second round gave everybody a little breathing space, but he really must have wondered why he was there. Eight strokes behind halfway leaders Jeff Sluman and Carl Paulson, he applauded those fans that shouted out words of encouragement but must have lost no sleep at the thought of moving on to the next tournament.

Switching to the longer shafted belly putter in an attempt to take any wrist action out of his putting stroke, he gave a solid performance at the Shell Houston Open, followed by a seventeenth-place finish behind Retief Goosen at the BellSouth Classic in Atlanta. Never an advocate of the left-hand-below-right style of putting favoured by players like Jim Furyk and Thomas Björn, Monty first tried out the longer-shafted club on the practice putting green after Fred Couples lent him a spare during the Williams World Challenge event at the end of 2001. Contracted to Callaway, who omitted to make them, he politely asked if they could supply him one in the hope that it would help him cope with the much faster greens found in the United States. They did and the results were encouraging, especially with the Masters coming up the following week. 'My putting is much improved and that can only augur well for not just this week, but the rest of the season,' he said prior to the first round. 'The fear of fast greens has been taken away, which is great. I've never gone into the tournament before feeling confident about putting well.'

For someone whose 'fear of fast greens' had been taken away, the Scot set his sights surprisingly low at Augusta – even with defending champion Tiger Woods vaunted as the shortest-odds favourite in the history of the game. Admitting that he would be satisfied with a top-ten finish, it seemed a downbeat statement from someone who only two years ago was ranked third in the world! Still in the top thirty, Monty said he was just being 'realistic' considering his start to the season, which included withdrawing from the Johnnie Walker tournament in Australia because of back trouble, tumbling out of the WGC Match Play in California in the first round and missing the cut in Dubai.

Recovering from a disappointing opening 75 to card rounds of 71, 70 and 71 at Augusta, Montgomerie ended the week tied in fourteenth place alongside Nick Faldo – eleven strokes behind the winner, Tiger Woods. After the rigours of the PGA Tour in the United States, Montgomerie hoped that a return to more familiar surroundings in Europe would improve his form. A week later he was in Ireland captaining Great Britain and Ireland to its third consecutive victory over a team from Continental Europe in the Seve Trophy at Druids Glen. Originally scheduled for the year in between the Ryder Cup, the only downside for the Scot was losing the captains' match against Seve Ballesteros, a source of much embarrassment and ribbing from his players. Monty seemed unable to defeat someone who, through his back problems, had hardly picked up a club in the previous few months!

Before the match got under way, the thorny subject of Montgomerie as a future Ryder Cup captain was brought up. Putting his name forward as a possible candidate for the 2006 match at the nearby K Club, Monty admitted that he had notified the Ryder Cup committee of his interest almost six months before, but had not received any response. The timing of his announcement raised a few eyebrows among the media. With Sam Torrance leading the European team at the Belfry in September in the rescheduled match from 2001, that left Bernhard Langer, Ian Woosnam, Nick Faldo or possibly Sandy Lyle in the frame for Oakland Hills in Michigan for 2004. Whoever was selected, it was assumed the remaining candidates would fight it out for the Ireland job two years later. Now with Monty throwing his hat into the ring – unofficially or otherwise – it caused a certain amount of frenzied debate. 'I can't say it's a goal of mine but of course it would be a great honour if it arose,' announced Montgomerie diplomatically. 'The last thing I want to do is start campaigning for that here and now. But yes, it is something I've thought about. I've spoken to officialdom about the situation and it's been taken on board . . . There won't be any announcement (about the 2006 captaincy) until after the 2004 match in October of that year. So there's a bit to go. Nick Faldo has been talked about for the next one and thereafter there is myself, Bernhard Langer and Ian Woosnam. That seems to be the roll call, if you like. But we'll all have to wait and see what happens.'

With Gleneagles in Scotland pencilled in for 2014 it was thought that Montgomerie would be an ideal candidate even at the age of 51 – but this did not fit into his plans. If not Scotland, where then? Valhalla in Kentucky in 2008? Celtic Manor in Wales in 2010? In typical fashion, Monty would not be drawn into the debate except to say somewhat cryptically, 'You wouldn't want to do it somewhere that you feel uncomfortable?'

A promising performance at the Novotel Perrier French Open in May, including a five-under-par 67 to share the first-round lead at Le Golf National, prompted Montgomerie to say that he would now focus on *his* game rather than anyone else's. 'Instead of trying to hit the ball further to be like whoever,' said Monty. 'I've taken a step back to go forward. It's what got me to a position of strength in Europe. I've decided to think about me for a change instead of everybody else.'

One change he did make the following week was to dismiss his long-time bagman, Alastair McLean, who had been on the bag for all of his seven Order of Merits. The pair first met back in 1991 while the Fife-born Scot was working for Welsh World Cup golfer Mark Mouland at the German Open. Steady, reliable, with a quick mind and equally sharp sense of humour, McLean was a modern-history graduate of Dundee University and had a job working for his local government planning department. A single-figure handicap golfer from Lundin links, he began caddying for former Scottish amateur champion Sandy Stephen. Over the next couple of years, McLean worked for a number of journeymen players including Phil Harrison and Denis Durnian. Learning his trade at the poorly paid end of the caddy shed, his first tournament on Monty's bag was in Valencia in 1992. Missing three consecutive cuts in the run-up to the Masters in April, both men must have wondered what they had got themselves into. Deciding to stick it out, the pay-off was ten years of almost unbroken success.

Described as an 'amicable' dissolution by Monty's manager Guy Kinnings, the pro-caddie relationship had become stale and it was probably time for a change for both men. Having made what must have been a difficult decision, quite how Monty would cope without his loyal bagman had the media rubbing their hands in anticipation of the fun to come. Diplomatic and tactful, with a skin thicker than rhinoceros hide, should be on any caddie's CV, but especially if you are employed by the seven-time European number one. 'You have to be diplomatic with Monty,' recalled Alastair in one of the few comments he ever made about his boss. 'He isn't the same every day. He has immense mood swings, and has to be constantly reminded how good he is. I'm not sure why that is: maybe he lacks self-esteem, I don't know. What I do know is that his record is fantastic. So he should believe in himself more.'

Montgomerie was not in the mood for looking back. 'It's just a professional decision,' he said matter-of-factly. 'The sole reason is to see if it can bring me more success. I'm looking forward to the new challenge. It's been a very difficult thing to do, but we will remain very good friends.'

Without a victory since the Scandinavian Masters in August 2001, Monty appeared desperately short of inspiration. His golf was solid if not spectacular and in an effort to get his number-one position back from Lee Westwood, he had changed his schedule, ditched his coach and now his caddie. Enlisting South African Jason Henning as a temporary replacement caddie for the Benson and Hedges International Open at the Belfry the following week, the change looked to have made a real difference as Monty made a sustained challenge. At least he did until a loudspeaker announcement almost 450 yards away disturbed his concentration!

Playing the final hole, Monty was tied for the lead after a gritty fightback following a double-bogey at the tenth. Then, right at the top of his back swing, the Scot heard the course announcer welcome six-time major winner Nick Faldo on to the green ahead of him. Confirming the nickname of 'rabbit ears' given him by top coach Butch Harmon, he pushed his tee shot and was unable to reach the green in two at the difficult par-four. Making bogey on a hole where a birdie would have got him into a play-off with the eventual winner Angel Cabrera was galling for the Scot. (Cabrera had walked away from his ball when he heard the announcement.)

In contrast to José Maria Olazábal, who celebrated a birdie on the last green with a handstand, Monty harrumphed off towards the scorer's post complaining bitterly about the interruption. 'The quiet signs went up and everyone else was quiet apart from the announcer,' he complained after his round of 69. But by the time he faced the media Montgomerie had calmed down considerably. Finishing tied fourth at one of European golf's flagship events was a move in the right direction and he knew it. 'There was much to be encouraged about,' he explained before setting off on a run of high-profile tournaments he desperately hoped would turn his season around.

The signs looked good at the Deutsche Bank-SAP Open the following week. Faldo's diminutive former major-winning caddie Andy Prodger was now signed up as bagman, and he was enthusiastic about his new post. 'I've just celebrated my fiftieth [birthday] and, realistically, I've got another five years left in this job,' he opined. 'So I really hope I can help Colin win his first major – it would be a great way to go out.'

Unfortunately Prodger's former employer was not quite as enthusiastic, having been informed by the media that Monty had 'bagged his bagman!' Speaking a week later, Phillip Price, a quietly spoken Welshman, was understandably upset that he had not been informed by the pair. 'I don't mind him joining Monty at all,' he said. 'But it was the way it was done that I didn't really like.'

Resisting the temptation to pour soothing oil on the situation, Montgomerie simply brushed away criticism, explaining that he, at least, was not at fault. 'There's no animosity between Phillip and me,' said Monty. 'It's unfortunate, but if there is a problem, it's between Phillip and Andy Prodger.'

Despite the controversy, the new partnership made a positive start in Germany. Striking the ball wonderfully well from tee to green, his twenty-under-par total was enough to take the mighty Tiger Woods into a play-off on the Monday. Then problems began as Monty revealed how his painful back problems had resulted in a sleepless night and inevitable defeat at the hands of the American. 'I was proud of how I competed considering I had no sleep whatsoever,' he said afterwards. 'I kept moving about the [hotel] room watching DVDs until six a.m. when the sun came up. I went to the course an hour later. I then practised for two and a half hours to get as loose as possible. After all that, you can imagine how knackered I was afterwards. As it turned out, four rounds was the limit for me – the extra holes were three too many.'

Back problems had forced him to pull out of the Johnnie Walker Classic in Australia in January 2002, a reccurrence of a problem that had first flared up in June 2001 at the English Open at the Forest of Arden. Even so, Montgomerie was a strong favourite to collect his fourth PGA title in five years at Wentworth. Then the problems really started when he cut short a practice round after just five holes. Complaining of severe back pain, he demanded a buggy to ferry him back to the clubhouse. Rumours about him pulling out of the tournament quickly began to circulate after Guy Kinnings cancelled Monty's official press conference on the Wednesday before sending his apologies to the Tournament Players Committee, who had a meeting that evening. 'Yes, I think I will be able to play but to what standard I can compete remains to be seen,' Monty said before leaving for specialist treatment on his ailing back. 'I'm seeing a chiropractor and an osteopath to try and get some flexibility into my back.'

With rain and cold weather predicted for the week the signs were not good for someone with back problems. Returning for the first round Montgomerie explained how he was now spending two hours per day swimming in his pool at home to strengthen his muscles. 'I have got to get my stomach muscles strong or else my career will be shortened, it is as simple as that,' said the Scot somewhat dramatically.

Montgomerie's last-minute decision to play ultimately proved the right one. 'At the moment,' he admitted, 'every week is a bonus.' Two shots behind the halfway leader, Dane Anders Hansen, his concentration was badly affected after poleaxeing a spectator with a pushed drive on the par-four sixteenth in the second round. He stayed with the victim until the ambulance arrived, and the blood-soaked individual tried to offer a few words of encouragement, but the effect was obvious. 'Colin is very upset and shaken by what happened,' reported Guy Kinnings afterwards.

The final two rounds were no less dramatic as pouring rain hampered Montgomerie's efforts to make inroads into Hansen's lead. The Dane won by five shots with a final round of 70, but Montgomerie appeared satisfied with his runner-up performance and score of fourteen under par. Not that he hung around to celebrate. His back problems had become increasingly acute and the following evening he was examined in London to see if surgery was necessary to relieve the pain. Thankfully it was not deemed serious enough to warrant an immediate trip to the operating table, but it was still a problem.

Following a fourth-place finish at the British Masters at Woburn, Montgomerie had now come third, second, second and fourth in his past four tournaments. A combined 56 under par, he was now in second place in the money list and looking forward to the upcoming US Open in New York.

Fresh from a family break at Loch Lomond in Scotland, Montgomerie declined the opportunity for a second practice round over the treacherously difficult Bethpage Black course on Long Island. 'I'm not really fit enough to manage two,' he said. 'It's a difficult walk and my back's still not that great, though I wouldn't have made the trip here if I didn't think I could win.'

Satisfied with his game, he obviously felt it would be 'reckless' to practise more than necessary, which was a huge pity for the thousands of American golf fans who wore 'Be Nice to Monty' badges throughout the practice days. The brainchild of American magazine *Golf Digest*, the idea was to promote good behaviour among the notoriously volatile New Yorkers, who had a reputation for blunt speaking. 'It's a fun way of making a serious point,' said a spokesman, 'but this year's US Open is a terrific opportunity to improve player and fan relations.'

Monty was not convinced. 'The badges are terrific and the crowd today were very friendly,' he said after his practice round. 'The big test will come if I start off with a sixty-five or something like that.' Indeed, when he declined to sign autographs because he needed a massage to relieve his back, there was a distinct ruffling of Long Island feathers. 'You can come back and sign on Friday,' said one fan, 'after you've missed the cut!' So much for being nice to Monty.

He may not have worried Bob Hope in the humour stakes but the fan's predictive powers were spot-on as Montgomerie crashed out of the second major of the year along with Ryder Cup team members Lee Westwood, Phillip Price, Pierre Fulke and Jesper Parnevik. With increasing pressures off course, his on-course performances were also beginning to suffer.

15. UNWANTED RECORDS AND PRESS PACK BLUES

Without a win all year, Montgomerie's disappointment at missing the cut at the US Open in June had bitten deep. Now, the week before the Open Championship in July, his confidence was beginning to erode as he struggled around in 72 and 71 at Loch Lomond in the Barclays Scottish Open. Stamping off the final green on what he had previously described as 'one of his favourite courses', Montgomerie reacted angrily as one unfortunate journalist congratulated him for holing a snaking fifteen-foot putt to make the cut! Asked if he was happy at the way he battled on to the end, he rounded on the gathered media, saying sarcastically, 'It wasn't a good finish at all, actually!'

Admitting that he did not anticipate making the cut, it must have thrilled the tournament sponsors to hear that he would now use the final two rounds as 'a practice session'! (On Wednesday he was astonished at the suggestion that Americans would only play at such a prestigious tournament as a warm-up to the Open the following week.)

Returning to the parlous state of his own game, Montgomerie was almost inconsolable. 'This has been a problem for months and right now I don't see any light at the end of the tunnel,' he lamented. 'I don't know what the problem is, really. But I know I'm not playing the golf I used to play, that's for sure. So I've got to get back [to my former game] as soon as I possibly can.'

Exactly what this 'problem' was eluded most of the journalists. His back problems seemed to have eased, his putting was better than ever and he had barely been outside the top twenty in any tournament since the Qatar Masters in March. Playing with Darren Clarke in the third round he scored 66, but even this failed to lift the dark cloud he seemed to be under. 'That was a bit a better,' he said grudgingly, before falling away in the final round. Upset at his distance control all week he bemoaned his luck, saying, 'You can't play an Open without knowing how far your five iron is going.'

Alternately snappy and smiling and ultimately 'very, very tired', Monty had let his fans witness the full gamut of his emotions over the weekend. Criticising the weight of expectation that Scottish crowds put on him he said, 'They expect me to do better but I haven't done. That's one of these things. I can't perform and be on the leader board all of the time. I've had a good run at it. Seems I've not been on it this week and won't be. I just have to head over to Muirfield.'

It was an astonishing outburst from someone who had received nothing but fantastic support north of the border. In 2000, he complained about such an important tournament for Scottish golf being scheduled the week before the Open. 'However easy it might look to score sixty-four, as I did on the last day a year ago, the truth is it wasn't easy and took a lot out of me. Then you head off to the Open at Carnoustie and it just doesn't happen for you . . . Put it this way, if the Tour event wasn't at Loch Lomond and we had one somewhere else, I would seriously think about having the week off. I can't do that at Loch Lomond, as you know, because of all my obligations. This is a very demanding time for me – more tiring mentally than physically. There's so much to cope with on and off the course.'

Continuing the same theme in 2002, Montgomerie hinted that his poor record in the Open – he had missed the cut in three of the past five championships – might be down to the

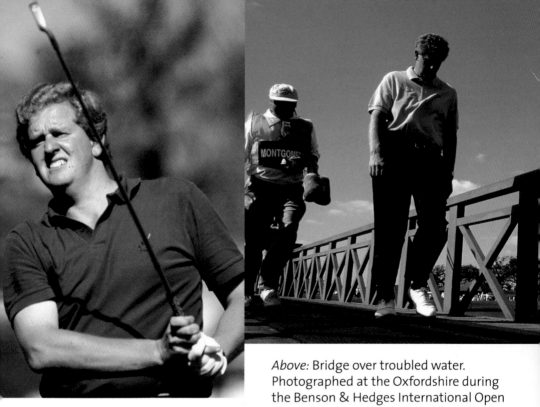

Above: His first full season on the European Tour, Montgomerie stares down an iron shot at the Spanish Open at Las Brisas in 1988.

Above: Bridge over troubled water. Photographed at the Oxfordshire during the Benson & Hedges International Open in 2001, he gives the impression of having the weight of the world on his shoulders.

Below: When do you think I will win a major? Chatting with manager and long time confidant Guy Kinnings in 1996.

Above: Monty rules: Top European Tour official John Paramor shows Montgomerie where to drop his ball during the World Match Play at Wentworth in 1999.

Right: Sand Storm: Known for wearing his heart on his sleeve, Montgomerie shows his displeasure at a poor bunker shot during the US Open at Pebble Beach in 2000.

Above: With a growing reputation, Montgomerie has designed more than twenty golf courses worldwide.

Left: On top of the world. Monty is lifted aloft by team-mate Costantino Rocca after Europe's historic Ryder Cup victory at Oak Hill in 1995.

Top: Quiet Please! Montgomerie does his own marshalling during the final stages of the US Open at Congressional Country Club in 1997.

Above left: Up for the Cup. Known for his legendary Ryder Cup exploits, Monty raises the trophy high at Valderrama in 1997.

Above right: Me and my shadow: Montgomerie and caddie Alistair McLean working closely together at the World Match Play Championship at Wentworth in 1996.

Top: Mind games: Montgomerie explaining what it takes to be a top tournament professional during a corporate day at Turnberry in 2003.

Above left: All things bright and beautiful. Montgomerie shares the spotlight with his family after winning the PGA Championship at Wentworth in 2000.

Above right: Eimear Montgomerie, shortly after her marriage to Colin in 1990.

Above: Montgomerie approaches the 72nd green at the 2006 US Open. Moments later a disastrous double bogey would rob him of victory.

Above: A putt slips by at the delayed Ryder Cup at The Belfry in 2002.

Below: An essential tool of the modern golf pro, high-flying Monty boards a private jet at Frimley Airport in Surrey in 1998.

Top: Sharing a joke with Ryder Cup partner Bernard Langer at the 2002 Ryder Cup at The Belfry.

Above left: Casting a long shadow: As eight time European number one, Colin Montgomerie was among the most dominant professionals of his era.

Above right: Two heads are better than one: Montgomerie advises Ryder Cup partner Paul Lawrie during the 1999 Battle of Brookline at Brookline, Massachusetts.

Above: Eye of the Tiger: Watched by opponent Tiger Woods, Montgomerie strikes the opening tee shot at the 2004 Ryder Cup at Oakland Hills.

Below: Scotland forever: Passionate about his Scottish roots, Montgomerie remains one of the few players to represent his country in both the Walker Cup and Ryder Cup.

strains of competing the week before at Loch Lomond. The media was singularly unimpressed, especially after he rebuffed a light-hearted suggestion that he should have followed Tiger Woods' example and gone fishing in Ireland for the week *whatever* his commitments.

The simple truth was that Montgomerie had failed to land the big one and the strain was beginning to show. Questioned about his future plans he explained that he was not 'in any sort of mood to think about stopping'. Patently at odds with himself, he explained that his primary concern was now coping physically with the rigours of the professional game. 'I just wish I was playing a bit better,' he said cryptically. 'It takes care of everything really.'

With everything that had happened at Loch Lomond, the portents were not good for Muirfield. At his official press briefing, a look of deep regret swept across his face as he spoke about not capitalising on his 65–70 start at Royal Lytham the previous year. In a carry-over from the black mood that pervaded his words at Loch Lomond, he described his tied-thirteenth finish as 'an opportunity missed'. Now in his fortieth year, he accepted there might not be many more opportunities to challenge for golf's top honours. Getting older was a fact of life, but as he walked out of the media centre Montgomerie looked like he had the weight of the world on his shoulders.

With everything that had gone before, it was anyone's guess how the next four days would play out at Muirfield. Tiger Woods was odds-on favourite as usual with Montgomerie a 66–1 outsider. That seemed a fair price after a bad-tempered display during the first round of 74 saw him down the field among the also-rans. Approached by a radio reporter, he was innocently asked if it had been a difficult day? 'Been a difficult day?' Monty replied with as much sarcasm as he could muster. 'No, it hasn't. It's been a very simple day. I hope this is not live. You start your questions better and I'll start answering them better.'

Amazing what a difference 24 hours can make. With another missed cut in the Open Championship beckoning,

Friday saw his game take flight with a magnificent record-breaking score of 64 – his best ever in a major. Described by former Ryder Cup player turned BBC pundit Ken Brown as 'the type you don't have very often in your career', it launched him up the leader board. On a bright breezeless day, his game plan was both simple and effective. Taking the safe option off the tee with a three wood, Montgomerie could play to his strengths by being extra aggressive with his iron play.

Everything seemed set for a meaningful challenge over the weekend, but as the dark clouds rolled in over the Firth of Forth on Saturday afternoon, Montgomerie simply imploded. Battling against the high winds and lashing rain, he splashed his way around Muirfield in a score of 84 – twenty strokes worse than the day before! Never mind Jekyll and Hyde – this was more like Laurel and Hardy. Sending journalists scurrying to the record books, few could recall such a turnaround in fortune at the Open Championship. (Jack Nicklaus followed up an 83 with a 66 at Sandwich in 1981, while Ian Baker-Finch improved with a 69 after shooting 86 at Turnberry in 1986.)

Beating a record that had stood since 1923 when Albert Tingey followed up a 94 with a 76, it came as no surprise when manager Guy Kinnings described Monty's mood at dinner that night as 'unusually subdued'. It was a disaster and, after racing around in under three hours for a quick-fire final round of 75, the Scot made matters worse by petulantly lashing out at a group of golf writers looking for a few short quotes before he headed for the exit. Berating them for what he saw as unfair reporting, he spent a full ten minutes behind the eighteenth green lecturing them on what was acceptable comment and what was not. (Contrast this with his humorous aside with Tiger Woods on the practice putting green before the final round. 'I kicked your ass yesterday, Monty,' said Woods, referring to his own weather-wrecked score of 81. 'Well, it's the only one you did kick,' replied the Scot.)

Returning to his own horror round on Saturday, Montgomerie railed at the suggestion that he had stormed off after his round and refused to talk to the media. Enforcing the belief that he tends to say the wrong things at the wrong time, usually to the wrong people, he was upset at what he considered was an unfair slur on his character.

'I played in very difficult circumstances yesterday,' said an incensed Montgomerie to his astonished audience, 'and I'm very disappointed the way you [the media] keep on trying to believe that I have a bad temper on the golf course! I haven't shown a sign of bad temper on a golf course for five years and I'm very, very disappointed . . . I would've spoken on Saturday but Tiger Woods was here and you were more interested in him. I left five minutes after his round. I was off after him. I left here and no one wanted to speak to me. I didn't storm off. I didn't go off in a temper – OK? I'm really hurt by it. Really hurt. So I've pulled out of golf tournaments for the next two weeks. I can't handle it any more.'

Meat and drink to any pressman worth his pay packet, the story of his bizarre behaviour raced through the media centre like wildfire. Many rubbed their hands in anticipation at the MONTY GOES NUTS! headlines while others shrugged their shoulders in a seen-it-all-before kind of way. As for his assertion that 'I haven't shown a sign of bad temper on a golf course for five years,' that had the press pack laughing into their 'house red' all evening!

For the past decade, the relationship between the former European number one and the media – especially the British golf press – had been a mutually beneficial one. When the mood took him, Monty was a bright, insightful individual who was eminently quotable and wonderfully entertaining company after a good round. Flip the coin over and he could be petty, rude, aggressive and immature, all depending on how poorly he had played that day. The British golf media for their part had been hugely tolerant of his moods. Now it was open season on the Scotsman and he only had himself to blame.

Award-winning columnist Paul Forsyth voiced the opinion of many when he wrote in *Golf World*:

The periodic threats Montgomerie throws forth in the wake of a poor performance have come to be taken with the same pinch of salt that his major prospects are consumed. Over the course of the past week he has managed to combine his two least endearing qualities by falling apart at the Open Championship and later responding with the confession that he couldn't handle it anymore . . . Last week was no watershed in the career of a diminished force, no crossroads or nadir in his history of self-destruction. It was just another sad and rather pathetic episode in the continuing saga of Montgomerie's uncontrollable emotions, the volcanic nature of which provoke eruptions of hot air that are credited with undue significance.

Over the weekend Montgomerie informed his manager Guy Kinnings that he needed an indefinite break from tournaments. Not entered for either the TNT Open in Holland the following week or Wales the week after, he was committed to crossing the Atlantic for the PGA Championship at Hazeltine National, Minnesota from 15–18 August and the NEC Invitational at Sahalee in Washington a week later. This was not a problem, as most pundits believed he would have got over his spat by then. The real issue was whether or not he would defend his Scandinavian Masters title in Stockholm in three weeks' time. Something had to be done quickly and it fell on Kinnings to pour oil on troubled waters. 'We'll have a chat on Monday,' he informed the media, 'and take things from there . . .'

The prospect of a family holiday off the coast of Naples did not help matters. Montgomerie appeared determined to keep his word, provoking all manner of speculation about his current state of mind. He outlined the schedule that had caused him so much stress: 'The two tournaments in Ireland, one of which I was defending. Then Loch Lomond and the Open! There is not a worse month for pressure and expectation and everything that goes with it.'

After the sunshine of Italy the world seemed a slightly less depressing place. 'I needed the holiday to recharge the batteries, they were pretty low,' said Montgomerie on his return to competitive action in Sweden. Proving you cannot be a seven-time European number one without being tougher than your average pair of old boots, Monty had considered taking three weeks off but was persuaded by wife Eimear that, metaphorically speaking, he needed to jump back on the horse that had so publicly thrown him. It was probably the right choice but his decision to return to competitive golf was not without its risks.

Describing his inability to lose enough weight over the past few months as a 'real problem', Montgomerie commented how his lack of discipline could be the 'difference between having an operation [on his back] or not.'

Thankfully this diagnosis was downgraded after Montgomerie saw an osteopathic surgeon in America the week before the PGA Championship. Monty confirmed that not only could he complete his busy schedule in America but he would definitely not require surgery in the near future. His words came back to haunt him during the second round of the NEC World Championship tournament at Sahalee Country Club in Seattle. Struggling at the wrong end of the elite field on four over par, he pulled out with severe back pain. 'I'm very disappointed,' said Monty afterwards. 'It's a real pity because I was looking forward to coming here and competing. My back has been causing problems all week and if you compete with others who are physically fit then there is no point carrying on.'

It was the same story at the BMW International Open a week later near Munich. Consulting yet another specialist in London, his last-minute decision not to travel to Germany must have been of huge concern to European Ryder Cup captain Sam Torrance. With the match at the Belfry less than a month away, contingency plans had already been put in place should Montgomerie's back injury stop him from playing all five sessions of the contest – something he had done since 1991. Or, indeed, if he was not playing at all!

Both the Linde German Masters and WGC World Championship event at Mount Juliet were also thrown into doubt. Sam Torrance was philosophical about losing his most experienced team member at such short notice but remained upbeat. 'It might be a bit much for Colin to play in every series,' he said, 'but I had already taken that into consideration.'

Montgomerie had a different view. Finding some relief, he showed his best form in months with a final-round 67 to finish ninth in the Linde German Masters in Cologne. Then, in typical Monty-style, he announced that he would pull out of Europe's Ryder Cup team if his back injury prevented him from taking part in *all five* matches at the Belfry. 'There's nothing wrong with the golf,' said Monty. 'It's just if I can play – and if I can't play five times for Sam I won't go, whether he wants me to play or not.'

Entered to play in the American Express Championships in Ireland the following week, it was now a race against time to get fit for the Belfry. Playing through the pain in Germany, he offered to telephone Torrance after his trip to Mount Juliet with the verdict, but his 'gut feeling' was that he would play. In the end, Montgomerie not only played but also dominated the 34th Ryder Cup as only he can. Winning four and a half points out of a possible five in the delayed match, he was singled out by Sam Torrance as the 'King of the Castle' at the Belfry. No wonder he got the biggest cheers of the day when Torrance introduced him to the crowd at the opening ceremony simply as 'Monty'.

His form in practice was less than impressive, but all that changed once the match started. Leading from the front, he partnered both Bernhard Langer and Padraig Harrington, before demolishing his old adversary Scott Hoch in the opening singles. Cheered on by expectant crowds, the Americans had no answer to Montgomerie as Europe ran out winners by 15½–12½.

Even as Irishman Paul McGinley was tossed unceremoniously into the lake fronting the eighteenth green, Torrance lost no time in praising the vital part Montgomerie, his so-called 'rock', had played in the historic victory. 'I have never seen him like that in any event,' he said. 'He's always been a great team man but this week he was incredible . . . He has so much experience that it makes it a very easy job to be his captain.'

His opposite number Curtis Strange agreed. 'Seve was their leader for a long time, now it's Colin,' said the US captain. 'Every team needs a leader, not only for their play but also for the way they handle themselves . . . He led by example and the others took their cue from him. He certainly did not disappoint this week.'

Lionised by friend and foe alike, Colin Montgomerie had once again been rescued by the Ryder Cup in a season with very little to celebrate.

16. MOONLIGHT PLAY-OFFS AND LAST-GASP VICTORIES

As satisfying as victory was for the European team at the Belfry in September 2002, it must have been especially sweet for Colin Montgomerie.

Struggling to mount a telling challenge in any of the four majors, the battling Scot came good at exactly the right time against a USA team that included half a dozen major winners. Boosted by the plaudits he received, the Scot enjoyed a rich vein of form over the next month including a joint-third place at the Dunhill Links Championship the following week. From the east coast of Scotland to southern Spain, his rapid climb up the money list was further enhanced after finishing equal first in the Volvo Masters at Valderrama in October.

It was the first 'shared' title on the European Tour since 1986 – when Bernhard Langer and Seve Ballesteros tied for the Lancôme Trophy – and the German was involved once again. Montgomerie had finished tied with Langer in regulation play on three under par. In fading light, the former Ryder Cup partners then halved both the eighteenth and tenth in the play-off before taking up the offer by European Tour executive director Ken Schofield to share the title. 'There was no way we could continue,' said Langer as the option of lighting the way with car headlamps was even discussed. 'I couldn't see how far I was standing from the ball and I saw that Colin felt the same way . . . It was really getting ridiculous. We both agreed [sharing] it was the right thing to do.'

Chasing his first tournament win since the 2001 Scandinavian Masters, Montgomerie agreed enthusiastically. 'There was no way we could play on,' he said. 'So when Ken Schofield came on the radio, we very quickly shook hands.'

Either way it was an anticlimax, but both players believed it was the right decision – especially Monty, whose seven previous play-offs had all ended in defeat. 'Nobody lost, and bearing in mind how we both had such a wonderful Ryder Cup together, I think that was right,' he said afterwards. 'I could not think of a better guy to share a tournament with. And don't forget I hadn't won any of my seven previous play-offs. Now I can finally add an entry to the win column.'

Langer agreed: 'When you remember what happened in the Ryder Cup, perhaps it was fitting that we should go on to share this title. We both played tremendous golf and neither of us deserved to lose.'

Not that Montgomerie was ever satisfied with a share of anything. Losing out to Lee Westwood in 2000 and now finishing fourth behind two-time winner Retief Goosen, his desire to win his eighth Order of Merit was stronger than ever. 'Of course I can be European number one for the eighth time,' he said, 'but only if I perform. I haven't played so consistently well over the past couple of seasons as I did when I won seven in a row. This year I've performed OK, but only in fits and starts.'

Without labouring the point, his back problems had played a significant part in his lack of consistency throughout the year. 'May was good, September was good and October wasn't bad,' said Monty. 'But at the same time I didn't play so well in other months and that's what I did when I won the Order of Merit for seven years.'

Before the Scandinavian Masters, Montgomerie's last win in a stroke-play event was over fifteen months earlier in the Irish Open. A week later, Monty made it two in a row at the

TCL China Classic at the Plaza golf club in the Dongguan Province of southern China, taking him back into the world's top ten for the first time in a year. He now had two wins and a tied-third finish from his last four stroke-play events. Two more long-haul trips to the Million Dollar event in South Africa and Tiger Woods' tournament in California saw the year out before heading back to Eimear and his children for a lengthy Christmas break.

It had been a whirlwind year with more highs and lows than your average spring forecast. The season began with him still looking for his first major. After the PGA Championship in August, he shifted his focus to looking for his first European Tour tournament victory of the year. With back problems making that look more and more unlikely, his goal was to be fit enough to play all five sessions of the Ryder Cup in September. In the end that was the key, as his season was then transformed by winning twice in the space of two weeks.

'I found very early on in my career that I could cope,' he told the BBC's *Breakfast with Frost* in November. 'I could cope with certain pressure situations, as some footballers can cope with taking a penalty, I suppose, and some snooker players can finish off a great break.'

Amid the champagne-popping celebrations at the Belfry, Montgomerie was in a surprisingly reflective mood. It had been a time of change, a time of transition. During the past six months, he had changed his caddie and his putter, reunited with coach Denis Pugh and employed an ex-army fitness trainer in the hope of extending his career through a new fitness regime. He even teased the media, saying how he might retire should he win a big European Tour event by the end of the year. Two weeks later he won the prestigious Volvo Masters in Spain and guess what? No retirement. The British golf media were now used to such tongue-in-cheek prognostications and it came as no surprise when his management company announced that he had actually added *extra* tournaments to his schedule for the next season!

With his fortieth birthday looming large on the horizon in 2003, it was inconceivable that Montgomerie would just win and go. Unlike the legendary Bobby Jones, who retired from competitive golf aged just 28 after winning the Grand Slam in 1930, Monty was just not that way inclined. As the media speculated, imagine the hugely competitive Scot passing up the opportunity to win the Open Championship a week after he had won the Loch Lomond tournament, for example.

It was never going to happen. After his dramatic end to the 2002 season, where he led Europe to a brilliant victory over the USA in the Ryder Cup and won twice in Spain and China, the golfing world had high expectations of Colin Montgomerie. Yet Monty's overwhelming feeling was one of disappointment and frustration. He had spent more time in the United States than ever before, yet the trophy cabinet was still looking a touch bare. Another year had gone by and he still had no major championship and still no wins on the PGA Tour. In fact, the Scot was finding it hard to win even the most low-key European Tour events. For the seven-time European number one, it was time to reflect on the mistakes he had made and try to learn from them.

As the 2003 season dawned the clamour became a clarion call as the media continually grilled Montgomerie about his inability to win one of the 'big four' major championships. As someone who regularly put the Americans to the sword in the Ryder Cup, why did he not play in the same swaggering way when the heat was on in the Masters, US Open, Open Championship and PGA Championship?

There was an obvious question mark over his fitness, but that had not stopped him competing in all five sessions of the Ryder Cup. Nor had it prevented him from finishing second in the PGA at Wentworth or the Deutsche Bank-SAP Open in Germany when his back pain was reputedly at its worst. So just how bad *was* the injury that saw him pull out of a number of tournaments this year? Was it career-threatening as reported, or merely a protection mechanism he employed to release some steam from the pressure cooker his life had become? Only Montgomerie knew for sure and he was determined to remain upbeat about his chances of breaking his major hoodoo.

As someone who had changed his diet, his caddie, his coach and taken up the belly putter in an effort to land the big one, Montgomerie lost little sleep dumping his long-time club sponsors in favour of Ben Hogan equipment. Bringing to an end a hugely successful seven-year involvement with Callaway, he had already used the Hogan Apex Tour ball in his matches with Bernhard Langer (a Hogan staff professional) at the Belfry, and teed up the same ball up in his singles against Scott Hoch.

Montgomerie rejected an early-season trip to Australia on the European Tour schedule in favour of six weeks on the PGA Tour in America. With Guy Kinnings dismissing the idea that Colin had switched allegiances, it proved a frustrating start to the year. Ring rusty after spending ten weeks at home with his family, Monty hoped all the work he had done on his fitness would pay off as his season got under way in California. Swimming every day to strengthen his back muscles, it was a big disappointment when he missed the cut in his first tournament at the Nissan Open in Los Angeles in mid-February.

Struggling with his forged Hogan irons with their standard shaft fitting (he was used to a bored-through shaft in a cast-iron club) Montgomerie followed it up with another poor performance in the WGC World Match Play in San Diego at the end of February. Suffering a first-round knockout against Germany's Alex Cejka, he was annoyed at a complete lack of distance control – the hallmark of his golf game. With a face like thunder, he was asked whether he was playing in the Dubai Desert Classic the following week? With the tournament under threat because of possible conflict in Iraq, his reply was typically forthright: 'I'm not interested in next week – OK?' (In fact, he had already made the decision to withdraw the week before.)

Taking up an invitation to compete in the Ford Championship in Miami, his unhappy start to the season continued as he missed the cut at Doral after rounds of 72 and 74. Deciding to tough it out in the United States, his miserable run of form extended into the Honda Classic in early March with yet another missed cut. Described as a 'pivotal season' by Montgomerie, this was definitely not the start he expected. The following week he paid a private trip to Augusta National with friends as a 'mini practice round' prior to the Masters. Resisting the temptation to fly back home and cut his losses, he invited Eimear and his children to fly out to America for three weeks as he warmed up at the Bay Hill Invitational in Orlando in late March. It seemed to work, because he made his first cut of the year to finish in 31st place.

Then it all went wrong at the Players Championship in Florida. Another missed cut made it five out of six stroke-play tournaments with not a single round below 70. In the worst run of his career, Montgomerie promptly withdrew from the BellSouth Classic in Atlanta the week before the Masters. Heading home to England to 'recharge his batteries', the entire trip had proved a frustrating waste of time. For years, players like Nick Faldo and Tony Jacklin had advised him to spend more time playing tournaments in America in the run-up to majors and now he had. For Monty, it would not be something he would be doing again in a hurry!

Back in Surrey with his coach Denis Pugh, Montgomerie knew that mistakes had been made. Regretting his extended New Year break when he hardly picked up a club for ten weeks, he also blamed his lack of practice with his new bladed irons for his lack of form. 'I'm getting used to some new equipment that I started using,' he admitted at the Players Championship, 'and I felt I could get used to it more quickly than I have.'

He returned to Augusta for the Masters, but really should have saved himself the trip. With the course playing longer than normal after some unseasonably bad weather, his coach was concerned from the start. 'The measure of the test in front of him is he'll be hitting five irons into greens when someone like Tiger is using a nine iron,' said Pugh. Missing the cut after rounds of 78 and 76, it was Monty's second-worst performance in 46 major appearances.

Thankfully there was no sign of Tiger Woods as Montgomerie made his first appearance of the season on the

European Tour at the Italian Open in Brescia in April. Back on more familiar territory, the Scot seemed happier. 'If I play relaxed golf I play good golf,' he said. 'I don't feel I have anything to prove here. In America I always have the tag that I've never won there and you're always trying to prove something. Here you don't have to. It is much easier for me here.'

Admitting that he had spent longer in the States than perhaps he needed to, at least the days when he was continually heckled and abused by American galleries were behind him. 'Although I didn't play all that well in the States earlier in the year,' said Montgomerie, 'the bonus was the good reception from the crowds . . . I feel I can now come up the last hole [at major championships] one ahead and have a chance to par. Six years ago that would have been tough. I don't expect to receive the level of support I have in Britain at the Open, of course not. But maybe the last two Ryder Cup matches have done something for me. All I ever wanted . . . was a level playing field – I can't ask for any more than that.'

It was in Italy that Montgomerie made the brave decision to ditch his Hogan blades in favour of the company's cavity-back irons. Using them in the pro-am, the impact on his confidence was immediate as he went round in ten under par. 'Having reflected on it, I think I stayed in America for a couple of weeks too many,' he said before the first round. 'In retrospect it was a mistake. I think I was digging myself a deeper hole each week. No one ever talked about my clubs when I was winning seven European Order of Merit titles, now they do because I'm not. But I'm so glad that I've got back to something I was using before and I'm very happy with it . . . I'm looking forward to scoring as opposed to the doubts about "Is it me, or is it the equipment?" '

Any doubts Montgomerie had about his career going into free fall after his confidence-sapping eight-week trip to America were dispelled after a final-round 65 in Italy. Claiming a share of second place behind tournament winner Matthias Gronberg of Sweden, it was now full steam ahead, but it was not long before controversy struck once again. Having caused a rift with Ryder Cup colleague Phillip Price when he was accused of 'poaching' his caddie Andy Prodger in the run-up to the 2002 match at the Belfry, it appeared Monty was at it again at the PGA Championship at Wentworth in May, when he was accused by Stephen Leaney of pinching his bagman Steve Rawlinson. The 34-year-old Australian was understandably aggrieved. 'I had an inkling that Monty wanted my caddie but it wasn't until five-thirty last night that I heard about it,' said Leaney after the first round. 'It was unfortunate that I didn't get to hear about it until the deal was already done. I'd have preferred Monty to have had the courtesy to call and tell me what was going on.'

In typical style, Montgomerie was unrepentant, saying that everything had been arranged after his telephone call to Leaney before the tournament began: 'I thought I was doing the right thing and, if I haven't, I apologise. But at the same time I don't feel I have to.' Explaining his split with Prodger, who stayed on the bag at Wentworth, he added, 'I just wanted a change, it just wasn't gelling very well.'

Building up a full head of steam, Montgomerie turned his attention to what he saw as the unseemly 'bidding war' to become Europe's next Ryder Cup captain. 'I see that Nick Faldo has put his name forward for 2006 and it looks like we are getting into a bidding war,' warned Montgomerie. 'There seem to be three people up for the next one – fine – but two are going to lose. I would hate for Sandy [Lyle], Bernhard [Langer] or Ian [Woosnam] to feel like they've lost out. Then what happens? Do they bid again and give themselves the opportunity to lose again?'

With the match scheduled for Oakland Hills in September 2004, the name of the new captain would be announced after the Open Championship in July. Having declared his interest in becoming a future Ryder Cup captain, you could sense his frustration at being pushed down the list for years to come. 'I've said before, that if I qualified in ninth or tenth [in the Ryder Cup points list], I'd be better off as captain rather than playing just once or twice,' declared Monty, before adding diplomatically, 'Of course, I'd be honoured to do it anywhere and any time.'

Competing in the Wales Open shortly after, Montgomerie described how having Rawlinson on his bag would help him relax more. 'A little joke at the right time' was the key to maintaining a positive demeanour on the course, he announced. 'He is a real character,' said the 39-year-old Scot, who also promised to shed the grumpy, self-absorbed image the media portrayed of him.

You could practically hear the hacks choking with laughter as he ended up by saying: 'I think you will see me smiling a lot more on the golf course because he is so funny.'

17. BACK TO THE FUTURE FOR THE FALL MONTY

Announcing that the British public would see 'a new, easy-going Monty' in May 2003, the old, uptight version was still in view as the second half of the season unfolded in the same frustrating manner.

Missing consecutive cuts in Europe for the first time in five years, he entered the US Open at Olympia Fields in June with a new mental approach to the game. In an effort to counteract the dominance of Tiger Woods, the Scot explained how he had been 'screwing with the successful formula' that had brought him seven Order of Merit titles. Having spent the last two years experimenting with a raft of new drivers and shafts in the hope of hitting the ball 'further and further', Montgomerie enthusiastically declared to the press that he was now going back into the past to rekindle his former glory. Accuracy rather than distance would be his mantra for the week. 'I'm going back to doing things the way I did during that spell,' said Monty about his golden era in the American majors from 1990 to 1997, 'rather than the frame of mind where, truthfully, I was trying to play other people's games rather than my own.'

Quite what 'frame of mind' Montgomerie was in was anybody's guess as he explained his new debriefing method prior to the opening round of the US Open in Cook County, Illinois. Unlike most players, who have a chat with their coach after the round, Monty now chatted with two coaches after every nine holes he played in practice! Add to that a liberal sprinkling of positive reinforcement and the media had all the headlines they could wish for!

Talking up his chances around a course he saw as a typical American major set-up, Montgomerie said he felt the rest of the field was already 'one down' to him before a ball had been struck! Perhaps someone should have told the winner, Jim Furyk, because he hardly noticed the Scot back in joint 42nd place as he paraded the famous trophy for the cameras late into Sunday evening. (In a curious turnabout, Stephen Leaney finished tied second with a new caddie on the bag.)

One year on from the 'Be Nice To Monty' campaign at Bethpage, the Scot needed all the help he could get. Returning to Scotland and the Diageo Championship at Gleneagles, his world ranking of 21 was under threat as his form slipped even further in the run-up to the Open Championship at Royal St George's. With his fortieth birthday falling on the Monday following the tournament, Monty was in a surprisingly positive mood about the immediate future. 'I am coming here to win,' said the home favourite. 'I am going to Loch Lomond to win, and I am going to the Open to win. So I am not thinking that time is running out. I am here to compete at this level for the next five or six years.'

The record books show that he did not win at Gleneagles, neither did he win at Loch Lomond. In fact, he had not won a stroke-play tournament in over eight months since the TCL China Classic in October 2002. And, despite ranking his chances of winning the Open at Sandwich as 'ten out of ten', he not only failed to win, his decision to pull out after just seven holes of the first round ignited for some fevered speculation in the press!

Arranging to meet Denis Pugh and Hugh Mantle, his sports psychologist, for breakfast on Thursday morning, he described how he broke a fall with his right hand after tripping over a step at the Walletts Court hotel near Dover. Choosing to tough it out, he played seven holes of the first round before giving in to the pain of his throbbing right hand. 'My wrist is swollen and I am on my way to get it X-rayed to see if anything is broken,' said the Scot to waiting reporters.

Montgomerie admitted that he would definitely not have attempted to play through such pain if it was any other competition. With the chance of winning the Open proving too hard to resist, he said, 'I knew it was bad right away and after hitting only about five shots on the practice range I was about to say forget it, but because it's the Open and because of my competitive nature I wanted to give it a go. It was no good, though. I couldn't strike the ball with any authority . . . It's frustrating because I was hitting the ball very well and the course was set up superbly for a straight driver, which is what I am.' Philosophical about his latest injury setback, Montgomerie pulled out of the Irish Open and ended up taking three weeks away from the game.

For all his self-belief, Montgomerie's recent form had been pretty dire even before he headed north to London citing a hand injury. One top-ten finish, five missed cuts and two failures to qualify in fifteen previous assaults on the Open Championship hardly qualified Montgomerie to describe himself as one of the favourites to win. Add that to his poor form coming into the week and the fact he was four over par at the time, and rumours that he had exaggerated his injury started to gain momentum.

He had been dubbed 'The Fall Monty' by the British tabloids, and the story sparked into life after his playing partner Brad Faxon denied any knowledge of the injury until Montgomerie was driven back to the clubhouse. Offering a robust response, Monty admitted that he was hurt by the suggestion that he had not acted honestly. 'If someone has that opinion, that's fine,' said the Scot at his return at the inaugural Nordic Open in Copenhagen. 'If you go and see my MRI scans and my doctor and how bloody sore it was, that opinion would change and change in a hurry. There is no way I would ever pull out of a tournament after seven holes because of the fact that apparently I didn't want to be there – that's not me

... Whoever wrote that doesn't really understand me as a person and the competitive spirit that I have.'

Hoping that he would be fit for the 85th PGA Championship at Oak Hill Country Club a week later, his confidence was boosted by a runner-up finish in Denmark. Complaining that his hand was 'still not a hundred per cent', he was encouraged by the prognosis that there was definitely no fracture or ligament damage. The problem now was mental. From the fairway there was no pain but coming out of the rough it was a different matter. 'I went to see the doctor on Monday and he said if it doesn't hurt, then go with it,' confirmed Montgomerie. 'It doesn't hurt when I hit an ordinary shot, only when I'm in the hay.'

Heading out to Rochester, New York, in confident mood, the Scot genuinely believed this could be his week. The course was a personal favourite after Europe's 1995 Ryder Cup victory and if his wrist held up, this could be the week that he finally rid himself of the unwanted tag of being the best European golfer never to have won a major. 'I would not be surprised at all to see him in contention here,' said Bernhard Langer. 'You don't get to be number one in Europe for seven straight years unless you're a great player and, straight hitter that he is, any set-up where there's lots of rough and makes it so important to hit the fairways should suit him.'

Then, almost before he had unpacked his suitcase, Oak Hill became 'choke hill' for Colin Montgomerie after a disastrous opening round of 82. Not unlike the British Masters in June when he brandished a club at press photographers before calling them 'amateurs', the former European number one lost his cool completely. Mumbling throughout his round, he berated marshals for not keeping better order and was even accused of tossing a ball at another snapper who upset his concentration! (Following up a complaint by an official, Guy Kinnings asked Monty about the incident and he told him he had merely lobbed the ball to his caddie Steve Rawlinson and missed.)

Whatever the truth, it was his highest ever competitive score in the United States and left him major-less for yet another year. A month later, Montgomerie was down to his lowest world ranking for more than a decade at 32nd, his worst since he joined the rankings at number 36 in 1991. There was even the possibility that he might lose his multimillion-pound equipment deal with the Hogan Company. (In a curious turnaround, his former sponsors Callaway had bought out the TopFlite Company of which Hogan was a subsidiary.)

Montgomerie was also concerned how his form might impact on the upcoming Ryder Cup qualification process. With everyone starting on zero points after the European Masters in Switzerland in August, his success at the Volvo Masters the previous November now meant nothing in terms of ranking points. As someone who had once suggested that the European team should be made up of twelve captain's picks, the Scot immediately entered the next five consecutive tournaments in the hope of improving his situation.

Looking to turn his season around, other changes were made. Ditching the belly putter that had served him so well during the Ryder Cup, he went back to a standard-length blade in the last round of the Lancôme Trophy in September. Placing at least some of the blame for his poor form at the feet of his 'amiable' caddie, Steve Rawlinson, they parted company a week later. He enlisted the temporary services of family friend Colin Cotter from Royal Troon, a former university colleague of Eimear and brother of BBC radio and television presenter Andrew Cotter. It was his third change of caddie in five months, but it failed to arrest Monty's run of poor form as he missed the cut at the German Linde Masters in Cologne. Worse still, Monty then slipped on a step coming out of the scoring hut behind the eighteenth green at Carnoustie after signing for a one-over-par 73 in the first round of the Dunhill Links Championship. At least this time there was no permanent damage other than his pride, but it summed up a year that was getting away from him fast.

The season's frustration threatened to boil over at the Volvo Masters at Valderrama in October. Missing a birdie putt on the ninth green in the second round, Montgomerie upset playing partners Thomas Björn and Brian Davis after slamming his errant ball into the concrete buggy path near the green they were still putting on! Rebounding like a rocket, it narrowly missed a window in a nearby apartment building and, by the time Björn and Davis holed out, Monty was impatiently waiting on the tenth tee over 100 yards away! All this in a week where the Royal and Ancient Golf Club unveiled the latest guidelines on etiquette, one of which included the advice that: 'All players should conduct themselves in a disciplined manner, demonstrating courtesy and sportsmanship at all times, irrespective of how competitive they may be.'

Something had to change if Montgomerie was to keep up his record of winning at least one tournament per year since 1993, and change it did at the Macau Open in China in mid-October. Racing through the field with a final-round 68, he not only caught tournament leader Scott Bar of Australia but beat him at the first hole of a sudden-death play-off with a birdie four. 'I've kept the winning streak alive,' said a delighted Monty, 'but I am leaving it later and later. It's getting difficult. I am leaving it too late. October is late, I'd rather win in January.'

Finishing in 28th place in the Order Of Merit, the 2003 season had been a miserable one by his standards. His worst result since his rookie year in 1988, he had failed to win a single European Tour event, triumphing only once in an out-of-season tournament in Macau. Having lost ten weeks at the beginning of the year, his best results were second places in the Italian and Nordic Opens. Lacking any real consistency, he missed the cut at the Masters and the US PGA and retired hurt from the first round of the Open after injuring his wrist in a fall. Three caddies in five months had not helped his cause either.

Having spent eight frustrating weeks in the United States in 2003 where he barely made a cut, his decision to play more in Europe was twofold. First, he needed to boost his world ranking position so that he could have automatic entry into the US Open in June. And second, with the Ryder Cup scheduled for Oakland Hills in September, he needed to gain more points so he did not have to rely on a wild card from his former fourball partner and European captain Bernard Langer. 'We're always learning and I won't go again [to the PGA Tour], not for that length of time without a break,' said Monty.

No longer under contract to the Hogan company, Montgomerie had been experimenting over the Christmas break with different makes of clubs before settling on a contract with Yonex. Encouraged by his victory in Macau, he had worked hard on his fitness and flexibility in the hope it would pay dividends in the year to come. 'I feel a bit like a rookie having worked hard on my game and fitness over the winter,' he said.

Never one to talk down his own importance, his world ranking of 57 barely six weeks into 2004 was a harsh reminder of how far he had slipped from his pedestal, but Montgomerie remained philosophical. 'Am I the fifty-seventh best player in the world over the past two years?' he mused. 'Probably, yes.'

Determined to get back into the top ten by the end of the year, his first tournament was the South African Open at Erinvale golf club in mid-January. 'I don't set goals for the [individual] weeks any more, as you can easily find yourself in trouble,' he said. 'For the year my goal is now to get back in the top ten in the world. Whether that happens this year or takes a couple of years we will see, but that is my goal. I spent about twelve years in that top ten and I intend to get back into it.'

Getting his season under way much earlier than normal, he arrived in Cape Town armed with a new set of graphite-shafted, cavity-back Yonex irons and Mark McNulty's former caddie, Andy Forsyth. 'It is not necessarily an earlier start because it is a Ryder Cup year,' said Monty. 'I think I have taken too long off in the past to be honest. I am about a month and a half earlier than usual. I normally begin in the first week of March.'

The importance of moving up the world rankings was not lost on Montgomerie. He knew that unless he managed to make it back into the safety net of the top fifty, it threatened to keep him out of the lucrative World Championship events along with the Players Championship, the US Open and even the Open Championship. Even his invitation to the Masters in April was not an absolute certainty. 'Sometimes I get back to my room in the evenings and wonder how and why I'm in this position,' moaned Monty.

There was not much 'Ryder Cup camaraderie' when Montgomerie clashed with former team member Thomas Björn at the Johnnie Walker Classic in Bangkok in late January. Playing the sixteenth hole of their second round, the Danish star was forced to back off a chip after catching sight of the Scot coming over a bridge next to the green he was on. Monty had hit his ball into the lake and was in the process of taking a penalty drop. Totally oblivious to anyone else as he harrumphed around, Monty incensed Björn with his lack of etiquette. Never one to hold back his feelings, Björn missed his par putt and angrily pointed his putter towards his former Ryder Cup colleague like a matador facing down a rather unco-operative bull!

The incident might have ended with a brief apology, but Monty took exception to the Dane's actions and the heated comments that followed. Once they had handed in their scorecards Björn, the halfway leader, demanded to speak to tournament director Miguel Vidaor, despite Montgomerie's suggestion they deal with it in private. When the trio finally emerged from their behind-closed-doors meeting, the fiery Dane refused to divulge what had been sorted out between the pair. 'We have shaken hands and we are as good friends as we were before we went out,' he said unconvincingly.

The latest in a series of similar incidents between the two, it rekindled memories of the Volvo Masters at Valderrama a few months earlier when Montgomerie upset Thomas Björn after stamping off the ninth green before his playing partner had putted out. Sensibly, the Dane now insisted on letting the matter rest. 'I know you really want to hear what that was all about, but I'm sorry,' said Thomas to inquisitive reporters in Bangkok. 'This is staying between me and Monty and the

European Tour. I have the utmost respect for him and things happen once in a while on a golf course, where players that are as competitive as we are have a difference in opinion on some things. I did some things wrong and Colin did some things wrong. You know us well enough that we've both got our tempers and we both want to play well ... It's not a question of saying sorry. It's a question of saying what we felt happened out there ... We've got to make sure it doesn't happen again.'

With both players competing in the WGC Accenture World Match Play Championship a few weeks later in February, Montgomerie had yet to find any real form. The pressure was building if he wanted to gain automatic entry into the prestigious Tournament Players Championship at Sawgrass in March. The maths was painfully simple: Montgomerie must rank inside the top fifty, but the odds were not good. After the WGC at the La Costa Resort in California he was scheduled to play in the Dubai Desert Classic the following week. Both tournaments had exceptionally strong fields, including world number one Tiger Woods, and Monty needed to finish no worse than fourth in either event to gain the points he needed. 'I need to perform well,' he calculated. 'Very well in one, quite well in two.'

Admitting that getting back into the top fifty in the world was a huge priority, Montgomerie revealed that he had rarely checked the rankings when he was number two in the world behind Greg Norman back in 1997. Now he was forced to reschedule events because his ranking was not good enough to enter them! 'I check more regularly than normal,' he admitted at Carlsbad prior to his opening match against his buddy, Nick Price.

Part of the reason for his downward slide in the world rankings had been his injury worries – most significantly his back problems, which had seen him withdraw from a number of events over the past eighteen months. Unfortunately his health hoodoo struck again at the Accenture Match Play. After easy wins over Nick Price and Stewart Cink (including seven birdies and no bogeys in fourteen holes for a 6 and 4 victory) he lost to Australian Stephen Leaney in the third round. Looking tired and drawn, the bug he had picked up from his trip to the Far East the previous week finally took its toll. 'I was tired at the end. I never got over Malaysia last week where I had flu and diarrhoea and all sorts and that's never the best preparation for trying to play golf,' said Monty, who admitted that playing 36 holes of golf in a day was 'no fun'.

Scheduled to play three more events in America, Montgomerie made the decision to head home to England to rest before yet another long-haul trip to Dubai and Singapore. It proved to be an inspired choice because he finished fourth in the Dubai Desert Classic and moved up one place to 56th in the world rankings. Tantalisingly close to a coveted spot in the world's top fifty, Monty confirmed the secret of his success was the thirty pounds in weight he had shed since mid-2003. 'Basically I'm on the Atkins diet,' explained the svelte Scot. 'But I was bored with chicken, and I wanted to keep away from beef to keep an eye on my cholesterol, so a girlfriend recommended I go for elephant instead. She had already tried it, and it's absolutely delicious when it's well prepared.'

The thought of Montgomerie tucking into jumbo fricassee amused the press corps, especially when he explained the technique involved. 'You can eat an elephant, but you have to do it bite by bite,' said an unrepentant Monty. 'You can't do it all in one go.' It was a typically tongue-in-cheek comment by Monty that hardened golf hacks brushed off with a knowing smile, but the more serious task of getting his career back on track was an elephant-sized problem.

After his hugely encouraging performance in the United Arab Emirates, Montgomerie moved on to the Caltex Masters in Singapore where claimed his 28th career victory with a sixteen-under-par total. Managing to overturn a four-shot overnight deficit with a stunning final round of 65 at Laguna National, the Scot managed to carve out a three-stroke victory over American journeyman Greg Hanrahan. Following a superb 67 on Saturday, it was his first European Tour title in sixteen months and his delight was obvious. Having failed to win an event in Europe the previous year for the first time in more than a decade, it was the right win at exactly the right time. 'There is a sense of relief to win as well,' he told the media afterwards. 'Finishing in the top ten is OK but to win is slightly different and it's nice to go back up the rankings because I was falling rapidly and hopefully now I'll get into all the tournaments I have taken for granted for so long.'

It also answered a lot of questions, especially for European Ryder Cup captain Bernhard Langer, who heard about his win while competing in the Bay Hill Invitational in Florida. 'That's fantastic,' said the German. 'It's great for him to be in the winners' circle again. I always thought he would play his way onto the team and, hopefully, he will.'

Moving him back into the top fifty in the world rankings, it secured his qualification for the Tournament Players Championship at Sawgrass the following week. Indeed, getting into the TPC was the inspiration for his victory in Singapore. 'The Players had been on my schedule for the past twelve years,' said Montgomerie about the tournament often labelled the 'fifth major'. 'When I spoke to Jane, my PA in the office, about where I'm staying, it was a real jolt when she said, "Actually we haven't booked you in anywhere because you're not in it!" It's like anything in life, you don't know how good things are until they're taken away from you.'

It would prove a prophetic statement in more ways than one, with the Masters at Augusta National less than one month away.

18. MAJOR CONCERNS

A part from his third-round exit in the WGC Accenture World Match Play tournament in California, Montgomerie had played seven times so far in 2004 and his worst finish was sixteenth. Even with a disappointing 42nd-place finish at the Tournament Players Championship in Florida in March, he remained fortieth in the world rankings after his victory in the Singapore Masters earlier in the season. With confidence flooding back, Montgomerie headed back to America in preparation for the Masters. Arriving at Augusta National in confident mood, he would leave it a week later with his game in shreds and his marriage to Eimear in serious jeopardy.

In a sad echo of what happened at the Open Championship at St Andrews in 2000, the *Sun* newspaper reported a 'blazing row!' between Colin and Eimear after a bad-tempered round of 80 saw him crash out of the Masters at the halfway stage. (His one-under-par 71 the day before was not much happier.) Heading for the parking lot and a quick exit, he left his embarrassed wife stranded and shaking her head as he drove back to their rental property alone. The day ended with a shouting match that stretched well into the night and, one newspaper reported, 'awoke at least one of the neighbours!'

It may not have done the couple's reputation for marital harmony any good but it was certainly the stuff that tabloid dreams are made off. What sparked this latest row is unclear. Listen to the tabloids and it could have been anything from Monty raging at his inability to win a major to Eimear informing her husband that she wanted a divorce! One laughable report even suggested that Montgomerie ended the week apoplectic with rage because Phil Mickelson, his rival for the unwelcome tag of 'best golfer never to win a major', finally broke his own duck by winning the Masters! Monty has always sought to explain these frequent tantrums as part and parcel of being the competitive animal he is. Whatever the truth, something had gone very badly wrong in what was generally accepted to be one of the most enduring relationships in golf.

Could things get much worse? Sadly for Colin Montgomerie, they could. A holiday in Barbados the following week failed to heal the marital stress that had steadily grown more acute since Christmas. With rumours of another split on the cards, it was left to the loyal Guy Kinnings to try and keep a lid on things. 'There will be nothing from anyone – Colin, Eimear or myself – other than no comment,' he answered in response to the persistent rumours. 'When that situation changes, we'll let you know.'

Ever since he had turned professional in 1988, Montgomerie had been a driven individual when it came to achieving what he wanted out of golf. Uncompromising, dedicated and determined, he made the absolute maximum of the talent he was born with. Lacking the charismatic nature of Seve Ballesteros, the natural god-given talent of Sandy Lyle or the competitive nerve of Nick Faldo, Montgomerie's seven European Order of Merit titles bore testimony to his high level of consistency – something very few players have matched in the history of the game. At no point in his career was he the longest hitter, greatest iron player or even the best putter, but the combination of a silky-smooth swing allied with the ability to squeeze every last shot out of a golf course was his best, perhaps most underrated asset.

Many players have been more dedicated than the Scot when it came to practice but nobody felt failure quite as deeply as Montgomerie. His albatross was that he hated to lose more than he enjoyed winning and that was ultimately the root of the problem. Long ago he realised that only 100 per cent commitment would suffice if he wanted to realise all his golfing ambitions. Mentally he had to be so much stronger than the far more naturally gifted golfers he often competed against. Often that was enough, but having to work twice as hard as anyone else was exhausting.

Back in 2000, Eimear blamed his single-minded pursuit of the majors as the reason their relationship had broken down. This was a crushing accusation for such a thin-skinned character as Colin Montgomerie but, having accepted the reality of his situation, he changed his attitude and managed to win his wife back. Consulting his friend and mentor, sports psychologist Hugh Mantle, he endeavoured not to bring his disappointment home or become worked up when things did not go his way. It even worked for a while, but for someone as competitive as Monty it was like walking a tightrope.

As for tennis legend John McEnroe, competition was all-consuming. Not a matter of simply turning up and playing, the process of trying to win a major or Ryder Cup match involved every fibre of his being. If he was not playing in a tournament he was thinking about playing. During tournaments, his well-publicised spats with the crowd helped sharpen his focus, pinpoint his concentration. And, like the former Wimbledon champion, Montgomerie would often provoke such spats because he needed a something to trigger his competitive nature.

In an interesting exchange at the 1992 Bells Scottish Open, Montgomerie was asked by Jock Howard of *Golf World* magazine: 'Would it be fair to say there is part of you that needs to get annoyed with someone or something in order to focus?' After an uncomfortable silence, Monty reluctantly admitted, 'Yes, I suppose there might be something in that.'

At 41, the Scot instinctively knew time was against him. Redoubling his efforts, his growing obsession with winning a major had cost him a great price. In truth, it was only a matter of time before Montgomerie returned to his bad old ways and by the time of the Masters his 'obsession' had returned bigger and stronger than ever.

After the traumatic breakdown in their relationship at Augusta the couple agreed to keep a low profile. But in late April, Montgomerie suddenly pulled out of the VW China Masters in Hong Kong and flew back to London after the *Sunday Mirror* ran a story linking Eimear and actor Hugh Grant. (According to the *Sun* he returned for MONTY'S DIVORCE SUMMIT.) A strong friendship had built up between the two men after Grant began taking lessons with Montgomerie's coach, Denis Pugh, at the Wisley golf club in Surrey. Honing his skills at the Leslie King Golf School in Knightsbridge over the winter, Grant had played with Montgomerie in the Dunhill Cup Celebrity pro-am in October 2003. 'Colin has been showing me where I'm going wrong,' said the star of *Four Weddings and a Funeral*, before admitting that playing with the seven-time European number one was 'the biggest treat of the year'.

Montgomerie in turn described how he and Grant 'get on splendidly', but the tabloids were not going to let the truth get in the way of a great story. Desperate to link the dashing 42-year-old movie star with Eimear, they hinted strongly at a romantic relationship, using lines like 'sources close to the couple' and 'a friend of the family' in an effort to give credibility to the rumour. Referring to Montgomerie, one story described how not many men would put up with 'a good-looking movie star supporting your wife through your marriage rift ...' while another had Monty sounding like Arnold Schwarzenegger, telling Grant to 'Back off and let me get close to her again!'

The pressure became intolerable for both Colin and Eimear, and a statement was released on their behalf by IMG: 'We have sadly decided to separate, with a view to divorce. This has been a desperately difficult decision for us both and is a painful time for the family. We particularly wish to protect our three children. We dismiss current media speculation.'

In the end, Eimear simply stopped trying to make excuses. She was his wife, his best friend and mother to his three children – what she could not give him was the peace of mind winning a major would bring to this highly complex individual. In the end, she could not compete with a dream, and it was this realisation that led her to instigate the end of her marriage. 'The cracks which we both tried to paper over were becoming impossible to ignore,' she admitted later. 'I was emotionally and physically fatigued. I told Colin that it was over.'

Unfortunately, the tabloid press did not see it that way as interest in the celebrity 'threesome' reached fever pitch. A spokeswoman for Grant refused to comment, referring simply to the statement issued by the Montgomeries. Even James Montgomerie, Colin's father, responded to the reports that his daughter-in-law was having a relationship with Grant as 'totally untrue, absolute rubbish'. (When the story did finally subside, Hugh Grant was quoted as saying: 'I play golf and I'm quite embarrassed to say I don't think of anything else!')

Over the next weeks and months, Eimear's name was romantically linked to a host of high-profile celebrities including a married soccer star turned TV pundit, and she was photographed in a romantic clinch with an Oxford-educated barrister. 'We're just friends,' she told the *Daily Mail*, but the stories kept coming as the 35-year-old girl-about-town continued to dine out at fashionable London eateries frequented by the paparazzi. EIMEAR'S FORE-PLAY EXCLUSIVE reported the *Sunday Mirror* before detailing her 'kisses and cuddles with lawyer love'.

Not that 'Misty-eyed Monty' escaped the scandal sheets attention. Described as being 'devastated' over his wife's 'secret affair', he was portrayed in the press as a cuckolded spouse sitting quietly at home while his wife was out painting the town red with a series of romantic suitors. Neither was true, but that did not stop one lurid headline after another appearing in the press. 'I guess my faith in human nature had curdled when my marriage was covered in such detail,' said Montgomerie. 'It's then that you wish there weren't so many national newspapers in this country.'

In the aftermath of their previous break-up, Montgomerie had speculated on the devastating effect divorce would have on his life: 'I would have seen it as a failure and not wanted to be around people who were successful when I was a failure. I would have found it very, very difficult to compete, thinking all the time that I was a failure.'

Almost two years later, Montgomerie no longer felt the same way. The past four months had been spent running around between Europe, America and Asia, picking up world ranking points and qualifying for September's Ryder Cup in Detroit, Michigan. With the news that his fourteen-year marriage had come to an end, qualifying for the biennial match suddenly lost its importance. While he was out chasing tournament victories, his private life had crumbled around him, so nobody really expected him to turn up for the British Masters at the Forest of Arden in Warwickshire barely a week after his split with Eimear was announced.

But turn up he did. Travelling from the London apartment he had moved into after his split with Eimear a few days earlier, he arrived an hour before his tee-off time. In his first competitive round since missing the cut at Augusta in April, he signed his scorecard for level par before inviting questions from a small group of golf writers behind the grandstand on the eighteenth green. In a statement the week before, Montgomerie said the separation had 'been a desperate decision for us both and a painful time for the family'. Visibly upset, he answered each question with honesty and dignity. Describing his competitive return to action, he confirmed that it was better 'sooner rather than later'. As for the support he received from the fans, he said, 'I didn't know what the reaction might be and walking onto the first tee with all the support was a delight for me. That was fabulous and something I'll remember for a long time . . . It was a very important day for me to get back out there and play golf. It was an opportunity to put all the other parts of my life to one side and get on with what I do best – my job.'

Comparing his reception with the one he had received at the Ryder Cup a few months earlier he said, 'I think the golfing world, if you like, the spectators and whoever else, wish me well. I certainly hope so, and it seemed that way.' Asked if he had enjoyed his round, Montgomerie replied with surprising humour: 'I suppose I did in the sense of being away from everything. It was nice to have my mobile phone turned off for six hours.'

It had been an honest and forthright interview. Describing his opening round at the Forest of Arden as 'the first day of the rest of my life', the only thing Monty asked from the media was a level of privacy in their reporting. Sympathetic to his anguish, the journalists, many of whom had known him since he was an amateur, would keep their word, leaving the Scot to get on with the rest of his season.

Under the circumstances his sixteenth place in the British Masters was a miracle of mind over matter. Playing in a haze of public sympathy, he often appeared close to tears but somehow made it through to the end. 'Colin knows the challenge in front of him,' said his coach Denis Pugh, 'and now this is out of the way the rest of his golfing life starts tomorrow.'

A week later he made a nostalgic return to the St Leon-Rot course in Heidelberg, Germany where he had run Tiger Woods so close two years earlier in the Deutsche Bank-SAP Open. Back then he had been plagued by back pain that left him awake for most of the night before losing in a play-off. This time the pain was emotional but no less acute as a subdued Montgomerie crashed out on Friday in 128th place after scores of 75 and 78, his worst performance since his very first European tour start in 1987 at the Swiss Open. Montgomerie promised to 'try again next week, then I'll try again, then again the next week and the next week, until I can perform to my true ability'.

Unfortunately, golf scorecards do not paint pictures or allow for personal tragedies and his world ranking dropped to 49th on the back of this result – perilously close to the top fifty cut-off that would make him exempt for the next two majors. 'If I'm in the US Open, the Open and the Ryder Cup then fine,' said an unconcerned Montgomerie. 'If I'm not, then also fine. I have my health and I've competed in these events before and if I'm not in them then I'm not in them – I will have a week with my children . . . It's the furthest thing from my mind right now.'

With a place in the US Open at Shinnecock Hills the following month as the prize, Montgomerie was hoping for 'a little bit more luck' in the Volvo PGA Championship at Wentworth the following week. In desperate need of a good performance to keep him inside the top fifty, he could not afford to fail – but he did. In a week where Eimear was said to have briefly banned her husband from the family home, it was a bad-tempered display from start to finish. Not much went right and his final two-under-par total was never going to be good enough to keep him in the world's top fifty. Finishing seventeen strokes behind winner Scott Drummond, automatic entry into the US Open was looking further away than ever. Worse still, his place in the Open Championship at Royal Troon was now in jeopardy and it came as no surprise when his management company took the precaution of entering Montgomerie in the international qualifying round for the Open at Sunningdale in the first week in July.

Facing the more immediate prospect of having to qualify for the US Open at Shinnecock Hills on Long Island, New York, Montgomerie hoped that he would receive a last-minute invitation from the United States Golf Association as a two-time runner-up. 'I'd go if that happened, but it doesn't concern me this year,' he told BBC Sport. Describing his confidence as 'very, very low', the Scot was not keen to go through the qualification process that meant heading back to America in the middle of a run of European Tour events. 'Going to US Open qualifying would be difficult,' he said. 'Unfortunately, it all happened at the wrong time.' The invitation from the USGA never materialised.

Everything *was* happening at the wrong time for Montgomerie. His private life was regularly being picked over for the masses in the national newspapers, while the Open Championship and the Ryder Cup were just around the corner. In June, Montgomerie described how the painful split from his wife had impacted on his career in a candid interview with the *Scotland on Sunday* newspaper. Determined not to 'fold' after the break-up of his marriage, he explained: 'You have two choices most of the time; in the situation I am in, I can either jump off a bridge, which would be no good for the kids, or I can get on with it. And I'm trying to get on with it.' After all, he said, 'I'm forty years old. I'm healthy. And I'm a wealthy man.'

On the same theme Montgomerie was asked in May if it would hurt to miss out on an Open Championship played over his home course? 'Not really,' was his terse reply, before admitting that his days worrying about whether he won a golf tournament or not were long over. 'I always used to be conscious of where I was on the leader board,' he said. 'What I had to do to catch up, or, if in the lead, what they would have to do to catch me up. Now, looking back, I think, "Christ, what a waste of time".'

There was even speculation in the media that Montgomerie was considering retirement after the Ryder Cup in September. 'Did retirement cross my mind? Yes, for a brief moment,' he told BBC Radio 5 Live's *Sportsweek* programme some months later. 'Then I was advised not to ... I was given two options, really. One was give up, the other one to get off your backside and do something about it and that is what I did, and it all paid dividends in the end.'

In a season of emotional stress, the importance of competing in the Open at Royal Troon grew ever more important. Few things had gone his way since his victory in the Caltex Masters in Singapore three months earlier and he needed to stop the rot. 'There are a few ways to go, and I'll be trying my damnedest to get in through Loch Lomond and also the European Open,' he opined. 'If that doesn't happen, there is qualifying down at Sunningdale and I think I'll go down there.'

Montgomerie then predicted that his next tournament win would be the most important of his career: 'It will beat all the other thirty-seven,' declared the embattled Scot. He may even have been right as he teed it up at Sunningdale desperate to qualify for what was probably his last 'competitive' Open Championship over his home course of Royal Troon. 'I missed the US Open and I did not want to miss the British Open,' said Montgomerie. 'It could be the last time I play an Open at Troon. It might be nine years before it is back there and I would be fifty then.'

Offering the former European number one a final opportunity to get in, qualifying rounds are usually fraught with difficulty but this one was especially tense after Montgomerie lost his cool after spotting another so-called 'friend' of his wife Eimear near the ninth tee in his second round. 'I can't believe he's here watching,' said Montgomerie audibly. Even with that unwelcome distraction, the Scot came through a dramatic twelve-man play-off after a bogey by Argentina's Cesar Monasterio on the second extra hole. Joining 16 other qualifiers from an elite field of 120, Montgomerie had put his considerable reputation on the line and it had paid off. 'This is the first decent thing that's happened to me for a long time,' he told the media after rounds of 68 and 69 left him at six under par in regulation play.

Invigorated by his performance, the experience seemed to restore his appetite for the fray in the weeks leading up to the Open Championship. Unfortunately, the problems restarted off the golf course, with the tabloids continuing to haunt his every waking hour over the summer as they investigated the so-called 'Riddle of Monty's Stalker . . .' Even his normal 'grumpy' on-course demeanour was used as a stick to beat him with as he was labelled 'Troubled Monty' (the *Daily Mail*) and 'Gloomy Monty' (the London *Evening Standard*). Stories linking his ex-wife to other men were commonplace. One journalist even detailed a breakdown in the relationship between Eimear and Colin's father, the former golf club secretary at Royal Troon. The fact it was completely untrue hardly mattered by the time Montgomerie returned to his home town in July for the Open.

Determined to remain upbeat in what could easily prove the most emotionally difficult major he had ever played in, Montgomerie spoke candidly about the obsession that had driven him to win seven consecutive Order of Merit titles in the 1990s. 'What I achieved on this Tour for those infamous seven years nearly – well, it did – it broke me and I'm sure it aided breaking a marriage,' he said. It was quite an admission and his message to any player looking to break his record was equally forthright: 'I suggest they come and have a chat with me and I'll tell them not to bother.'

Back in April at the Masters, Montgomerie had asked fellow professional Nick Price for advice over his disintegrating marriage. 'Do your best to keep things together,' said the popular Zimbabwean, 'and if it doesn't work out, don't blame yourself.' They were wise words but nobody was harder on Montgomerie than himself. It was a case in point at Royal Troon where he ended the week in tied-25th place after a frustrating final round of 76. DREAM TURNS TO NIGHTMARE WITH MONTY'S DYING CIRCUS was the imaginative headline in the Scottish *Daily Record* the next day.

Under the circumstances it was an admirable effort, but having begun the final day just five strokes off the lead, Montgomerie's initial reaction was one of disappointment. That had changed by the time he spoke to the media as he concluded just how beneficial the trip to Troon had been. 'I'll think about the whole experience this week,' reflected Monty, 'and the support I have had not just from the Scottish public, but from the British public as a whole.'

On Tuesday evening, after most of the crowds had meandered away, Colin had walked the course with his father. No doubt bringing back memories of their many rounds together over the Ayrshire links, it must have been a period of reflection for the enigmatic Scot. 'This Open could not have come at a better time for me,' he admitted during the week. 'I don't feel as alone as you might think.'

So what did the future hold for Colin Stuart Montgomerie? Would he ever win the major championship he craved? Would he ever regain that level of consistency required to win an eighth Order of Merit?

Only time would tell. For now, his main concern was how to make it into Bernard Langer's European Ryder Cup team to face the Americans at Oakland Hills in Michigan in September.

19. OAKLAND HILLS VIA THE DIVORCE COURTS

Halfway through the 2004 season, Colin Montgomerie's most pressing on-course problem was how to qualify for the Ryder Cup that September in Detroit. With just two months before the team was finalised, Monty instinctively knew how difficult it would be. What he needed now were one or two good results to impress captain Bernhard Langer in the hope that he would pick him as one of his two wild cards. At the end of July, Monty had been fitted for his Ryder Cup uniform (a standard procedure for any player in contention for a place in the team) and told the press that he would gladly accept a captain's pick if he needed one. Confirming that he had heard the rumours that Langer was saving a place for him should he not make it automatically, the Scot sensibly added a caveat to his comments: 'I haven't heard it from the guy that counts and I don't really expect to. But if he feels I can help his cause I'll be gladly on that plane. If he feels differently that will be entirely up to him.'

Montgomerie was still relying on that all-important captain's wild card by the end of August but there was one particular ray of sunshine – the return of his former caddie Alistair McLean. When the surprise split from Monty came in May 2002, McLean was temporarily unemployed for the first time in fourteen years. After seven weeks he accepted a job from Australian prodigy Adam Scott and had stayed with him for much of the intervening period – winning a Players Championship along the way. 'It was very different with Adam,' he admitted in a candid interview with John Huggan of the *Scotland on Sunday* newspaper and *Golf World US*. 'He has a different nature and character. And he played very differently. He hits it miles. It took me weeks to get used to not having to ask if he could carry a bunker three hundred yards away!'

Although they had kept in regular touch, the offer to work for Montgomerie was still a surprise. With Monty struggling with life both on and off the golf course, McLean could probably have found a more lucrative bag, but it was the possibility of attending another Ryder Cup that swung the deal. Not that Monty was completely sure he would be playing. He was frustrated by his lack of form, and even McLean noticed the difference in his play now compared with over two years earlier. 'He never used to see the rough and wondered why golf courses were difficult for players,' he continued. 'Now he has a better appreciation for how tough some places are.'

That was certainly true of Firestone in Akron at the NEC World Championships in August where two weekend rounds of 75 effectively ruined his chances of making the European Ryder Cup team automatically. With just one more event to play – the BMW International Open in Munich at the end of August – the Scot arrived in Ohio requiring a top-nine finish in the $10m tournament to have any chance of grabbing one of the ten automatic places. In the end he finished tied for fiftieth – sixteen strokes behind the winner, Stewart Cink. So it was an apprehensive Colin Montgomerie who flew from Akron to London then on to Munich, wondering if he had played his last Ryder Cup.

But the Scot need not have worried. With McLean guiding him around the Nord-Eichenried course he finished joint-third after wonderfully consistent rounds of 67, 70, 67 and 68. In reality, anything but a complete disaster would have seen him on the plane to Detroit as far as Bernhard Langer was concerned. Pulling him aside one hour before the official announcement on Sunday afternoon, the German gave him the good news that he and Englishman Luke Donald were in the team. Montgomerie was understandably moved. 'I was obviously thrilled to hear the news,' he recalled. 'But what was more thrilling was what he told me after that. He said he asked all of the players that were already qualified about me and they all said they wanted me to play. In a way, that means even more to me than being picked by Bernhard.'

In a year of professional frustration and private heartbreak, Monty could now plan for the future and especially a trip to Oakland Hills in Detroit, Michigan from 17–19 September. The Scot had never needed a wild card to make the team before but all that was quickly forgotten. For much of the last six months he had struggled with his game against a background of emotional upheaval. His form was patchy and for the first time since 1991, he was forced to miss the US Open after dropping out of the world's top fifty. Fortunately, the last month had seen a significant upturn. Top-five finishes at the Scandinavian Masters and the BMW International in August had given Langer a free hand to pick him over younger players like Freddie Jacobson without any debate.

'When I looked at the golf course at Oakland Hills, I had to come to a decision who would serve the team best, and I came up with Colin Montgomerie and Luke Donald,' Langer told the media. 'Colin has given us a great performance this week. To play that well knowing he still had to show me something . . . I gave nobody the nod and I did that for a reason. And Colin brings some leadership.'

Montgomerie also brought a wealth of experience to the team. As seven-time European number one, his record of 16 wins from 28 Ryder Cup starts, including being unbeaten in six singles matches, was hugely impressive. Certainly Phil Mickelson thought so. 'Colin's a really good player who is able to bring out his best game at the most critical moments,' said the reigning Masters champion. 'Nobody was more impressed than I was in '99 when he took a lot of ribbing and was able to perform at the highest level of anybody there. So maybe that's kind of a word to the wise that maybe we shouldn't piss him off. Maybe we should just downplay it a little bit and not agitate him so much.'

Not that Montgomerie was playing that well coming into the match. Questioned whether his marital problems had disturbed his preparation, the Scot said that had he felt unable to play a significant role at Oakland Hills he would have withdrawn as Sandy Lyle did in 1989. 'I was never a hundred per cent sure that I would be selected,' admitted Monty. 'But he [Langer] felt I could help his team.'

Not quite so welcome was the news that his divorce hearing had been moved up three months earlier than expected. Montgomerie had hoped it would have been dealt with over the winter, but now the news had broken just days before the Ryder Cup. With Montgomerie competing in the Linde German Masters at Gut Larchenhof in the second week in September and Eimear unable to attend court, neither of them heard District Judge Helen Black of the High Court Family Division declare their fourteen-year marriage at an end. According to court papers, Mrs Montgomerie had been granted a so-called quickie divorce on the grounds that the marriage had irretrievably broken down because of her husband's 'unreasonable behaviour'. In a written statement in support of her divorce petition, Eimear was asked if she considered that her husband's behaviour had affected her health. 'Yes,' she replied. 'I have suffered from anxiety and depression from which I believe I have now recovered.'

Asked if the behaviour was continuing, she replied: 'No.'

Perhaps it was pure coincidence but Montgomerie stumbled to a second-round 76 on the day of the hearing. Whatever the reason, it was certainly not what the 41-year-old Scot planned on the eve of his seventh Ryder Cup. 'Not a problem,' he said, after missing the halfway cut in Cologne. 'I've been in this position before and there's nothing wrong.'

Bernhard Langer picked Colin Montgomerie as one of his two wild-card choices because the former European number one was someone who knew how to win a Ryder Cup match. The only question mark was his form coming into the match at Oakland Hills; despite good showings in both Sweden and Germany a month earlier, Monty had not been inside the top ten of the European money list all season.

Wallowing in 28th position before the final qualifying event at the BMW International in late August, the proud Scot must have considered the possibility that he might not be playing. Rarely will a captain go down the list beyond the top fifteen places. But as Langer was to prove at Oakland Hills a month later, he was no ordinary captain and Monty was definitely no ordinary wild card. Montgomerie was in the team and, for many seasoned observers, he was the difference between winning or losing – how right they were.

In a European team that bristled with youthful confidence, Montgomerie was seen as the veteran of the team both in terms of age and experience. Smiling and relaxed in the company of twenty-something stars like Luke Donald (the second wild card) and Sergio Garcia, he took his fair share of gentle ribbing as the two teams gathered on a sunlit practice ground for the team photographs. 'I think he likes it,' observed Irish star Padraig Harrington. 'I think he feels it's his calling. He's that sort of personality. He loves to lead; he loves to be that person out there. You can see he's got an air of confidence about him in the team room. He carries himself and his confidence rubs off on the rest of the players. I'm sure he feels that's what he was destined to be. It feels very natural for him to be that sort of leader. He's very comfortable in that position.'

Montgomerie was perhaps less comfortable with the extravagant opening ceremony at Oakland Hills. With such a high profile given to players' wives and girlfriends, it must have been a sharp reminder that he did not have Eimear present for the first time since he made his debut at Kiawah Island in 1991. Still, he took it in good humour and spoke warmly of how much emotional support he had received from everyone in the run-up to the match in Detroit. 'Coming to a Ryder Cup on my own is a new experience,' he admitted. 'And

I must admit there have been one or two moments since we got here when I've felt a little bit strange. When we got into our rooms at the team hotel yesterday there were cuff links laid out for the guys and a bracelet for their wives or partners. Since I'm here by myself, there were only cuff links in my room.'

Typically, Irishman Darren Clarke expressed amusement that the newly single Monty was now rated one of Britain's most eligible bachelors! Understandably, the Scot did not seem in the mood for any levity on that front. 'I just feel a little bit better about myself,' said the slimmed-down Montgomerie, 'and self-esteem is huge in this game, especially when you're out in public an awful lot.'

The Americans looked tense and pressured. Taking turns to be photographed with captain Hal Sutton and the trophy, many grasped it tight as if that might be the nearest they would come to it that week – for many of them it was!

Revealing the type of organisational expertise he had brought to his own career, Langer arranged his European team into specific pairings for the practice rounds. Often changing partners around after nine holes, the German also suggested – unlike the Americans – that his European team ignore pre-tournament instructions not to fraternise with the paying public. Realising the last thing he wanted was a hostile American crowd baying for his team's blood, his team, including Montgomerie, set about leading a charm offensive, signing autographs and posing for impromptu snaps. In hindsight it was an absolute masterstroke.

Another masterstroke was his gentle kid-glove treatment of his most fragile star. Montgomerie once predicted that American Brad Faxon would be unable to focus during the 1997 Ryder Cup because of his recent divorce. It was as crass as it was potentially true and Monty was berated for his searing honesty. Now it was Monty in the middle of a divorce and Langer, the master psychologist, knew exactly what to do. During practice, he quietly urged his team to throw a blanket of emotional security around the thin-skinned Scot. 'Bernhard suggested we big him up,' admitted one European star. 'We were asked to keep encouraging him. Keep telling him how great he was and how the Americans were frightened to death of playing him. You could see him grow in confidence the more we talked to him.'

Then came the pairings for the opening day. Putting Montgomerie out first with Padraig Harrington was exactly the seal of approval he needed – but whom would they play? The answer surprised everyone as Sutton paired Tiger Woods and Phil Mickelson together. It was exactly the type of bold move that was expected of 'cowboy' Hal, but what a risk he had taken putting his two biggest guns out together. Currently ranked number two and number four in the world, what if they got beaten?

The opening fourball was among the most eagerly antici-pated games in Ryder Cup history, setting the tone for everything that followed. The players were completely aware of what was at stake as they set off down the opening hole that crisp September morning. If the 'Big Dog' American partnership steamrollered Europe's top pairing it could start a tidal wave that would be hard to hold back. But, as Sutton found to his cost, Montgomerie is a tough player to beat under any circumstances. 'The key to all of this is Monty's pride,' said his coach Denis Pugh. 'He just feels like he doesn't want to let anyone down, including himself.'

Admitting his match against Woods and Mickelson was really 'worth two points', Montgomerie made the perfect start against the Americans. Driving first with the honour, Harring-ton found the right-hand fairway bunker with his opening tee shot. Montgomerie in contrast hit a perfect drive, then a perfect approach to six feet before holing the putt for a winning birdie. After another birdie at the short third from Harrington, Europe were now two up. It would prove an unassailable lead as the Europeans ran out winners by 2 and 1. American golf's 'dream team' pairing had been beaten and once again it was the big Scot who had given them night-mares. 'It was an honour for me to be selected for this team,' he declared. 'I wanted to do as well as possible, get points on the board and prove that Bernhard made the right decision.'

Not that he was content to finish there. Demolishing Fred Funk and Davis Love III 4 and 2 in the afternoon set the seal on an inspirational first-day performance by Montgomerie and Harrington. With Woods and Mickelson beaten by Clarke and Westwood, the Ryder Cup was turning into a rout as Europe raced to a five-point lead after day one. 'As a team, we tend to perform all the way through, and not just rely on any one individual,' said a delighted Lee Westwood afterwards.

Sadly the 'vast improvement' demanded by Hal Sutton on the second day proved as elusive as a John Daly veggie burger. At his own request an 'exhausted' Colin Montgomerie was rested in the afternoon after he and Harrington lost to Stewart Cink and Love 3 and 2 in the morning fourballs. Even then, the Scot spent much of it supporting his fellow players as they extended their overall lead going into the singles.

With Europe now six points ahead, Monty was given a pivotal role in the middle of the singles by Langer. Sutton sent out his players strictly in the order they qualified, from Tiger Woods at number one, Mickelson at two and Love at three, right down to wild-card pick Stewart Cink being given the anchor role as last man out. The US needed to get points on the scoreboard early, but as Woods, Mickelson and Love had so far earned only one point each, Sutton had long since run out of options. Asked if he thought his team could still win, he replied, 'I believe in my heart that they can . . . Whether they will or not is another story.'

With Europe needing three points to retain the Ryder Cup, it was somehow inevitable that Montgomerie would play his part. Edging closer and closer to victory, Garcia beat Mickelson, while Clarke fought out an amiable half with his close pal Davis Love III. Even wins for home players Woods, Furyk and Chad Campbell only delayed the inevitable. Barely ten minutes later, Westwood closed out Kenny Perry to retain the Ryder Cup, leaving the door open for Colin Montgomerie to grab the winning half-point.

Arriving at the eighteenth green with a one-hole advantage over 2001 PGA champion David Toms, Montgomerie found his ball fifty feet away on the right edge of the green with a massive spine between him and the hole. Toms was short in two and his nervously executed chip then came to rest about four paces away. The stage was set – two putts from Monty and Europe would win the Ryder Cup on American soil for only the second time in the event's 77-year history.

Back on Friday, from a similar position on the eighth green, he almost holed what Harrington called 'an impossible shot'. On Sunday, he did equally well to coax his slick right-to-left putt too within five feet of the cup. It was greeted with huge cheers from the predominantly pro-European crowd, and even Toms' par-saving putt could not spoil Monty's moment of glory. Resting his belly putter into his midriff, he calmly slotted it home for a one-hole victory and the celebrations could begin. 'It's been a long four, five months of mine personally and I've come a long way in that time,' said a reflective Monty. 'It doesn't matter who holed the final putt because this is a team event. But this means more to me than most.'

'When word came to me that Monty had won it, I was delighted,' said Irishman Paul McGinley. 'It was almost his destiny to do it this time. No one is more deserving of holing a winning putt in the Ryder Cup than Monty. His contribution to the Ryder Cup down the years and again this week has been phenomenal.'

'It was just perfect for Monty of all people to make the winning putt,' said an elated Paul Casey. 'David Toms had made a tremendous fifteen-footer and that meant Colin had to hole his putt as well. It was just perfect – and you knew he wouldn't miss. Absolutely nothing else in golf compares to this.'

Interestingly, Montgomerie teased the media by hinting that he did not know his putt was to win the Ryder Cup! Yes, dear old Monty apparently had no idea. 'Bizarrely, there was no scoreboard on the eighteenth and I didn't know what the situation was,' revealed a smiling Monty. 'I'd heard a cheer for Lee Westwood up ahead at the green but I didn't know whether he or Sergio [Garcia] had won their games or that Darren [Clarke] had got his half. My reaction when I made that four-footer was not that I'd won the Ryder Cup but only that I'd beaten David Toms and won a point for my team. It was only when I went up to Bernhard [Langer] and he said, "You've done it" that I realised.'

No wonder the first person the elated Scot sought out after holing his winning putt was his German captain. 'Being a wild card was a new experience for me,' said a grateful Monty. 'I qualified every time before, so when you look at the list and see I wasn't close to qualifying, and that Bernhard had to go a long way down to find me, that means a lot.'

Another Ryder Cup had come and gone with Colin Montgomerie firmly centre stage. He was catapulted from 'brokenhearted ex-husband' to national hero in the space of three days, and British tabloid newspaper the *Sun* summed up the feelings of many when it wrote, 'He may have never won a major but on a late sunlit afternoon here in the great Midwest, Monty enjoyed the finest moment of his long career.'

Montgomerie might even have agreed. As the dust settled on Europe's historic 18½–9½ victory at Oakland Hills, golf fans could now look forward to the K Club in 2006 with eager anticipation. Whether the Scot would be playing or not was a different question entirely. Perhaps he might be there as captain? At the moment, anything was possible as he lapped up the plaudits that came his way after such an historic victory. Described as a 'National Sporting Treasure' by some newspapers, Monty showed that the Midas touch had not deserted him on his return to the UK. Scheduled to appear at Staines Magistrates' Court the day after flying in from Detroit to defend a speeding ticket, the case was thrown out after the arresting policeman failed to attend!

In recognition of the role he had played in both the Ryder Cup and for European golf in general, Montgomerie ended 2004 with a special award from the Professional Golfers' Association for his outstanding contribution. Following in the footsteps of inaugural winner Nick Faldo, it highlighted a career that included thirty-plus tournament victories, seven consecutive Order of Merits and seven Ryder Cup appearances. 'Colin has proved one of his generation's most recognisable and endearing sports stars and is a true statesman of golf,' said PGA chief executive Sandy Jones.

Who could disagree? Well, the people who select the Ryder Cup captain for one! If a week is a long time in politics then a month proved a lifetime in golf as far as Colin Montgomerie was concerned. Within days of holing the winning putt at Oakland Hills, the clamour for him to stay on as a player grew apace. 'I'm sorry, Colin,' said his former Ryder Cup team-mate Andrew Coltart, 'but if you wanted to captain the team in Ireland, I'm afraid you've just shot yourself in the foot. I would drag you kicking and screaming to the first tee at the K Club if I had to.'

A member of the European Tour's influential Tournament Players committee, which helps choose the new Ryder Cup captain, he voiced the opinion of many of Monty's European Tour colleagues. A victim of his own success, it was just too soon for him to be captain and it surprised nobody when Montgomerie ruled himself out as captain in mid-December. 'I have been told I am too young,' said the 41-year-old Scot. 'After hearing what they have all said I agree with them; if I can maintain my form, I can be there as a player.'

Like many team members from the match at Oakland Hills, Montgomerie believed Bernhard Langer should be given the opportunity to captain the Europeans again in Ireland in 2006. Speaking as he donated his seventh Ryder Cup golf bag to his Academy at Turnberry, he was certain that was the right way to go. 'If he does want to do it again,' he said, 'then there's your captain.'

Langer ended the speculation that he would take on the job early in the New Year, saying he wanted to 'play his way on to the team in 2006'. In March 2005, the PGA and European Tour announced that former US Masters winner Ian Woosnam had been made European captain for Ireland. In a complete change of protocol, Nick Faldo was then awarded the job for the match at Valhalla in 2008. It was a quick, clean and popular move, and it seemed that Colin Montgomerie would have to wait a little longer for his turn.

*   *   *

In the months that followed Europe's historic win over the USA in the Ryder Cup at Oakland Hills, Colin Montgomerie was looking for some much-needed individual success. In mid-December, he let slip a two-shot overnight lead in the final round of the Target World Challenge at Thousand Oaks golf club in California. Finishing runner-up to the tournament host, Tiger Woods, the Scot shot 71 to finish tied with veteran Jay Haas on thirteen under par. Taking heart from his performance, Monty announced that his ambition for 2005 was to climb back up the world rankings. Number-two ranked player in 1997, he currently occupied 81st place and that was simply unacceptable.

The world rankings that had become so important in players' careers were introduced back in 1986. Endorsed by the PGA Tour in America, the European Tour, the Asian Tour, the Japan Golf Tour, the PGA Tour of Australasia and the Sunshine Tour in Africa, it was considered the most accurate way of identifying the world's best players on a month-by-month basis. With entry into all four majors depending on how high a player was placed, the system worked closely with the R&A, Augusta National, the United States Golf Association and the PGA of America plus the lesser Canadian, Nationwide and Challenge Tours.

Admitting that he rarely looked at his ranking position when he was winning the European Order of Merit back in the 1990s, Montgomerie rarely missed it these days. 'I have just got to try to get my own ranking up to where I feel it should be,' said Monty, 'at least in the top twenty-five in the world, if not higher. I spent twelve years of my seventeen as a pro in the top ten in the world and I want to try to get back there.'

Away from the golf course, success in the Ryder Cup had only compounded his bitterness over the failure of his marriage to Eimear. Like many top sportsmen, Montgomerie believed that he had managed to combine his career and family pretty well. 'I was number one in Europe from 1993 to 1999 and my three children were all born from '93 to '98,' said Monty. 'It seemed as if my wife and I were going for the same goals.'

In October, Montgomerie admitted missing regular contact with his three children (eleven-year-old Olivia, Venetia, eight, and Cameron, six) who continued to live in Oxshott with their mother. (One of the first texts Monty sent in the minutes after his winning putt was to Olivia to let her know he would be home in time to take her to school.) Like many single fathers, he treasured the time they had together and went out of his way to make their lives as 'normal' as possible under the circumstances. 'A marriage contract can be ripped in two,' he said, 'but the bond you have with your children endures.'

Montgomerie also said that winning seven successive Order of Merit titles had 'taken their toll' but insisted that it 'wasn't the reason for the break-up'.

Eimear disagreed. Asked whether her marriage could have been saved if Colin had won a major instead of being seven-time European number one, she replied, 'I don't think it would have made much difference. I married a man – not a career. That was the problem.'

20. JAKARTAGATE

A warded an OBE to add to his MBE in the New Year
Honours List, Montgomerie had resurrected his career
with victory in the Ryder Cup in Detroit. Working hard on his
fitness over the winter months, Monty took his inspiration
from another Ryder Cup hero, Seve Ballesteros: 'Seve told me
to keep playing as long as you can, because you're a long time
retired.'

Starting his season in mid-January at the South African
Airways Open in Durban, Montgomerie spent the first quarter
of the year jetting all over the globe from Australia to China
and all points in between. Without a confirmed place in the
game's elite events, he was forced to play more tournaments
than usual in his hunt for that elusive podium finish that
would catapult him back into the top echelons of the world
rankings. 'My life has changed over this last year,' said
Monty. 'I don't have three- or five-year plans right now. I'm
living week-to-week and seeing how I get on.'

Failing to make it inside the top fifty in the rankings after
the BMW Championship at Wentworth at the end of May,
Montgomerie's growing frustration with the world around
him was obvious. Struggling with the financial implications of
his split with Eimear, he was also forced to reduce the £6m

price tag on 'Nairn', his Surrey mansion, to attract a potential purchaser. Angry and frustrated at having to sell the home he had shared with his wife and their three children for seven years, the Scot was visibly upset when the FOR SALE signs went up in January. 'I put many, many years of strife and pressure and all my job into this house,' lamented Monty. 'It is all I could have wished for and now I have to leave.'

Besides that visible reminder of his glory days, his growing resentment towards Eimear and her lawyers' financial demands was starting to grate. 'She had so many clothes, she used to fill all the cupboards,' said Montgomerie in an unguarded exchange with a journalist posing as a buyer. 'This big new dressing room was only finished last year. That really does annoy me ... Perhaps I should have earned half the money and spent double the time at home with my wife and kids.'

Speculation was now rife as to the size of the amount Montgomerie would pay Eimear, after he reduced the house's price in May. According to the tabloids, Montgomerie was worth an estimated £25m and the expected sale would help fund an estimated £12m divorce settlement. Whether this was true or not, it must have made uncomfortable reading each morning when he looked at his newspapers over breakfast.

It was obviously time for a change. Armed with a new set of Yonex golf clubs, Montgomerie made the surprising decision to discard the belly putter that had served him so well in the Ryder Cup. Experimenting briefly with the left-hand-below-right grip at the US Open at Pebble Beach in June 2000, he went back to a more traditional style at the Caltex Masters in Singapore in late January. Looking for a method that he could rely on under pressure, he made a strong defence by chasing the eventual winner Nick Dougherty all the way to the finish line. Indeed, the five-stroke winning margin would have been much closer had it not been for a controversial ruling three holes from home in the final round.

Dougherty pulled his drive into a fairway trap on the par-four sixteenth, and the green was taken out of range because of the height of the large wooden sleepers that made up the face of the bunker. One stroke behind at this point, Monty nailed his drive down the fairway and looked to have the advantage. However, because the wooden sleepers technically impeded his shot, the 22-year-old Liverpudlian was allowed a generous free drop, from where he struck his ball to within three feet from the pin! Disturbed by the incident, Montgomerie three-putted for a bogey five on the same hole. Dougherty then holed for a simple birdie and the tournament was effectively over. 'The ruling was the turning point,' complained the Scot. 'I was one behind and in the middle of the fairway and he is in the bunker left, up the face of the bunker. Next minute you know he's three feet away.'

Finishing tied second with Dutchman Maarten Lafeber, it would not be the last time that Montgomerie would have a tangle with the rules that year.

Two weeks later in Los Angeles, Monty had another opportunity of boosting his world ranking and earning a potential call-up to the Masters in April. Playing in the Nissan Open, his poor luck continued after he was forced to settle for fifth place at the Riviera Country Club when the tournament was reduced to 36 holes because of the weather. On the course where he had lost a play-off for the 1995 US PGA Championship, his second-round 64 was his lowest-ever competitive round in America but he was looking for more. With weather-related problems all week, including a complete washout on Saturday and a further two-hour hold-up on Sunday morning, only two rounds could be completed before the tournament was called off later the same day, leaving joint second-round leaders Adam Scott and Chad Campbell to play off for the title on the Monday morning. Monty's frustration was obvious as he headed back to London having also missed out on a place at the lucrative 64-man Accenture World Match Play in San Diego a week later.

Without a confirmed berth in either the Masters or US Open, Montgomerie now knew how an accountant must feel. Constantly scanning the world rankings, he needed to climb twelve places from his current position at 62nd to qualify for the Tournament Players' Championship in Florida in mid-

March. How times had changed. Three years earlier at the Match Play in La Costa, there had been a lot of discussion in the media about the complexity of the world rankings. Asked by respected Canadian journalist Lorne Rubenstein if he understood the rankings, Monty replied, 'Do you?'

'I have some idea,' said the plucky writer, 'but I really thought you as a player would know.'

Monty became defensive as the packed media centre fell silent. 'My wife knows,' he said abruptly. 'She tells me.'

With Eimear no longer around, it was left to Guy Kinnings to do the maths. Faced with missing both the Masters and US Open, Montgomerie had to win either the Dubai Desert Classic or the TCL Classic in China a week later to have an outside chance of breaking inside the top fifty. 'My next time in America might not be until the US PGA in August,' explained Montgomerie in Dubai. 'That's the situation I'm in – I just don't know at this stage.'

Things looked up after Desert Classic. Describing it as a 'golden opportunity to win', Montgomerie finished fourth behind the eventual winner, Ernie Els. If he could just win the TCL Classic at Yalong Bay Golf Club in China against a weakened field, he would be heading off to Florida. A second-place finish in China would leave him with an anxious wait on performances at the Bay Hill Invitational in the same week. Only then would he know whether he would be heading out to America or returning to the golfing backwater of Jakarta for the Indonesian Open.

Rarely had the pressure been greater for so little reward for the seven-time European number one. In the end he finished sixth, just two strokes behind the winner Paul Casey. Having missed out on the Tournament Players Championship, now it was a trip to Indonesia, where only outright victory would give him enough ranking points to avoid missing the Masters for the first time since 1989. In Dubai, Montgomerie explained that his divorce from Eimear last September had 'simplified things because I'm thinking more about myself . . . I don't mean in a selfish way, it's just the reality of my life.'

The reality of life now involved a long plane journey across Asia to a tournament he would rather not have to play in. As the rest of the world's top players were in Sawgrass preparing for the Tournament Players Championship, Montgomerie acknowledged the significance of playing at Jakarta's Cengkareng golf club in a tournament dedicated to the victims of the previous year's Asian tsunami. Currently 54th in the world, he was also realistic about what was required. 'If I win here, I know that I'll qualify [for the Masters] so that's the main goal,' he told reporters. 'Then everything else will take care of itself.'

The first European Tour event ever played in Indonesia, winning the first prize of £87,000 would certainly take care of a lot of problems for the anxious Scot. Even second place might be enough to get Montgomerie back into the top fifty. Not that any of this mattered if he did not play all four rounds! Montgomerie was right on the cut mark with five holes remaining in his second round when the threat of lightning brought an immediate end to play. Faced with a tough chip to the fourteenth from a bank near a greenside bunker, he was left with no option other than coming back the next morning.

Failing to mark his ball, the Scottish professional returned to find it gone. Conferring with playing partners Thongchai Jaidee and Arjun Atwal, he located the point where his ball had been and replaced it. Chipping to within inches of the hole, Montgomerie saved his par before picking up birdies on the sixteenth and seventeenth for a round of 69. Making the cut by a single stroke, he completed fourteen holes of his third round to end the day nine shots behind the eventual tournament winner, Thailand's Thaworn Wiratchant.

Even a superb ten-under-par 60 in the final round – including nine consecutive birdies – would not be enough to claim the victory he needed to climb back into the world's top fifty. Tied for fourth place – seven shots behind the winning total – a place in the 101-strong Masters field now looked a forlorn hope for the disappointed Scot. Sadly for Colin Montgomerie, there was far worse to come as film of the incident near the fourteenth green in the second round showed him replacing his ball in the wrong place! The visual evidence was damning. In a before-and-after sequence, the tape showed him struggling to get a comfortable stance, shaking his head and generally unable to play the chip in the direction he wanted. The following day, he was able to get a stance and executed the shot with precision to within inches of the hole. As the cameras closed in, it became increasingly obvious that the ball was at least twelve inches away from the original spot!

The error might not have even been noticed if his fellow competitors Soren Kjeldsen and Gerry Norquist had not been watching live coverage of the tournament in the clubhouse on Saturday afternoon. The contrast could not have been starker. Aware that Montgomerie faced an impossible chip after watching the highlights the night before, both men were astonished as the former European number-one laid his ball stone dead from the side of the fourteenth green to save his par! One moment he was struggling to take a stance with one foot in the bunker – now he had both feet above ground. Shortly after, the two players notified tournament referee José Maria Zamora and Montgomerie was asked to explain the anomaly. The Scot simply explained that it was a genuine mistake and, correctly, the official took him at his word. No penalty or disqualification was levied, everyone got on with the rain-affected tournament and that was thought to be the end of the matter.

Unfortunately, that would not be the end. As the videotape of the incident emerged, it took on a life of its own as sport shows replayed it over and over again. Labelled 'Jakartagate' by the British tabloids, the storm of controversy would haunt Montgomerie over the next few months, but it was not the first time he had become embroiled in a rules controversy.

At the Volvo Masters at Valderrama in 2002, his play-off with Bernhard Langer was delayed because there was a question mark over what Monty did or did not do with his belly putter on the tenth green in the final round. One stroke off the lead, the Scot rushed a downhill birdie putt past the hole. Moving quickly, he casually placed the putter head behind the ball looking to roll it in for par. It was then that the ball appeared to move a quarter-inch to the right and back uphill towards the hole. Montgomerie, who showed no reaction, did not step away from the ball or appear to hesitate before tapping it in.

The matter may have been left there except for a request from former Ryder Cup golfer and television analyst, Ken Brown. Having spotted something during play, he asked the chief referee of the European Tour, John Paramor, to take a look at some VT footage taken for The Golf Channel. (Neither of the on-air commentators, Renton Laidlaw and Warren Humphreys, had noticed the incident when it happened live.) While the ball did appear to move, it was not immediately clear whether Monty had actually grounded his putter or not. If he had, then it was a two-stroke penalty and possible disqualification if his scorecard had not been amended before he signed for his score.

Paramor caught up with Montgomerie on the twelfth fairway to explain the situation. Clearly annoyed, Montgomerie denied touching the ball and asked to look at the tape after the round. 'Well, I'll tell you this,' said Laidlaw while Monty was shown animatedly discussing it with playing partner Bradley Dredge. 'If Colin Montgomerie had touched the ball with his putter, we would have known all about it. And he would certainly not be saying, you know, "I don't know what that's all about." There's an honesty with Colin Montgomerie.'

That was the consensus as Montgomerie and Eimear were whisked off on a buggy to the TV compound to review pictures of the incident. Not that he was happy about the accusation or being told about it during the final round of such an important tournament! After a bogey at the 72nd hole cost him outright victory, Monty vented his anger in the scorekeeper's trailer. 'He was kicking chairs and throwing pencils,' said Paramor to reporters. 'He was upset that he had been told about the possible penalty during play. I asked him, "Colin, what would you have had me do – not tell you, and then come to the last hole thinking you had three putts to win, when you might have actually needed two strokes less?" After that, he was fine.'

Then came a moment of confusion as Paramor and Montgomerie disagreed about something that was said in the buggy. 'He had a feeling the ball was going to move, so he made a point of *not* addressing it,' said the referee. The Scot, however, said he most emphatically did not tell Paramor that he thought the ball was going to move before it did: 'What I said to him was: "The ball might have moved – but I didn't make the ball move."'

Daylight was fading fast in southern Spain and the matter was resolved to everyone's satisfaction. 'What happened was I was asked to go down to the TV van to have a look at what happened on the tenth green when the ball appeared to move,' Montgomerie commented afterwards. 'The key question was – had I addressed the ball or not? Between us, John and I found out that I hadn't done so. That was why I was able to take part in the play-off.'

Incredibly, there was a similar incident weeks later at Nedbank Challenge in South Africa. Playing his opening hole of the tournament, Monty recorded a triple-bogey seven en route to a two-over-par 74. Approached by an official, he was informed that he had breached the rules regarding a moving ball and a one-shot penalty had been levied, making it an eight. Obviously annoyed, the Scot refused to attend the post-round press conference and it was left to tournament rules official Dennis Bruyns to explain the mix-up. 'The ball rested against a leaf or a twig and Montgomerie was unsighted once he addressed the ball,' reported Bruyns. 'So he didn't see the ball in the bush and he took his back swing and made some sort of contact with the ball. The scorer who was accompanying the group reported to us that, as Colin took his shot, the ball moved and Colin continued with the shot and hit the ball ... Rule Eighteen states that you do not get penalised for hitting a moving ball unless you have done something to cause the ball to move. We believe he did cause the ball to move because of his back swing through the leaves and bush.'

After fifteen years as a professional without a problem, Montgomerie had been pulled up twice in six weeks. The last top player to be put under the rules microscope was two-time major winner Mark O'Meara. As with Monty in Jakarta, a tape was produced that appeared to show he had replaced his ball closer to the hole on a two-foot putt during the 1997 Lancôme Trophy in France. 'If I had seen the film before I signed my scorecard, I would have given myself a penalty,' said a repentant O'Meara. 'But four months later, what could I do? All I could say was that it wasn't intentional, which it wasn't. It was one of the worst times of my life. To basically be accused of being a cheater was very hard.'

Rigorous self-regulation is what distinguishes the game of golf from all other major sports. A game policed by those who play it, honesty and integrity have been the long-accepted norm. Regarding the incident at Valderrama, O'Meara was unswerving in his support of the Scottish professional. 'Am I going to look more closely at Colin Montgomerie when I play with him? No. He's a player I respect for his honesty and integrity,' said the former Masters and Open champion. 'Actually, I think a superstar like him is less likely to do anything that messes with the rules. You have so much to lose. And your good name is all you've got.'

Langer felt the same after seeing the video. 'I saw the tape, but it wouldn't be fair of me to make a judgement,' said the German, who was also winless that year. 'The angle I had might be totally wrong. You need two or three angles for that. I trust Monty. He has always been a good referee of the game. I'm fine with what happened. Anyway, it's history now.'

Fast-forward to 2005, and finishing in the top four of the Indonesian Open meant that Montgomerie now relied on a special invitation to play in the Masters the following week. Whether his remarkable 60 on Sunday would sway the green jackets in his favour remained to be seen, but his record at Augusta was far from impressive. Missing the halfway cut in three of the past four Masters meant he would hardly be top of the invitation list. So it came as no surprise when Augusta National decided not to hand the Scot a special invitation to the first major of the year. Being listed at 54 in the latest world rankings never seemed like being enough – and so it proved.

However, top-ten finishes in both the Johnnie Walker Classic in Beijing and the BMW Asian Open in Shanghai in late April boosted his chances of qualifying automatically for the US Open in June. Returning to England, Montgomerie now boasted the European Tour's lowest stroke average. It was his first opportunity to review the video footage from the Indonesian Open. Confirming that an 'inadvertent mistake' had been made, the Scot declared that he had no wish to benefit from what he believed was an innocent error. In a spirit of sportsmanship he announced that he would be giving his £27,000 prize money to the Asian Tsunami Appeal. 'I am upset that I could have caused my colleagues to question me,' he said, 'and with this in mind I will be making a donation.'

One of his colleagues who did question the drop at the time was 43-year-old Asian Tour member Gerry Norquist. 'Before the weather delay he was in a very difficult position,' said the talented American professional. 'The camera was right there, showing he was having difficulty taking a stance because of the bunker. I came back to the course the next day and wanted to see how Monty would finish. When I saw he made par, I thought to myself "Wow!" Then I saw the replay and I thought "Holy cow!" I was astonished, because the ball was nowhere near where it was the day before.'

There were also a number of European Tour players who were not satisfied with his explanation. Industry gossip about the 'Monty incident' travelled like a brush fire. Something had to be done and a meeting was quickly scheduled by the fourteen-strong Tournament Players committee prior to the British Masters at the Forest of Arden in mid-May, attended by newly appointed European Tour executive director George O'Grady and chief referee John Paramor. Montgomerie gave his fellow committeemen his side of the story for twenty minutes before answering any questions that were raised. 'I realised myself there had been an inadvertent mistake,' said Monty afterwards. 'I suppose I was worried what people were thinking but I'm very open about what was done and how it was handled.'

The subject of a sustained locker-room whispering campaign, Montgomerie hoped his appearance before the Tournament Players committee would put the matter to rest. Andrew Coltart, a member of the committee, agreed completely and insisted it was now time to draw a firm line under the matter. 'It's up to others to decide whether Colin's good name has been tarnished by all this,' said his former Dunhill Cup partner. 'Monty is a legend on the European Tour and a talisman for the European Ryder Cup team. There's also a fair chance he will be a Ryder Cup captain one day. We all make mistakes and this should be the end of the matter.'

A statement was quickly issued to all 154 players competing in the British Masters effectively exonerating the former European number one of any blame. Despite expressing the committee's 'dissatisfaction' with Montgomerie's explanation, it was hoped that would be an end to the matter.

Waking up to I'M NO CHEAT! headlines at the Forest of Arden, Montgomerie kept his sense of humour during his opening round of 72. On a day when Spaniard Miguel Angel Martin was disqualified for illegally treading down a sapling, he responded to a tongue-in-cheek rules query from playing partner Lee Westwood with: 'Sure, I'm good on the rules!'

It was open to debate just how many of his fellow professionals agreed with him. The decision not to pursue the matter any further had annoyed a significant number of European Tour members, including Gary Evans. Unhappy that a more open discussion had not been held, Evans, who came close to winning the 2002 Open Championship at Muirfield, demanded the issue should be brought up again at the annual meeting of the European Tour at Wentworth before the start of the BMW Championship at the end of May.

It was at Wentworth that Evans made a searing attack on Montgomerie. Visiting the media centre to look at video footage from Jakarta, Evans was incensed at what he saw as a blatant infringement of the rules. With his comments plastered all over the Sunday newspapers, he claimed to speak for '98 per cent' of his fellow players who were unhappy at the decision to clear the Scot of blame. Demanding that he hand back his world ranking points by belatedly disqualifying himself from the Indonesian Open, Evans described Montgomerie's decision to give away his prize money as an obvious admission of guilt! 'There has been smoke around Monty before,' he said to journalists. 'Look what happened at Valderrama a couple of years ago. He got the benefit of the doubt there. And, of course, only he knows what he was really thinking in Indonesia, too.'

He was not alone in his criticism of Montgomerie. The media were equally sceptical about his explanation, but few were brave enough to stick their head above the parapet. 'Monty's re-birth as a regular feature in top-tens across the globe has been achieved in the wake of his desperately disappointing descent into blatant rule-bending in Jakarta in March,' wrote respected columnist John Huggan in the *Scotland on Sunday* some months later. 'As the gap between Monty and his European Tour "chums" has widened again, so their eyes have collectively narrowed.'

Not surprisingly, Gary Evans' controversial attack on the former European number one infuriated the European Tour hierarchy, including executive director George O'Grady. Reacting to the comment about how the 'integrity of our game cannot continue to be compromised in such fashion', a furious O'Grady demanded a full apology from Evans to Jaime Spence, chairman of the influential Tournament Players committee, describing Evans' remarks as 'enormously disrespectful'.

'I would expect that player [Evans], if the remarks reported are true, to apologise to Jamie Spence and the other fourteen elected members for publicly undermining the leadership of the Tour,' said the long-time number two to Ken Schofield.

Jaime Spence seemed less bothered and, perhaps reflecting the feelings of his members, he said, 'I didn't expect Gary to apologise. I don't want his apology. It's a free world, but I think the timing of his comments was very poor ... I don't think he fully understood the issues involved. I think the players feel we should have taken some action but there is no action to take. Colin broke a rule and the referee at the time agreed he didn't incur a penalty. It's a misconception that he could disqualify himself after the event.'

Montgomerie admitted that his failure to mark his ball when thunder and lightning moved into the area was at the root of the problem: 'The question that was asked is "Why didn't you mark your ball?" As soon as you don't mark your ball and come back the next day to find it is missing, you're making a "guesstimate" of where the ball should be. But you have to remember there was a bolt of lightning and I wasn't prepared to stand around for any longer than I had to.'

John Paramor agreed: 'In my opinion, he did not replace the ball close enough to the original spot, as the bunker was there to help him as a visual reference. As soon as Colin saw the footage, he was mortified.'

After the meeting at Wentworth it was left to George O'Grady to bring matters to a close. In the spirit that used to underpin most major sports until the advent of television replays, he explained that the referees' decisions *must* be considered final, including the one made by José Maria Zamora in Indonesia. 'We have some of the best field staff in the world,' he said, 'and when they make considered judgements, which are fully and calmly explained to the tournament committee, these decisions should not be questioned.'

Montgomerie now considered the 'Jakarta incident' dead and buried, but his nemesis Gary Evans certainly did not. Accusing the Scot of acting unprofessionally by not marking his ball, he suggested that a review body should be established to scrutinise 'dubious' incidents like those found in Premier League football. 'We are playing for so much money now that the onus needs to be taken off the player,' he commented. 'It is unprofessional not to mark your ball. Are you really sure your ball is going to be there when you get back the next morning? You can't be serious. I have seen players mark their ball on the green and put two pegs on either side. The R and A seriously need to look at their rules. Cheating is almost acceptable in football. We must not let the integrity of the game fall by dubious situations.'

Falling just short of asking for Evans to be disciplined by the European Tour, Montgomerie admitted being upset by his fellow professional's comments. 'I was very surprised and very hurt,' said the Scot. 'I thought the issue was dead and buried. I think everyone is disappointed about what has happened here. Whether he should apologise or be fined is not my decision. That's up to George O'Grady.'

Montgomerie could afford few distractions in his attempt to book a place in the upcoming US Open in Pinehurst in June. With the new rankings calculated after the BMW at the end of May, he admitted entering the newly instigated international qualifying tournament at Walton Heath just in case he failed to qualify automatically. Missing one US Open was bad enough, but missing two in a row could have the golf obituary writers out in force sharpening their collective pens. 'I've got to get into the top fifty by the end of the BMW Championship at Wentworth,' said a determined Monty, 'and I'm very focused on doing that.'

In the end, qualification for the US Open at Pinehurst could not have been closer. Still outside the top fifty after a disappointing performance in the Nissan Irish Open the week before, Montgomerie finally came good at Wentworth after a final round of 66 in the BMW. Needing to get up and down from 100 yards on the final hole for a birdie to get into the world's top fifty and the US Open, he managed it under the toughest pressure imaginable. In 36th position at the end of the third round, he moved 25 places up the leader board for a final share of eleventh. Not surprisingly, Montgomerie later described his achievement that day as a 'milestone moment' in his career.

After a nervous wait, Monty received the good news that he had qualified automatically for the US Open via the latest world rankings. Such were the complexities of the ranking system, that when Kirk Triplett slipped out of second place in the St Jude Classic in Memphis on the PGA Tour the same week, the Scot had just enough points to reach number fifty! Such were the margins of success and failure when you were dancing on the edge of a precipice as Montgomerie had been doing for the last two years or more. Therefore it came as no surprise that the wafer-thin margin by which he qualified for the US Open reopened the debate regarding the world ranking points he had accrued at the Indonesian Open two months earlier.

Competing in the Wales Open at Celtic Manor in August, Montgomerie found himself answering even more questions about the Jakarta incident. Speaking to the media, Jamie Spence explained that Monty could not be asked to give back the world ranking points that had earned him a place the US Open 'after the event'. Forced to reiterate that his decision to give away his winnings was 'no admission of guilt', Montgomerie was frustrated that the matter had not been laid to rest. 'At the Forest of Arden tournament committee meeting, I thought it was dead,' he said tersely. 'At the players' meeting [at Wentworth] I thought it was dead. Hopefully this is third time lucky.'

Even the media considered the Jakartagate story old news until Darren Clarke inexplicably withdrew from the British team to face Continental Europe in the Seve Trophy in September – a team that Montgomerie would captain. A critic of Montgomerie's conduct in Indonesia, a strong bond of friendship had existed between the two Ryder Cup colleagues, but that had reputedly soured somewhat over the previous few months. Forced to deny a rift at the PGA Championship in August, the straightforward Ulsterman told the media they were reading far too much into his decision. Adamant that it had nothing to do with Jakarta or Montgomerie, he commented, 'My personal opinions make absolutely no difference whatsoever. It is a scheduling issue. It is just one of those unfortunate things that it doesn't fit into my plans.'

Montgomerie understandably had no comment. All he wanted to do was get on with his already disrupted season. Back in May at Wentworth, when the questioning about Jakarta was at its zenith, the former European Tour number one expressed his frustration saying, 'There have been times when I thought, "What the hell am I doing in this job?"'

After a stirring performance in the Open at St Andrews two months later, he would know exactly what he was doing in this job.

21. NEW HOPE AT THE OLD COURSE

With the US Open and, hopefully, an Open Championship at St Andrews to look forward to, Montgomerie was in a positive mood. His game was in good shape and even his putting was starting to come together. Content to return to a course where he had posted a top-twenty finish in 1999, his relief in the days leading up to the first round at Pinehurst was obvious. 'There's no doubt I missed being at Shinnecock last year,' he admitted. 'When you've missed one US Open, you don't want to miss two.'

Having expended so much effort to make it into the second major of the year, perhaps Montgomerie should have missed this one. Attending a memorial service on the eve of the championship for Payne Stewart, winner here in 1999, he was visibly moved as a Scottish piper played a lament for his former Ryder Cup opponent. Never quite coming to terms with the emotion of the week, he performed well below his best, finishing thirteen strokes down the field behind a first-time major winner, Michael Campbell of New Zealand.

It was a different story at St Andrews a month later. After struggling hard to improve his world ranking for the first half of the year, the Scot had progressed from 83rd in January to 40th place. In optimistic mood, he predicted that he would win one of the three tournaments he had entered between the US Open and the Open, and that almost came true at the European Open in Ireland when he finished tied runner-up with Graeme Storm, two shots behind Kenneth Ferrie. 'While I might not be playing quite as well now as I was in 1999, I am performing *almost* as well,' he said at the Barclays Scottish Open at Loch Lomond, where he finished inside the top twenty. 'I feel I'm just a putt or so away in each round from being where I want to be.'

Montgomerie must have been in reflective mood in the days leading up to the Open Championship a week later. Five years earlier, he had walked the empty streets of the 'auld grey toun' desperately searching for some peace of mind after a bitter argument with wife Eimear, causing him to shed tears during the final round of the 2000 Open. She had now departed, along with a substantial percentage of his fortune. Monty had returned to the Kingdom of Fife many times since for the Dunhill Trophy, but this was the Open and that brought pressures of its own. Describing himself as an 'underdog', he expressed the view that he had been held back from perform- ing at his best in the Open because of the pressure he was under as European number one. 'The pressure is off this week,' he said before the opening round. 'In 1995 I was one of the favourites and in 2000 not far from it. But I ended up in the middle of the pack both times. So this time I'm going to have a bit of fun.'

As the top Scottish professional of his generation, Mont- gomerie had always struggled with the weight of expectation – especially when the Open Championship returned to St Andrews – the 'Home of Golf'.

All the legends of the game had played here: from 'Old' Tom Morris to Harry Vardon, Walter Hagen to Sam Snead, Ben Hogan to Arnold Palmer, and Jack Nicklaus to Tiger Woods. Mary, Queen of Scots, a frequent visitor to the links, once described St Andrews as the 'most pleasing towne in my kingdom'. Countless thousands of golfing pilgrims who arrive each year would certainly agree, because nowhere on planet golf does sporting history come alive as it does here. Home to dozens of Open Championships and many other prestigious tournaments, the legendary Old Course has changed little since it was formed eons ago. Occupying a narrow strip of land between St Andrews Bay and the Eden Estuary, it stretches away from the ancient town like a shepherd's crook. At first sight it appears flat and uninspiring, with little of the majestic splendour of Augusta National or Pebble Beach. Resembling a moonscape in places, it offers a straightforward challenge in benign weather but is a monster when the wind blows from the north. Deceptively featureless, the first time Sam Snead spotted it from the window of his railway carriage en route to the first post-war Open in 1946, he asked a fellow passenger the name of 'the old abandoned golf course'.

'That, sir,' replied an indignant Scot, 'is the Old Course at St Andrews. Home to golf for over six centuries, and has never been, nor ever will be, abandoned!'

Like breakfast whisky and haggis, the Old Course has to be experienced numerous times to appreciate its subtle eccentricities. It's the most fiendishly bunkered golf course in the world, the bunkers ranging in size from dustbin lids to hazards large enough to rate their own par! Many are hidden from view by slopes and hollows but once they have swallowed up the ball, they rarely let the golfer escape without exacting a severe penalty. Boasting high, almost vertical riveted faces, they also have names that stimulate the imagination, like Lion's Mouth, Coffin, Grave and, most intimidating of all, Hell. Some of the links' most recognisable features are the massive double greens that serve a number of holes.

St Andrews is also home to the Royal and Ancient Golf Club – the rule makers of the game. Founded back in 1754 by 'twenty-two noblemen and gentlemen being admirers of the ancient and healthful exercise of the Golf', the stone clubhouse that stands behind the first tee became their home a century later. When they first began, the Old Course was made up of twenty-two holes with a typical round consisting of eleven holes 'out' to the sea and eleven back to the town, but it was reduced to eighteen holes shortly after William St Clair went round in the sacrilegious total of 121 strokes in

1764, and that has been accepted as the standard round ever since. St Andrews Opens have produced their fair share of Scottish winners. Starting with Tom Kidd back in 1873, the list includes notables like Hugh Kirkaldy in 1891 and five-time Open Champion James Braid in 1905 and 1910. However, even if you count St Andrean-turned-US-citizen Jock Hutchison in 1921, there has been a dearth of Scottish winners ever since. No wonder the pressure on Montgomerie to perform was greater than ever in 2005. The only question was how he would respond.

Since the 2000 Open Championship at St Andrews Montgomerie's career had seen more lows than highs. There had been the occasional tournament victory but they were far less frequent than before. As for winning an eighth European Order of Merit, that seemed as far away as ever. The last few months had proved a real struggle both on and off the golf course. Coming to terms with putting his Surrey mansion up for sale to fund an increasingly acrimonious divorce, missing the cut in the Masters and an unwelcome slump in form around the US Open all contributed to his anxiety. Add to that 'Jakartagate' and ask yourself, how much worse could it have got? 'There are a hell of a lot of knocks in this game,' Monty had commented earlier in the season, 'definitely more downs than ups, but this has been the worst time I have ever experienced. There have been knocks all over the place.'

Resilient as ever, the seven-time European number one admitted that it was his hugely competitive nature that kept him going. In typical Monty-speak, he described how 'I am learning to really celebrate the ups I have because I didn't before – I'm encouraged by them. If I win three times in a year it's great. I play thirty times a year so there are twenty-seven knocks.'

Of course, winning the Open Championship at the legendary 'Home of Golf' would round his career off perfectly. 'I did say five years ago I'd die a happy man if I won at St Andrews,' said Montgomerie. 'And I feel exactly the same way now.' Portraying a far more positive image, he appeared determined to shed the 'Mr Grumpy' label given to him by the media.

'Yes, I hit a bad shot,' he told reporters in the lead up to the Open, 'but away from the course I actually do quite enjoy my life.'

Describing these as 'exciting times', an upbeat Monty said how much he now looked forward to the future. 'Everyone who has been through what I've been through,' said the Scot, 'whether it's in business, sport or their private lives, comes out of it a lot stronger.'

Nominating Tiger Woods as his pick for winner, his relaxed attitude worked wonders over the first few days at St Andrews, having spent, in his opinion, 'three years in the wilderness'. After balmy conditions earlier in the week, which saw temperatures in the eighties, it was back to typically Scottish weather as the Scot opened up with rounds of 71 and 66 in woolly-hat conditions. Better weather returned over the weekend as Montgomerie set his sights on consolidating his fine start. Four strokes behind championship leader Tiger Woods, he had halved the deficit by the turn and it got better. Birdie on the par-four tenth brought him within a shot of his playing partner and the Scottish crowds began to dream. Then, like Icarus flying too close to the sun, Montgomerie undid all his good work on the back nine. Beginning with three putts at the short eleventh for bogey and ending with a visit to the Road Hole bunker on seventeen for another, Monty saw Woods accelerate away to put daylight between him and the chasing pack. Even a birdie on the final hole still left Monty three strokes behind the American in joint third place with Retief Goosen. 'I got one shot back out of the four,' he said afterwards. 'All I need now is to get back the other three!'

Halfway through the last round on Sunday, that looked almost possible. Partnering Goosen, Montgomerie burst out of the blocks with birdies at holes three, five and nine – once again closing the gap on Tiger Woods to a single shot. But if the gateway to golfing immortality was a tunnel, this one had a train coming from the opposite direction. As briefly as the door opened, Woods slammed it firmly shut. Not many golden opportunities of this kind appear when the American is around and Montgomerie was unable to take his chance. Once again, his problems began on the treacherous par-three eleventh, with its gaping Strath bunker guarding the front half of the green. With the wind picking up, Montgomerie overclubbed to leave his tee shot above the hole. His downhill chip was poor and the penalty levied by the course was a dropped stroke at a crucial stage of the round

Seizing on the Montgomerie error, Woods quickly opened up a two-shot gap. Like a noose around the Scotsman's neck, the pressure became increasingly tight as the championship moved to its inevitable conclusion down the closing holes. 'On the eleventh tee the wind suddenly switched and when I hit the wrong club that threw me a bit,' said the downhearted Scot. 'I didn't get the same momentum after getting halfway to my target of six under for the round. That would have won.'

The reality was that Monty *might* have won if he had not been quite so defensive on the back nine. Putt after putt came up short as if he was locked into the idea that par might win. Playing against the number-one player in the world, the Scot struck the ball wonderfully off the tee but desperately needed to abandon his customary caution on the greens. 'Woods is in a different league from anyone on the greens,' said former European Ryder Cup captain Bernard Gallacher. 'But Monty is as good as anyone from tee to green.'

From the reachable par-four twelfth onwards the battle was always for second place as the patriotic crowd assailed him with calls of 'Get your chin up, Colin'.

'I thought the crowd were phenomenal,' said a grateful Monty afterwards. 'When the fans realised I wasn't going to win and my task was to finish second they helped me do that.'

Carding an even-par 72 for a nine-under-par total of 279 was never going to be good enough despite Monty's assertion that 'anything could have happened'. Within minutes of receiving the silver salver for finishing second, the former European number one was trying to convince anyone who would listen that he could have won if things had gone his way! If only he had not overclubbed on the eleventh hole . . .

if only he had not three-putted two consecutive greens on the back nine ... if only ... if only.

Boasting about getting to within one stroke of the American at the turn, he omitted to mention that both Fred Couples and José Maria Olazábal did the same before a succession of bogeys on the back saw them slip back to joint third. While few will remember their contribution to the 134th Open Championship, the Scot's place in the hearts of those present was assured.

'Montgomerie gets under Scotland's skin,' wrote Scottish journalist Alasdair Reid in the *Sunday Herald*. 'He engages the nation as a whole. And in an era when sports writers have a better chance of getting snappy quotes from a sand wedge than any number of star players they might interview, Montgomerie is a welcome exception – refreshingly distinguished as an interesting bloke.'

Of course, when Woods wins a major by such large margins – five shots this time over Montgomerie – it raises the question whether the American is that good or if his competition is not up to the task. A five-stroke margin of victory may seem small change compared with his record-breaking fifteen-shot win in the 2000 US Open at Pebble Beach, or his twelve-shot victory in the 1997 Masters or his even his eight-shot win at St Andrews in 2000, but Tiger Woods still remains at the head of an elite group of runaway major winners. Nicklaus managed it twice in his career, by nine strokes at the 1965 Masters and by seven at the 1980 PGA Championship, leaving only Arnold Palmer, Ben Hogan and Nick Faldo as the other players to have won a major by at least five shots. As gracious as he is talented, Woods took time out from his busy schedule parading the silver claret jug to congratulate Montgomerie on his estimable effort. Then he said it. Oh, why did he say it? Those fateful words that had haunted the Scot for the past dozen years or more. 'There's no reason why he can't win a major championship,' said the nine-time major champion.

It is hard to recall any top player from Jack Nicklaus to Bernhard Langer who has not uttered those disabling words at some point. In truth, Montgomerie should place his hands firmly over his ears and walk away as quickly as possible. Unfortunately, the opposite was true as he feasted on each syllable like a blind man searching for the light. As seven-time European number one, the Scot had enjoyed one of the most successful careers in modern golfing history *without* winning a major. It should have made him extremely content as well as rich, but it obviously had not as the divorce testimony of his ex-wife plainly illustrated.

As someone who really did carry their heart on their sleeve, Montgomerie had spent fruitless years chasing some major-filled Valhalla. Why did he bother? Only someone with the drive and stubbornness of Colin Stuart Montgomerie could answer that. For now he could bask in the intoxicating limelight that major runners-up enjoy for a week or so after the real winner has headed home with the trophy in his hand luggage.

For Montgomerie, the next few weeks were spent talking up his chances in the majors to come. Indeed, so upbeat were the British tabloids about his performance at St Andrews, you really had to refer back to the record books to check he did not actually win it! No, there it is: 'Tiger Woods (USA), winner, Open Championship, 2005'.

Golf, like life, can be fickle sometimes and Montgomerie would have done well to remember that. Throughout his career he had worked hard to override the negative aspects of his personality: the doubting Monty that made him question whether he was good enough to turn professional back in 1987; the insecure Monty that drove him to win the European Order of Merit time and time again when his greatest rivals were happy winning it just once and moving on; and the highly unpredictable Monty that made him wonderful copy in the pressroom one moment and an arrogant bully the next.

Compensating for his faults, he had gone overboard on positive reinforcement after his performance at St Andrews: 'There is no disgrace in losing to the best player of our generation, by far,' said Montgomerie. 'I'm taking a lot of positives from this result. It's been a while since I was a contender in a major and with my life better sorted out, I feel I can contend in the major championships again.'

It was nothing we had not heard before. At the start of each new season, each new major, he would assault the media with claims of how well he was going to do. At the 2003 Open at Sandwich he claimed that his chances of winning were 'ten out of ten' and expected hard-bitten hacks to take him seriously. His coach Denis Pugh put these 'Monty moments' down to the type of player he was. 'The "feel" golfer needs to be able to picture the shot and then have the confidence to pull it off,' said the respected coach. 'That's why with Colin you some-times hear him make what sounds like an outrageously confident remark. It's because he's trying to get himself up.'

According to many golf journalists, perhaps Monty should forget 'feel' and try a little humour and humility in his quest to win that elusive major he craved. Why? Because golf has a nasty way of humbling even the greatest practitioners of the sport. Tiger Woods had felt its sting during his rainswept round of 82 in the Open at Muirfield in 2002. The legendary Sam Snead never won the US Open he desperately wanted. Ben Hogan was denied the professional Grand Slam in 1953 because he was unable to make it back to America in time to compete in the PGA Championship. And who can forget Doug Sanders missing a short putt on the final green at St Andrews to win the 1970 Open. Even Jack Nicklaus was denied more majors than the eighteen he actually won. For all his achievements, Montgomerie had yet to win the big one – the major that would round his career off Cinderella-style. While he did not realise it, a little humility would come in useful, because less than a year on from all the back-slapping at St Andrews, Montgomerie would experience perhaps the greatest disappointment of his career. Significantly, it would be at a golf course named in honour of one of the ancient gods that shaped the destiny of mortals – Winged Foot.

22. EIGHTH TIME LUCKY AT VALDERRAMA

C oming second to Tiger Woods in the 2005 Open Championship at St Andrews had imbued Colin Montgomerie with a new-found self-belief.

With his highest finish in a major since he finished runner-up to Ernie Els in the 1997 US Open and best-ever result in the Open Championship (his previous best finishes in the Open being tied-eighth in 1990 and 1994), Montgomerie was brimming with confidence. The immediate reward for his performance at St Andrews was a significant leap up the world rankings to a new position of 22nd. Having achieved his goal of getting back into the top 25 by the end of the year he was in no mood to stop there. Two second-place finishes in the past three weeks had given him a boost and there was even mention of the dreaded 'M' word as he predicted making a solid challenge in the US PGA Championship at Baltusrol in less than a month's time. But for now he was content to discuss his meteoric rise in the world rankings from his early-season position at 83. 'I'm not saying I can get back to number two in the world as in 1996/97,' he said, 'but I believe I have got the talent to get back into the top ten, which would be a huge achievement.'

Buoyant after finishing runner-up to Tiger Woods, Montgomerie described his second-place finish to Nick Dougherty at the Caltex Masters in Singapore at the end of January as a huge turning point in his career. 'I came out and shot sixty-five the first day and led by three,' he recalled. 'That was the start of it. It put me on the map again. It put me on the scoreboards, put me on the leader board.'

Proving a month is a long time in golf, the Scot arrived in New Jersey for the US PGA Championship in confident mood, only to see his opening round blow up in his face as he finished seven over par.

After his appearance at the Johnnie Walker Championship at Gleneagles a week earlier, where he withdrew after straining his wrist attempting to hit a driver off the fairway midway through his opening round, Montgomerie's so-called Indian summer was turning into wet weekend in Blackpool. Needing a top-two finish to lead the European Order of Merit for the first time in six years, Montgomerie ended the tournament with swollen fingers and a visit to the same London specialist who had treated his hand after his accidental fall before the 2002 Open at Royal St George's. 'My fingers are heavily bruised and I'm going to see the specialist,' he said, adding optimistically, 'Hopefully I can rest up over the next three or four days and still go to America.'

His injury no doubt played its part in his poor performance over the testing Lower Course at Baltusrol. Following up a first round 77 with 71, the 42-year-old Scot refused to put the blame on his injured hand. 'I didn't have any timing from the word go,' he lamented. 'You can't hit it the right distance if you are not timing it.'

Despite his disappointing PGA Championship, Montgomerie was still in the hunt for a record-breaking eighth Order of Merit title. 'In 2004, I finished twenty-fifth and to think about winning money lists again was a long way off,' said the Scot. 'It's exciting talking about it, even to have an opportunity to talk about it. I'd wrap up the other seven and put them together and place this one ahead of them. Winning it this year would mean more than finishing second in the Open at St Andrews.'

Montgomerie might have been focused on the Order of Merit but he was still searching for his first tournament win since the Caltex Masters in Singapore in March 2004. Even with all-important ranking points on offer he lost 2 and 1 to rising Australian star Mark Hensby in the first round of the World Match Play at Wentworth in September after being four up after thirteen holes. Since the Open in July, he had registered only one top-ten finish and had missed the cut at the PGA. One bright spot had been in the Seve trophy. Despite losing his match against José Maria Olazábal, he led his Great Britain and Ireland team to their third consecutive win in the event.

In October, Montgomerie returned to St Andrews for the first time since finishing second to Tiger Woods in the Open Championship in July. Competing in the pro-am style Dunhill Links tournament over the Old Course, Kingsbarns and Carnoustie, he calmly rolled home a short birdie putt on the final green at St Andrews to claim one of the biggest cheques of his career, just under £450,000. Added to the £430,000 he picked up over the same course ten weeks earlier, it breathed new life into his hope of winning the Order of Merit for the first time since 1999. More significantly, it brought him closer to making his eighth Ryder Cup appearance at the K Club, near Dublin, now less than twelve months away.

'I said my next win would be the most important of my career and it is,' said an emotional Montgomerie afterwards. 'When I was winning seven Order of Merits, it was a bit of a roller coaster and you couldn't get off. I wouldn't say it was easy, but it was expected. And then it stopped. My life changed dramatically. And that's why I feel it's the most influential win of my career.'

With his season earnings now approaching the £1million mark, his narrow one-stroke victory over England's Kenneth Ferrie also moved him inside the world top twenty. Now second in the European money list behind Michael Campbell, winner of the US Open at Pinehurst, the Scot relished the dogfight to come. From St Andrews to San Francisco a week later, Monty's campaign for an eighth Order of Merit was boosted after South African Retief Goosen withdrew from the £4.2m WGC American Express Championship in San Francisco with a groin injury. Effectively turning it into a two-horse race, the opportunity to land a decisive blow was not lost on either Montgomerie or Campbell.

With just three ranking events to play after the American Express Championship – the Madrid Open, the Mallorca Classic and the Volvo Masters – a top-ten finish in California could make all the difference. Needing to finish seventh or higher to overtake Campbell, the Scot was in positive mood after a superb opening round of 64 at Harding Park. Leading after the first round, Montgomerie was elated, especially after following it up with two 69s. 'As the years go on you probably don't think you can be number one again,' he said. 'I didn't believe it but now I do. I am still a fair way behind and have to catch up. I want to gain as much as possible so I can go into the last event with an opportunity to win.'

Finishing with a solid round of 70 for a 272 total, Monty rarely looked like reprising the brilliance of the first round and a share of third behind Tiger Woods and John Daly was a suitable reward. Missing a number of putts over the closing holes, he eventually holed from twelve feet for a birdie on the seventeenth to lie just one shot off the lead before bogeying the last. Dropping him from outright third into a tie with Sweden's Henrik Stenson and Spain's Sergio Garcia, it cost him well over £110,000 in prize money – perhaps the difference between winning the Order of Merit or not! 'I played great on the back nine and got nothing out of it,' said Monty. 'I hit some great shots in there and played it level par. It's disappointing really but I would have taken third before we came so that's OK.'

Rising to fourteenth in the world rankings with the help of £199,856 in prize money, he overtook Michael Campbell at the top of the Order of Merit after the Kiwi finished way down the field in San Francisco. Now just over £90,000 ahead in their personal race, Montgomerie headed back to Europe to play in the Madrid Open the following week. Then came the surprise news that Campbell had decided not to play in Europe until the end-of-season Volvo Masters at Valder-rama.

A top-ten finish in Madrid stretched Montgomerie's lead to £102,000. Frustrated at times, the Scot looked tense and nervous as he missed putt after putt on the 'terrible' greens of the Club de Campo. He threw his putter over a fence en route to signing for a final round 66, and it was left to caddie Alistair McLean to retrieve it. Whether it would survive in the bag for Valderrama in two weeks' time was anyone's guess.

Ignoring the Mallorca Classic in favour of practising for the Volvo Masters, he calculated that Michael Campbell had to finish in the top five to beat him while Goosen, £224,000 behind, had to win or finish second (assuming Montgomerie finished outside the top thirty).

The mind games started early in the run-up to the Volvo Masters as Campbell insisted he would not swap his oven-fresh US Open title for all seven of Montgomerie's Order of Merit titles. 'We, as golfers, play this game to win majors,' said the New Zealander. 'Seven Order of Merits is fantastic but if I was in Colin's shoes, I'd definitely swap my seven for one major.'

Montgomerie cleverly rolled with the punches and answered without agreeing either way. 'Michael's got a major but hasn't got an Order of Merit, so he hasn't got a choice and neither have I,' said the Scot. 'I don't look back and think my career is not fulfilled without a major. I'm very happy to have won the league championship, if you like, seven years running.'

For the past month, Montgomerie's number-one priority had been to keep ahead of Campbell in the Order of Merit race. Now raising his sights, his stated aim was to win the Volvo Masters outright. 'Everything else will fall into place if I do that,' he said. 'It would be a great honour to win another Order of Merit title. To come back and win again after five years would mean an awful lot – more than all the others put together.'

The odds were definitely in his favour. If this were the *Mastermind* television show, Colin Montgomerie's specialist subject would be 'getting the job done at Valderrama'. Since the Volvo Masters returned in 2002, he had finished first, tenth and nineteenth and was level par for his last twelve rounds over the Andalucian golf course. Campbell, in stark contrast, was twenty over par for his last eight rounds, including an 82 on the final day in 2004.

Sergio Garcia, who lost in a play-off here against Ian Poulter in 2004, also considered Montgomerie favourite in the race. 'I played with Colin in San Francisco at the Amex [American Express Championship] where he struck the ball very nicely,' said the Spanish star. 'While I wouldn't say he was performing better than he did in 1999, I agree he is playing much better than a couple of years ago. Colin is in very good form and has some confidence back in his putting.'

In the end that was the difference. The record book shows that Irishman Paul McGinley won the tournament, but most eyes that Sunday were on Montgomerie as he scrapped his way around the tree-lined course.

In what proved a bad-tempered round at times, his girl-friend Joanne Baldwin kept him updated on what the New Zealander was doing. Not that brilliantly as things turned out, as the Scot moved inexorably towards third place in the tournament to secure the Order of Merit. Receiving the silver Harry Vardon trophy for the eighth time in his career, Montgomerie told the media that he was now playing the best golf of his career. 'I'm a better player now than I ever have been,' said Montgomerie. 'Every year that I won the Order of Merit I had to improve. Now, with a six-year gap, the improvement has to be so much more.'

It was only a matter of time until the 'M' word was brought up again by a member of the media. Expertly sidestepping a loaded question about whether this would help him 'in his quest to win a major', Montgomerie preferred to focus on the past few months. Crediting the 'huge boost' he had received from his runner-up position at the Open back in July, he would not be tempted to make any rash predictions regarding how well he would do in next year's major championships. 'Perhaps I won't go down in the record books for winning majors,' he admitted to the media, 'but I will go down for winning Orders of Merits and Ryder Cups.'

With the *next* Ryder Cup in Ireland eleven months away, Colin Montgomerie had built a solid platform in which to qualify for the European team to face the Americans at the K Club in Ireland. Banking £139,685 for his week's work at Valderrama, it had been a remarkable turnaround in fortune for the Scottish professional. In a season that had begun with him running up air miles all over Asia and the Middle East, Monty finished 2005 with official earnings of £1,888,613. Apart from winning the Dunhill Links he managed seventeen top-twenty finishes, thirteen top-tens and seven top-fives. Along with registering three top-ten finishes in five events on the PGA Tour in the United States, this was a first-class season by anybody's standards.

'If I was to show you a route map of the year,' said manager Guy Kinnings, 'the amount of ground he's covered was staggering. I can't tell you how impressed I was by the inner calm and resolution he found along the way.'

Ending the season more than £200,000 behind the Scot in second place after finishing fourteenth at Valderrama, Michael Campbell was typically magnanimous. 'I'm obviously disappointed but all credit goes to Colin,' said the smiling Kiwi. The difference in the end was that Montgomerie wanted the number-one spot more than anyone else – certainly more than Campbell or Goosen.

At the British Masters in May, Monty said that he already had the 'Order of Merit T-shirt' so why should he need another? At the same tournament he switched from the belly putter to a conventional-length one and saw an immediate improvement in his putting. In the end, that was the key. Arriving in southern Spain, Montgomerie probably did not *need* another Vardon trophy to put in his cabinet, but he definitely *wanted* it. Crediting his psychologist and friend Hugh Mantle with his unfailingly positive attitude that week, Montgomerie described how hard they had worked on maintaining the correct posture. 'I was strong enough to maintain the body language I learned from my training with

Hugh,' he said. 'I wasn't prepared to give any sign of weakness. I never backed off even when I made bogey. I would just walk to the next hole as if it was a birdie.'

Would it be churlish, asked the media, to suggest that Montgomerie should have tried this technique before – perhaps in the majors where he often appeared to spend all four days walking around like the weight of the world was on his shoulders?

'With any sportsmen at a high level, when it comes to slump-busting they have to re-birth, as it were. Go back to find some of the things which made them great competitors in the first place,' said Mantle after watching his best-known client win at Valderrama. 'It's important the competitor is independent and owns that sense of confidence. The phrase I use a lot with sports people is – "if it's to be, it's up to me".'

Even the media noticed how much his recent successes had contributed to his more relaxed attitude at Valderrama. 'Montgomerie's very demeanour suggested a level of inner calm that could never have been envisaged during the more incendiary moments of his competitive life,' wrote Alasdair Reid of the *Sunday Herald*.

Back in January his career had been in free fall. His stated goal was just to get back in the top 25 in the world rankings, and many in the media thought that objective was little more than the last ramblings of a spent golfing force, and took little notice until he scrambled into the US Open in June on the back of a run of good results. Then he finished a fortunate second at the Smurfit European Open at the K Club in Ireland and they really began to sit up. As for the Open Championship in July, they could not praise him highly enough. Three months later, he was number one in Europe. As the media speculated, you can forget 'Colin Montgomerie OBE' – it was now surely a case of, 'Arise Sir Monty' in the New Years Honours List!

'Colin transformed his fortunes by playing his way out of a difficult period,' said Kinnings after the Volvo Masters. 'He lives for being competitive. When his game was in a bad way, it took a big commitment to get back to the top of the rankings. A lot of people formed the opinion that, at forty-two, Colin's best years were behind him. That wasn't how he saw things and it isn't the way they've turned out.'

Montgomerie knew what he had achieved and was too long in the tooth to take unsolicited flattery from the media seriously. Never one to resist rubbing an unfortunate journalist's nose in the dust should the humour take him, the Scot was surprisingly diplomatic with those who had written him off at the start of the year. Unlike Darren Clarke, who professed to have a little black book with the names of golf hacks who had upset him written inside, Monty said diplomatically: 'Had I thought my best days were behind me and everything I'd achieved was in the past, then I wouldn't bother entering golf tournaments.'

Back in America, Tiger Woods described Montgomerie's eighth European Tour Order of Merit title as 'truly one of the remarkable feats of modern golf'. The Burghers of the City of Glasgow in Scotland made him their 'Sports Person of the Year' and he was made favourite to win the prestigious BBC Sports Personality of the Year. Accepting his OBE from the Prince of Wales at an investiture ceremony at Buckingham Palace in November, Monty credited the huge part his winning 2004 Ryder Cup team had played in him being honoured in such a way. 'It's nice to be rewarded again for one's accomplishments,' he said. 'This was awarded, I think, on behalf of the Ryder Cup team of 2004.'

Not that Colin Montgomerie MBE OBE was finished winning golf tournaments quite yet. With Asia proving a favourite hunting ground, Monty registered his thirtieth victory on the European Tour by winning the co-sanctioned UBS Hong Kong Open in early December. Taking advantage of a final-hole double-bogey by South African James Kingston to win by a stroke, his victory lifted him up another eight places to ninth in the latest world rankings. 'The goal at the start of 2006 is to try to get into the top ten in the world,' Montgomerie had said before the event. 'I am not saying I want to be number one in the world, I know that is not realistic, so I am sensible in saying the top ten is a good and realistic goal for me to achieve.'

Building a firm platform for 2006, at least Montgomerie could now plan his schedule without having to chase world ranking points in every golfing outpost of the European Tour. Now inside the elite top-ten golfers in the world, he had automatic entry into any tournament he wanted, including the four majors and all four WGC World Championship events. Planning out his schedule at the end of the year, Monty and his highly able manager Guy Kinnings must have passed a wry smile at each other when it came to which tournaments to choose and which ones to omit. As they announced the list prior to the Hong Kong Open, it surprised nobody that the Indonesian Open in Jakarta was definitely *off* the list. 'I know Colin has made a bit of a joke of how hard I've worked him this season,' said Guy. 'I understand we've overdone it. But if you remember how far down the rankings he was at the start of the year, everything turned out for the best.'

It certainly had and now, as Montgomerie prepared to take a well-earned Christmas break, he could do so in the knowledge that he was ready to take on the challenges ahead. And what challenges they would prove.

23. WOUNDED PRIDE AT WINGED FOOT

S hortly after winning an historic eighth European Order of Merit at Valderrama in October, one brave journalist asked Colin Montgomerie when he might win a major. 'April,' he answered back. 'I would love to achieve it one day and the second Sunday in April is on the agenda.' Turning up at Augusta National for the first time in two years, Montgomerie had the opportunity to make his prediction come true.

After 34 tournaments in 2005, Montgomerie described himself as 'tired – physically and mentally'. Negotiations with Eimear's lawyers and the Jakartagate controversy had taken their toll but, through it all, the Scot had maintained his competitive focus. Removing any lingering doubts concerning his ability to compete at the highest level, he had risen from 83rd in the world rankings to inside the top ten within twelve months. It was nothing short of miraculous and no wonder he looked forward to a distraction-free season in 2006. 'I've always managed to block things out when I'm out on the course,' he admitted. 'A round is only five hours long and that's not bad out of twenty-four. You can concentrate on the other horrible stuff for the other nineteen.'

Sadly the 'horrible' stuff came back to haunt Montgomerie during the first quarter of 2006. While his marriage to Eimear had been over since September 2004, the past eighteen months had been spent negotiating a mutually acceptable divorce settlement. Initially the split appeared to be friendly, if only for the sake of their three children. After the Ryder Cup in September 2004, Eimear had texted her congratulations and he had replied thanking her. With Eimear and the children settled into a new 'luxury barn conversion' near Burhill golf club in Surrey from November, Christmas came and went in relative harmony. Then in the New Year allegations suddenly surfaced in the media about the restrictions placed on Montgomerie visiting his children. Eimear denied it vehemently, saying that as a joint custodian, her ex-husband had as much access as he wanted.

She was increasingly portrayed as a gold-digging schemer out to ruin one of British sport's most popular heroes, and claims that she demanded at least half his £25m fortune were openly discussed in the tabloids. Eimear fought back, describing how her former husband had consistently refused to discuss *any* financial settlement relating to their divorce. Once again, the 'unreasonable behaviour' cited in the official divorce papers was raked over along with Eimear's assertion that her husband's obsession with golf had left her with 'anxiety and depression'.

It was stalemate as the tabloids went to town on the increasingly bitter relationship. Montgomerie, somewhat typically, proved stubborn to the last. With a court date set for the end of January 2006, a financial agreement was agreed at the eleventh hour as he made a hurried return from the Abu Dhabi Championship. With top London lawyer Raymond Tooth – affectionately known as 'Jaws' because of his ability to take huge chunks from the bank accounts of his clients' spouses – representing Eimear, the final settlement appeared to suit them both. Inevitably some details leaked out, revealing that Montgomerie had agreed to a £6m one-off payment to Eimear plus £2m towards her new family home in Walton-on-Thames. She in turn agreed to give up all claims on her former husband's future earnings including prize money and commercial endorsements. Considering his recent return to form it was probably a wise move by Montgomerie. (A recent landmark case in July 2004 involving former Arsenal and England footballer Ray Parlour established the principle that a wife could claim ad infinitum on her husband's future earnings if she could establish that she had materially contributed to her husband's success.)

As Montgomerie returned on the next flight to the Arab Emirates to play in the Dubai Desert Classic it was left to Guy Kinnings to give the media the good news. 'The couple have agreed a pre-court settlement,' he announced. 'That obviously means a financial agreement has been met through mutual agreement. I think people assumed that because he rushed out and played so well last year that all this was behind him. He played a year of terrific golf under unbelievably difficult circumstances, which was the result of incredibly hard work. Hopefully with this resolved, he can focus on working for the future.'

With no details about the financial settlement available, both parties confirmed that it was nowhere near the Fantasy Island figures dreamed up by the media. Unfortunately for Montgomerie, whether it was £8m or £18m, the money still had to be found from somewhere. Reducing the price of his house in Surrey to £5m for a quick sale in May, Montgomerie also sold his £2.25m apartment overlooking the Thames in Battersea. Deal done, they could both get on with their respective lives. 'Colin and I have settled,' said the former Mrs Montgomerie shortly afterwards. 'I am not allowed to discuss the details but I can say the settlement was nothing like the twelve million pounds that has been rumoured. I am very happy that it has all been resolved because it means my future as an independent person is assured and so is the future of our children.' Denying the rumours that she was seeing someone new, Eimear did at least admit to acquiring a new member of the family – a pet dog.

Ranked eighth at the end of 2006, Montgomerie slipped outside the top ten in the World Rankings despite finishing tied-sixth in Abu Dhabi in late February. (In terms of ranking points it was considered no more than a warm up event for the prestigious Dubai Desert Classic a week later.) Missing the cut in the Desert Classic, Montgomerie took the downward turn in his fortunes philosophically. 'It was final closure and I can move on,' said Monty about his divorce settlement in Dubai. 'But it will take more than one round of golf. It was important for me to come here, and if it worked – it worked. But if it didn't – it didn't. I'm not unduly worried at all. I'll get going again. It's more a matter of when rather than if.'

After Dubai, Montgomerie missed three more consecutive cuts at the Johnnie Walker Classic in Perth, the Bay Hill Invitational and the Tournament Players Championship in Florida. A temporary slump in form threatened to become a crisis and the Scot immediately pulled out of the BellSouth Classic in Atlanta the week before Augusta. 'He does not feel he's playing well enough for this week's tournament and he's hugely apologetic about it,' said Kinnings. 'He just wants to work on his game in private.'

At the Masters, though, Montgomerie had a different story. With the news that Eimear was dating a millionaire business-man less than a month after the divorce settlement had been finalised, he admitted that his torrid personal life had played on his mind during his opening round of 74 at Augusta National. He conceded that his recent dip in form had coincided with his break-up from girlfriend Joanne Baldwin, but nobody considered that it might also have a great deal to do with Eimear. Confirming the split, his reply to one inquisitive question too many at Augusta was a terse 'I'm single – how is that? Is that fair enough? I don't mind you printing that. Jo and I have split up and I'm free to meet and date other women. It's a shame, but these things happen.'

She had been with him throughout his successful campaign of 2005, after they had met the previous November on the local school run. With both his and her children attending the same private school in Surrey, they got on well. She was bright and vivacious and that appealed to him. At the time of their original courtship, Ms Baldwin was still married, although she and her husband were living separate lives and would later divorce. When his divorce settlement was finalised in late

January, their relationship was long-lived enough for Guy Kinnings to comment on how Montgomerie would be likely to let the 'dust clear' before he and Ms Baldwin discussed marriage. 'For the first time in a heck of a long time I feel I'm truly enjoying every day,' said Monty early in their relationship. 'I put that down to the happiness I have found with Jo. I don't need a crystal ball to see that we've got a future together.'

Montgomerie missed yet another cut at the Masters after rounds of 74 and 75. Switching back to the belly putter that had served him so well, he described it as a 'particularly barren spell'. Looking morose, the 42-year-old professional knew better than anybody that time was in short supply if he was to achieve his long-held ambition of winning a major championship. 'I'm just not holing enough putts at the moment,' he said, before adding. 'It's a hundred per cent mental rather than physical.'

By the time Montgomerie arrived in Mamaroneck, New York for the second major of the year, he had managed to turn things around. A fourth place in the Celtic Manor Wales Open at the beginning of June, followed by a top-fifteen performance in the BA-CA Golf Open in Austria, convinced him that he was coming back into form at just the right time. He also believed that Winged Foot, located less than one hour from New York City's Grand Central Station, would favour his game.

Designed by Albert Warren Tillinghast – the genius behind two other US Open venues at Baltusrol and Bethpage Black – Winged Foot stood on land which was originally home to the Mohegan Indians and a base for George Washington's troops in the Revolutionary War. An attractive corner of New York State, it was turned over to the gentler pursuit of golf in 1923. Named after Mercury, the fleet-footed messenger to the gods, the Winged Foot US Open roll of honour included the immortal Bobby Jones, winner here in 1929, followed by Billy Casper in 1959, Hale Irwin in 1974 and Fuzzy Zoeller in 1984, and Davis Love III had captured the last major held here in the 1997 PGA Championship. Americans all, there was pre-tournament press speculation that this was a course that European golfers simply could not handle. The press was practically handing over the silver trophy to Tiger Woods, Phil Mickelson or Jim Furyk before the first drive had even been struck, and Montgomerie was not alone in wanting to prove them wrong.

Set up at brutally tough par 70, the determined Scot recovered from a shaky start – dropping two shots in his first three holes – to end the day at the top of the leader board with a 69. The only player to break par, the conditions suited his game perfectly as a combination of narrow fairways, ankle-high rough and hard crusty greens saw the elite field decimated. 'It's got to be difficult,' said Monty. 'When you've got the world's best players and there's only one guy under par.'

Echoing Sam Snead's comment back in the 1950s that 'these greens are harder than a whore's heart', 22 players were unable to break 80 and 35 players failed to register a single birdie all day, including the defending champ, Retief Goosen. The toughest start to a major in years, another player who found it hard going was left-handed Masters champion Phil Mickelson, who opened with a level-par 70. Looking to capture his third consecutive major, he spoke for just about everyone when he said, 'I feel a whole lot better now that the round is over.'

Leading the US Open for the first time in nine years, the second day was all about holding on for Monty and Lefty. The Scot clung on gamely all day, shooting a remarkably consistent second-round 71 with seventeen pars and one bogey. On a day where it proved almost impossible to get near the hole for tap-in birdies, he was happy at starting the third round just one stroke behind tournament leader Steve Stricker. 'I've not competed here since 1997, that's nine years ago, and it's nice to get back in the frame,' said the Scot afterwards. 'That's the beauty of this game, you're never quite sure. I'm just glad I managed to hold on. We all think it could have been three shots better but it could have been three shots worse. A couple of seventies from here and you never know what can happen.'

Mickelson was also pleased with his effort, despite carding a 73. Running up three bogeys in his first nine holes he was still in contention at tied seventh and that was all that mattered. 'Guys are going to make bogeys,' said the double Masters and PGA Champion. 'Bogeys are OK. I just had to prevent the double – prevent the really big mistake . . . This is a very penalising golf course and the scores are just going to get worse.'

Paired with Stricker in Saturday's third round, it was nine years since Montgomerie had last played in the final group at the US Open. Looking apprehensive, he started badly by dropping five shots in his first four holes, before managing to steady himself for a 75. 'To be five over after four was a disaster so to be five over at the finish was a hell of an effort. A sixty-seven tomorrow and I've got a big, big chance of winning this thing. If I can drive the ball the way I know I can I will be OK. I am three behind and that's an opportunity. I have very few opportunities left at this thing and I want to give it my best shot.'

Keeping alive his faint hopes of a first major championship, at least he did not have to concern himself with what Tiger Woods was doing after he missed his first cut in a major since turning professional in 1996. (It was also the first major Woods had competed in since the death of his father, Earl.)

Montgomerie *did* have to worry about Phil Mickelson, though, who carded a superb 69 on a day when many of the leading contenders fell away in the hot weather, including Steve Stricker with a 76. Tied with Kenneth Ferrie on two over, it was the first time the 54-hole lead had been over par at the US Open since 1974 – the year that saw the infamous 'Massacre of Winged Foot' when Tom Watson led at three over par going into the final round. 'One time a year, we get tested like this. And I love it,' said Mickelson. 'I love being tested at the highest level of the most difficult and sometimes ridiculous golf course set-ups we'll ever see. I love it because I get to find out where my game is at, where my head is at, and it really challenges me as a player.'

Montgomerie, who would turn 43 the week after the US Open, knew what a testing final round lay ahead of him but even he could not imagine just how testing. Beginning the day tied for fourth, three shots off the lead, the Scot stood on the eighteenth fairway four hours later tied for the lead with Phil Mickelson at four over par. In what American baseball fans call a 'career moment', the Scot was left with 172 yards uphill to a right-hand pin. With his two biggest rivals playing behind him – Phil Mickelson and Australian Geoff Ogilvy, winner of the Accenture Match Play Championship in February – Monty had no way of knowing that a simple par would give him the major championship he had craved for two decades.

For the millions watching on television back in the UK, the drama seemed to play out in slow motion. Caddie Alistair McLean suggested a six-iron into the heart of the green on the testing 450-yard par-four hole. Montgomerie decided on a seven-iron to allow for the adrenaline racing through his system. It was the wrong choice. Slapping at the ball, he watched in disgust as it flopped down short and right of the green. Having made the cardinal error of short-siding himself, Monty had no room to pitch the ball and was forced to play well left of the pin and above the hole. Three putts later and his nightmare was complete – a double-bogey six. Ending the week at six over par, he finished a tantalising one shot behind Geoff Ogilvy who made a nerveless par at the last to win. Runner-up with Mickelson, who also had a disastrous double-bogey on the final hole, and Jim Furyk, who bogeyed it, his disappointment was obvious. 'This is as difficult as it gets to take,' said Montgomerie as he came off the green. 'You do wonder sometimes why you put yourself through it.'

It was the first time a US Open Champion had finished over par since Andy North at Cherry Hills in 1978 and the highest score by a winner since Hale Irwin was seven over at Winged Foot in 1974; it must have brought no comfort to Montgomerie that his opening 69 was one of only twelve rounds under par that week. The Australian winner failed to break par in any of his four rounds en route to winning. 'Other chances I've had, other players have done very well,' said Montgomerie. 'This is the first time I've really messed up.'

Drawing sympathetic laughter from the British press contingent, it was difficult to know quite what to ask the shell-shocked Montgomerie. He not only had one hand on the trophy, he could almost taste the champagne he would have filled it with that night. On the par-four seventeenth he had rattled in a massive birdie putt from across the green to tie for the lead. After the drive of his life at the last everything was set up wonderfully. 'I switched from a six [iron] to a seven. I thought the adrenaline would kick in and I hit it about ten yards further,' he said. 'I caught it slightly heavy and it went slightly right. It was a poor shot and I put myself in a poor position, there was no question about that.'

Montgomerie was not alone in feeling that he had blown his chance to win. Mickelson came to the final hole also needing a par for glory only to drop two strokes. 'I had it right in my hands, and I let it go,' said Phil. 'I just can't believe I did that.'

At least Mickelson hung around for the presentation ceremony, which is more than Montgomerie did. He was heading for the airport while Ogilvy was accepting the trophy, and USGA president Walter Driver mentioned his absence at the awards ceremony, though he was too much of a gentleman to point out that it was far easier to show 'the class of a real champion' when you had already won two majors like Mickelson. It was not the last criticism Montgomerie would face in the aftermath of his disastrous finish at Winged Foot.

Indeed, it was not the last criticism the Scot would face that day. A journalist picked up on an incident on the seventeenth when Montgomerie backed off his tee shot after a boy had kneeled down next to the tee box to get a better view. Glowering at the child, he addressed the ball once again before pushing it down the right. Plucking the broken tee from the ground, he threw it in the direction of the young fan, catching him on the shirt. Onlookers were understandably angry and berated Monty as he stomped off down the fairway. Up to this point, the crowd had been nothing but supportive of his efforts but now, suddenly, it was back to the bad old days. Forty minutes later, he was accused of barging a state trooper out of the way moments after running up his double-bogey at the last. Serious enough to warrant a statement from the local commander, this was not the ideal way to end his US Open challenge.

'A collision occurred between Colin Montgomerie and a state trooper as both moved through a highly congested area adjacent to the clubhouse next to the scoring area,' announced Captain Michael Kopy. 'Mr Montgomerie was then assisted into the scoring room by another member of the state police who was in the area ... the incident requires no further action.'

Whatever the truth, it was left to trusty Guy Kinnings to calm things down. Dismissing Walter Driver's criticism, he explained how it had all been a miscommunication and that his client had been given permission to leave early despite the long-accepted policy that 'all podium finishers are always encouraged to attend'. As for the trooper, Kinnings suggested that Monty would have been more scared of the state trooper than vice versa. 'I doubt that Monty would have tangled with him deliberately,' said Kinnings convincingly.

Not that Monty needed much defending. 'The state trooper bumped into me, not me into him,' he said, robustly dealing with each incident individually. 'Jim Furyk and I were asked to attend the presentation though we didn't have to. We'd flights to catch.'

As for the incident with the child on the seventeenth tee: 'I threw a tee *towards* somebody, but not at somebody,' he declared. Montgomerie was equally forceful when it came to explaining the reasons that stopped him from winning – especially the moments before he hit that fateful second shot into eighteen. Forced to wait while his playing partner Vijay Singh called for a referee after finding a temporary obstruction, he agreed with his sports psychologist Hugh Mantle that it had a detrimental effect on his concentration: 'It wasn't just a seven-iron to a green. There was a lot more involved and we've been through it all. I'm convinced that if I was to go up to that ball at my usual pace and hit it, *I'd have probably won.*'

Like a government minister explaining away yet another by-election disaster, Montgomerie was determined not to dwell on the negative aspects of his latest major cock-up. (Moments after Ogilvy was congratulated by USGA officials, Monty had turned to his agent Guy Kinnings and said, 'Let's take some positives from this, OK?') Turning negatives into positives had become a way of life for the Scot, especially when it came to the US Open. 'There is nothing negative at all,' he said to reporters. 'I probably played as well as anyone out there, I just didn't win. I'm determined now more than ever to get this thing done.'

Six-time major winner Nick Faldo had a different point of view. 'What happened at Winged Foot will definitely scar Monty,' he said. 'He had a great opportunity to finally nail that first major, possibly his best chance. He was standing there with just one shot to the eighteenth green but it went wrong. Whether he gets over it remains to be seen but it's not getting any easier for him.'

24. IFS AND PUTTS AT THE K CLUB AS MONTY CONSIDERS HIS FUTURE

Before the US Open at Winged Foot Montgomerie truly believed that it was just a matter of time before he won his first major. After all, if his fellow countryman Paul Lawrie was good enough to win the Open Championship at Carnoustie in 1999, why couldn't he? Long considered no more than a journeyman professional, the gulf between the two in terms of achievement was vast. Even Phil Mickelson, his former rival for the best-golfer-never-to-win-a-major title, had won two major championships out of the last three! His fifth runner-up finish in majors, a record for someone who has never won one – surely the golfing gods would not deny him much longer? 'I'm proud of what I achieved and I'm back in the world's elite,' said Montgomerie. 'We'll try again at the next US Open and at Hoylake in the Open.'

Montgomerie now had to regroup in the run-up to the Hoylake Open at the Royal Liverpool golf club in July, but it proved harder than he imagined. Seven days on from Winged Foot, he was the tournament host at the Johnnie Walker Championship at Gleneagles. Continuing his good form, he led for much of the week, before slipping back in the final round to finish tied fourth, two strokes behind the winner Paul

Casey. 'Every shot I hit I thought about the last one I hit at the US Open,' he admitted afterwards. 'And that's difficult. The birdie I made at the first was important because you try to move forward. But one round of golf won't get it out of my system. I might never get it out. If I never win a major, that will remain with me. But it doesn't stop me playing decent golf in between.'

He returned home to Troon on the Friday of the tournament to spend his 43rd birthday with his father James. It must have been a reflective time for both men. A few days earlier, Montgomerie expressed the belief that the emotional turmoil surrounding his marriage break-up and subsequent divorce had made him a far better player. Then, with typical honesty, he confirmed that it had had a more negative effect on his bank balance. 'I was financially secure for life,' he complained, 'and now someone else is.'

Third on the money list and thirteenth in the latest world rankings, it was unlucky thirteen at the French Open at Le National, Versailles the following week. Citing 'exhaustion', the Scot withdrew just over halfway through. Eight months earlier at the Champions Tournament in Shanghai, Monty boasted that he still had 'the same drive and ambition I had when I was twenty'. Now he was not quite so sure. Speaking at the European Open in County Kildare, Ireland in early July, he lectured the younger generation of European Tour stars about playing golf in the *financial comfort zone*. 'The money involved in sometimes making third, fourth or fifth places is a good living,' said Montgomerie. 'I've never been content with that ... The money now is exceptional and we're very lucky, but it does cause its own problems sometimes. Do people really want to win, or have to win? I always come away having finished second, fourth or ninth as last week in Ireland, thinking, "Damn! That was one that got away ..." I hate finishing second, knowing that you came so close to winning but didn't. That's when questions arise like why didn't I win? What went wrong?'

At the Open at Royal Liverpool two weeks later, even second place would have been preferable to missing the cut!

Following a lacklustre 73 on Thursday, he dropped five strokes in four holes during his second round of 75 to crash out of the tournament at the halfway stage. A huge disappointment for his fans who wanted a repeat of Winged Foot (without the disastrous finish), it made nonsense of Montgomerie's pre-tournament prediction: 'My celebrity status has made me more relaxed and, if I'm relaxed, I generally play better.'

More a case of *I'm a Celebrity, Get Me Photographed*, Montgomerie admitted being flattered by the attention he had received after being snapped at Wimbledon in June while attending the tennis championships with 26-year-old fashion model Alex Leigh. 'After the US Open and Wimbledon I'm getting recognised more, which is fine,' he said. 'I will drive up to Hoylake on Tuesday morning feeling relaxed, I'll go into my apartment feeling relaxed and on Thursday morning I'll bring that to the first tee of the Open. A number of other players won't be like that. If you took a heart-rate monitor of the 156 players you'd be amazed how high it would be. I will be one of the lowest.'

Quizzed by the press about his latest 'love interest', all he would say about Ms Leigh was an abrupt, 'She's a companion – that's all you need to know!' That would have been fine except that a message had been sent out to the media the previous day by some enterprising public relations type along the lines of: 'Famous golfer Colin Montgomerie ... New girlfriend ... Row J ... Centre Court ... Tuesday ... Bring a camera or a notebook ...'

It was nothing more than a tawdry publicity stunt: his 'date' proved to be happily married with a young child. The latest in a parade of pretty consorts brought in to establish his credentials as an eligible bachelor-about-town, it simply made him look a fool. The situation was probably made worse by his comment 'I don't think I am the sort of person who is going to be happy on his own ...'

The question seasoned Monty-watchers wanted answering was why? The media speculated that he was bitterly upset by the news that Eimear had found happiness in the arms of a

Surrey millionaire businessman barely a month after the ink had dried on their divorce settlement. Selling his former family home in May was yet another blow to his fragile ego. He was forced to accept £4.5m – £1.5m less than the original asking price – but at least it helped fund the £8m hole in his finances caused by his divorce settlement. Montgomerie, of course, dismissed such talk as nonsense. 'Right now I am concentrating on my job and my children,' he said. 'I need someone to look after me but a housekeeper, not a girlfriend. Besides, when can I fit in a woman? The day does not have twenty-five hours!'

With 'Monty-speak' moving into overdrive in the run-up to the US PGA Championship at Medinah in August, he described how he could realistically contend in twenty more majors over the next five years! (He had said the same thing prior to the PGA Championship in 2000.) In reflective mood, he admitted taking time to analyse what had happened at Winged Foot with his sports psychologist Hugh Mantle. 'I'll only stop thinking about it if I win one,' he concluded. 'We've been through it all and hopefully if that occasion happens again in the not-too-distant future I will be able to cope in a different way.'

Whether another gilt-edged opportunity like the one Montgomerie enjoyed at Winged Foot would present itself again only time would tell. It certainly did not happen at Medinah where he crashed out after rounds of 77 and 71. Now boasting three missed cuts in four majors in 2006, even the upbeat Scot struggled to put a positive spin on things. The Ryder Cup was only weeks away and, like so many times before, the competition would come to Monty's rescue just when he thought his season was falling apart.

Without a tournament win in 2006, his less-than-dedicated attitude was perhaps best summed up by a trip he made to a Robbie Williams concert in Scotland, right in the middle of the BMW International Open in Munich, a flagship event on the European Tour. He finished his third round at Nord Eichenreid before being whisked away by courtesy car. An hour later he was enjoying a glass of champagne on the executive jet he had hired for the ninety-minute flight to Glasgow. Accompanied by the Ryder Cup trophy (which he paraded on stage) and his new best friend, Gaynor Knowles, he arrived back in Germany in the wee small hours. Barely three weeks from the start of the Ryder Cup at the K Club in Ireland, it attracted understandable criticism from the media that he was not taking the tournament seriously. Contrast his behaviour with Padraig Harrington, they said. Turning down the opportunity to watch the Euro 2008 qualifying match between Ireland and Germany just two hours down the autobahn in Stuttgart, the Irish Ryder Cup golfer had a different take on matters. 'Unfortunately, when you are doing well you don't travel round the world for two hours,' said Padraig. 'You have to be disciplined and go to bed early and all that stuff.'

It had been the same story after Montgomerie pulled out of the WGC Bridgestone Invitational at Akron a few weeks earlier to captain the European team in the made-for-television *All Star Celebrity Cup* at Celtic Manor in Wales. A Ryder Cup-style event, he would play a significant part in the real one at the end of September in Ireland. Questioned about his rollercoaster season, he simply said, 'This is a tournament that my personal record goes flying out the window. I'm here for the team.'

Not that his record in the Ryder Cup was anything but hugely impressive: he was seventh on the all-time list for matches won, joint sixth in total points won with 21, and was still unbeaten in singles. Out of 32 matches he had won nineteen, drawn five and lost just eight! All were played under the most intense pressure imaginable. Monty was the player who had wrapped things up for the Europeans at Valderrama in 1997 and Oakland Hills in 2004. No wonder American wild-card pick Stewart Cink said before the start of the 2006 match in Ireland: 'Monty is the guy!'

Reflecting back to a time when he needed his own captain's pick to make the team, Montgomerie knew his presence at the K Club was due in part to Bernhard Langer's faith in him two years earlier. 'That [wild card] two years ago was, I think, vital for my career,' said the fourteenth-ranked player in the world. 'That pick saved me in many, many ways.'

Montgomerie would lead from the front as usual. There was no better example than his foursome match on Friday afternoon. Partnered by Lee Westwood, Monty arrived on the final green one down to the powerhouse pairing of Chris DiMarco and Phil Mickelson. With the Americans in the greenside trap for two on the par-five, Mickelson's bunker shot settled fifteen feet short of the hole. Moments later, DiMarco's birdie putt to win missed on the low side. Putting up from the front of the green, Westwood had run his long eagle putt six feet past the hole, leaving the eight-time European number one with a putt to win the hole and halve the match. It was a pivotal moment in the entire Ryder Cup. As the huge crowd around the eighteenth fell silent, the Scot calmly stepped up and rattled it home for a winning birdie. Pumping his fist in triumph, as did many of the European team watching from behind the green, it might only have been a half, but it was a half at *exactly* the right time. 'How many times have we seen him hole that left-to-right putt under pressure,' said the delighted European captain, Ian Woosnam. 'He's done it so many times in the Ryder Cup and he's got such courage. What a man to have on your team.'

What a man, indeed. It was made even more impressive by the fact that Montgomerie had lost his opening fourball match with Padraig Harrington against Tiger Woods and Jim Furyk in the morning. It had been highlighted as the main European threat by USA captain Tom Lehman before the Ryder Cup, so two defeats on the opening day would have brought enormous encouragement to the Americans. Now it was business as usual as Europe took control of the match.

On Saturday, Montgomerie was rested from the morning fourball matches as the European team extended their lead to three points. He reprised his successful partnership with Westwood against Chad Campbell and Vaughn Taylor in the afternoon foursomes, and the match also came down to the final green. This time the hole was halved in birdies to share the spoils and now all that was left was the singles.

The home team held a four-point advantage going into the final day, each one of the twelve European players having contributed to the points tally. It was a time for records and Woosnam was determined that his would be the first European team to win all five Ryder Cup sessions to complete an historic victory. Montgomerie was sent out by Woosnam at the top of the order and charged with the task of setting an example for those to come. Playing former PGA Champion David Toms – his same opponent from Oakland Hills in 2004 – it was always going to be a close battle. Back in June, he informed the media that his divorce had actually *improved* his golf and he set about demonstrating it by taking a one-hole lead after birdies at the third and fourth. Maintaining a one-hole advantage coming to the final hole, he pulled off a fantastic long-range bunker shot to seal a narrow win. 'I was never down and it was important for the team to see that [European] blue at the top of the leader board,' he said afterwards.

Unbeaten in the singles since Kiawah Island in 1991, his tally of six wins and two halves equalled the best in the event's eighty-year history. More importantly, it was first blood to Europe and one point nearer to retaining the Ryder Cup. Setting the standard for the eleven remaining singles, it was Henrik Stenson playing in match eight who hammered the final nail in the USA coffin with a 4 and 3 victory over rookie Vaughn Taylor. It came just minutes before Darren Clarke won his match against Zach Johnson on the sixteenth green, and the huge Irish crowd were denied the perfect denouement to a match played just weeks after the tragically early death of Clarke's wife Heather.

Amid some of the most emotionally charged scenes ever witnessed in a Ryder Cup, Montgomerie maintained a low-key presence even when the crowd chanted his name again and again in front of the clubhouse. For once, the glory was shared equally among the team and he was happy to play the elder statesman.

Winning 18 ½–9 ½, nobody had expected Europe to inflict yet another nine-point defeat on the USA. Speaking to Tom

Lehman's father behind the seventeenth green, the Scot agreed with him that this was indeed 'the best European team which had ever been assembled'. Ian Woosnam may have been captain and Henrik Stenson may have holed the winning putt but this was a 24-carat Monty-led, Monty-inspired and Monty-constructed victory. Asked if his fantastic record in the event made up for not winning a major, he replied, 'The Ryder Cup has been a bonus, so have the Order of Merits. I wouldn't give any of them away for a major – not one. But you never give up . . .'

After all the celebrations and champagne spraying he joined his European team in the media centre at the K Club. Inevitably, the questions turned to the next Ryder Cup in 2008. 'Of course I want to play in the next one at Valhalla if I can manage to qualify,' said the 43-year-old Scot. 'I would really like to play under Nick. Possibly the match at the K Club was my last on home turf. The next one on this side of the Atlantic is not until Wales in 2010. And that might be beyond my time. Don't forget, I'm not getting any younger.'

Asked if he wanted to be a Ryder Cup vice-captain in preparation for captaincy, the eight-time Order of Merit winner replied, 'No, I think I've seen enough. I feel like I know what to do.'

There was a time when Montgomerie thought that he might have been a Ryder Cup captain by now. Six years ago he put his name forward to lead the team in Ireland but had been rebuffed because he was considered 'too young'. Since then, his playing career had seen some ups and downs but had been rejuvenated over the past eighteen months by two major factors – his back problems had lessened and his divorce had inspired him to practise more. Describing himself as 'a better golfer than I was five years ago', Monty said that his playing career had probably been extended by five years because of his *lack of practice* in past years! 'I haven't practised the way some people do and so my body is younger than my age,' he asserted with a straight face after the Ryder Cup.

In October, Montgomerie handed his European Order of Merit crown to Irishman Padraig Harrington. Finishing ninth, he maintained his position in the top twenty of the world rankings, proving what a formidable force he still could be as he approached the twilight years of his playing career. 'I'm now back into playing the way I would like,' he said after the Ryder Cup, and that was certainly the case as he partnered the unknown Marc Warren in the WGC World Cup of Golf in Barbados in mid-December. Losing to the German pair of Bernhard Langer and Marcel Siem in a play-off, Scotland, which has never won the World Cup, now made it four second-place finishes in the tournament stretching back over five decades. Once again, it was a minor mistake by Montgomerie that cost him victory. Having made only one bogey all day in foursome play, he pushed his tee shot at the par-three eighteenth left of the green, then missed the short putt after Warren had played a superb chip to within four feet.

'It's just one of those things,' said Warren, who had earlier described his partner's play all week as 'awesome!'

Was it a final hurrah for Montgomerie? As competitive as ever, he stormed off without a word to the press on his way to yet another tournament. Nothing particularly new there, then.

Comfortable talking about life after tournament golf, the Scot dismisses newspaper reports suggesting that he might go into politics. Still one of Britain's richest sportsmen, with an estimated annual income in excess of £2m, he has assembled a tight-knit team who, through their expertise, enable him to concentrate on his first love of playing tournament golf. From caddie Alastair McLean to his long-time business manager Guy Kinnings, these are people who have his trust. 'Having good people around me is crucial,' explained Monty back in 2005. 'It has taken time, but now I've got the people I want, good people, around me. That is why I win.' Today, no top international golfer can run his career independently. From merchandising contracts to simple travel arrangements, 'Team Monty' help smooth the path for their boss.

Desperate to eradicate the hurt he experienced on the final hole of the US Open at Winged Foot in 2006, the desire to compete at the highest level burns just as strong. Whether his increasingly erratic golf game will sustain such desire is another question entirely. Mark McCormack, the brilliant entrepreneur behind IMG, used to tell all his top sports people, including Montgomerie, 'Love winning more than you hate losing because one is driven by joy and the other is driven by fear!'

It's a subtle difference in many ways. He believed the fear of defeat often clouded the mind and led to bad decision-making – while the joy and anticipation of winning filled the mind with positives. Take Arnold Palmer, for example: no player in the history of the game celebrated winning like him. The same can be said of Tiger Woods. Compare that with Montgomerie, who barely raises an eyebrow after winning a tournament. Some of this can be put down to personality and upbringing, but throughout his entire career, the pain of losing a tournament far outweighs the transitory pleasure in winning one. This is why Montgomerie performs so ably in team events like the Ryder Cup, the former Dunhill Trophy and, most recently, the World Cup. For that week alone, the fear of losing is somehow negated by his almost obsessive desire not to let his fellow team members down. Pride is everything to this remarkable sportsman, and who knows what great heights he might have achieved if he had taken McCormack's advice to heart.

Like everything in life, timing is everything and the question 'when to go' must also have occupied his thoughts in recent years. As for Nick Faldo and Ken Brown, the thought of pontificating on the next generation of golfers is enormously tempting, as it would provide the tournament 'buzz' Colin Montgomerie so obviously enjoys. Determined not to outstay his welcome, Montgomerie admitted consulting some former sporting legends in 2006 about what he should do. 'I'd like to go out at the top but I've spoken to many people about this, including world motor racing champion Jackie Stewart, and they all tell me how a competitor misses the competition,' said Montgomerie. 'It would be no different for me, in fact I'd probably be worse.'

Unlike former legends of European golf like Faldo, Lyle, Woosnam, Langer, Ballesteros and even Olazábal, Montgomerie is not able to rest easy on his laurels. The record books do not, as yet, record his major-winning triumphs and that is a pity. Apart from his own obvious disappointment, it leaves him open to criticism from those who believe his career has been one of unfulfilled promise. The evidence is damning, they say, in that despite being an eight-time European number one and appearing in five winning Ryder Cup teams, he has never been able to convert that dominance into a major win or even a single victory on the PGA Tour in the United States.

Montgomerie in turn believes that he has nothing to prove. What drives him is the simple need to win golf tournaments – any tournament. After two decades as a professional Montgomerie expressed his desire in 2006 to capture not only a ninth Order of Merit but perhaps even a tenth! Winner of more than 33 events worldwide and over £15m in prize money, his golfing prowess may be in decline but his competitive drive and desire are far from over. Away from tournaments, his design company has eleven courses in play with over a dozen more in construction all over the world. In typical style, he says, 'I want to design the best courses in the world.'

Inspirational, determined, stubborn and indefatigable, especially when it comes to the Ryder Cup, Montgomerie's career looks to carry on for a few more years yet. Whether it will include winning a major only time will tell. In truth, no modern-day professional deserves it more. After the last Ryder Cup in Ireland, the Scot showed little desire to walk off into the golfing sunset but, like most of us, he knows the clock is ticking on his glory days. 'As I get older, it gets tougher physically,' he admitted. 'That has to be the way it is. I look forward to competing as time goes on. I'm a competitor. That's who I am.'

What better epitaph could any professional sportsman have?

FOR THE RECORD

AMATEUR RECORD

1983: Scottish Youths Champion
1985: Scottish Amateur Stroke Play Champion
1986: (British) Amateur Championship Silver Medallist
1987: Scottish Amateur Champion

TEAMS (AMATEUR)

Eisenhower Trophy: 1984 (Hong Kong), 1986 (Venezuela)
St Andrews Trophy: 1986 (winners)
Scottish Youths: 1983–87
Walker Cup: 1985, 1987

TURNED PRO: 1987 (plus-3 handicap)

QUALIFYING SCHOOL: 1987
Sir Henry Cotton Rookie of the Year: 1988

EUROPEAN TOUR VICTORIES

Total: 30
1989: Portuguese Open – TPC
1991: Scandinavian Masters

1993: Heineken Dutch Open, Volvo Masters Andalusia
1994: Peugeot Spanish Open, Murphy's English Open, Volvo German Open
1995: Volvo German Open, Lancôme Trophy
1996: Dubai Desert Classic, Murphy's Irish Open, Canon European Masters
1997: Compaq European Grand Prix, Murphy's Irish Open
1998: Volvo PGA Championship, One-2-One British Masters, Linde German Masters
1999: Benson and Hedges International Open, Volvo PGA Championship, Standard Life Loch Lomond, Volvo Scandinavian Masters, BMW International Open
2000: Novotel Perrier Open de France, Volvo PGA Championship
2001: Murphy's Irish Open, Volvo Scandinavian Masters
2002: Volvo Masters (tied after abandoned play-off with Bernhard Langer)
2004: Caltex Singapore Masters
2005: Dunhill Links Championship
2006: UBS Hong Kong Open

EUROPEAN TOUR PROFESSIONAL CAREER RECORD

Year	Order of Merit			Stroke Average	Prize money (£)	
1987	164	4 (2AM)	2	71.77	2,871	2,051
1988	52	22	15	71.45	84,133	60,095
1989	25	30	19	71.80	170,901	122,072
1990	14	30	24	71.21	250,587	178,991
1991	4	28	20	71.43	691,351	493,822
1992	3	26	24	70.21	763,580	545,414
1993	1	24	20	70.81	1,117,403	798,145
1994	1	21	19	69.60	1,288,906	920,647
1995	1	20	19	69.70	1,454,205	1,038,718
1996	1	18	15	70.26	1,448,653	1,034,752
1997	1	19	19	69.37	2,217,466	1,583,904
1998	1	17	15	69.66	1,515,966	1,082,833
1999	1	20	20	69.59	2,066,885	1,476,346

2000	6	23	22	70.26	2,046,921	1,217,355
2001	5	23	20	75.31	1,684,989	1,047,657
2002	4	23	21	70.36	2,235,147	1,425,158
2003	28	22	19	71.06	883,806	616,198
2004	25	25	21	71.16	768,349	531,332
2005	1	25	22	69.83	2,926,774	1,978,205
2006	9	26	22	70.68	1,534,748	1,028,816

BIGGEST EUROPEAN TOUR PRIZE

€662,415 (£449,741) Dunhill Links Championship 2005

EUROPEAN TOUR APPROVED SPECIAL EVENTS VICTORIES

Total: 3
1997 World Cup of Golf (individual)
1997 Accenture World Championship of Golf
1999 Cisco World Match Play Championship

INTERNATIONAL TOURNAMENT VICTORIES

Total: 3
2001 Ericsson Masters (Australia)
2002 TCL Classic (China)
2003 Macau Open (China)

OTHER TOURNAMENT VICTORIES

Total: 3
1996 Nedbank Million Dollar Challenge (Sun City)
1997 King Hassan II Trophy (Morocco)
2000 Skins Game (USA)

TEAMS (PROFESSIONAL)

Ryder Cup: 1991, 1993, 1995 (winners), 1997 (winners), 1999, 2002 (winners), 2004 (winners), 2006 (winners)
Alfred Dunhill Cup: 1988, 1991, 1992, 1993, 1994, 1995 (winners), 1996, 1997, 1998, 2000 (tournament format changed)

World Cup: 1988, 1991, 1992, 1993, 1997 (individual
    winner), 1998, 1999, 2006 (runner-up)
Four Tours World Championship: 1991 (winners)
The Seve Trophy: (captain) 2000, 2002 (winners), 2003
    (winners) 2005 (winners)
UBS Cup: 2003, 2004

RECORD IN MAJORS

Year	Masters	US Open	Open Championship	US PGA
1988	FQ	62T	–	–
1989	FQ	MC	54T	–
1990	48T	9	8T	–
1991	26T	2	15T	–
1992	37T	3	MC	33T
1993	52T	33T	MC	MC
1994	MC	2T	8T	36T
1995	17T	28T	MC	2
1996	39T	10T	MC	MC
1997	30T	2	24T	13T
1998	8T	18T	MC	44T
1999	11T	15T	15T	6T
2000	19T	46T	26T	39T
2001	MC	52T	13T	76T
2002	14T	MC	82T	MC
2003	MC	42T	MC	MC
2004	MC	FQ	25T	70
2005	FQ	42T	2	MC
2006	MC	2	MC	MC

MISCELLANEOUS: Low Rounds and Course Records (CR)

60 (–10) Enjoy Jakarta Standard Chartered Indonesia Open
    2005
61 (–10) Canon European Masters 1996
62 (–9) Murphy's Irish Open 1997 (CR)
63 (–9) Portuguese Open 1989 (CR)
63 (–9) Murphy's English Open 1995 (CR)

63 (–9) One-2-One British Masters 1997 (CR)
63 (–9) Dunhill Links Championship 2002 (CR)
63 (–8) Murphy's Irish Open 2001 (CR)
63 (–7) Lancôme Trophy 1990
64 (–8) Scottish Open 1995 (CR)
64 (–8) Smurfit European Open 1997 (CR)
64 (–7) Open Championship 2002 (CR)
64 (–6) WGC American Express Championship 2005 (CR)
65 (–7) Dunhill Links Championship 2005 (CR)
66 (–6) Algarve Portuguese Open 1991 (CR)
67 (–5) Compaq European Grand Prix 1997 (CR)

PLAY-OFF RECORD

Won 0, Lost 8, Halved 1
1991: lost to Seve Ballesteros, Volvo PGA Championship
1992: lost to Sandy Lyle, Volvo Masters Andalucia
1994: lost to Ernie Els, US Open Championship
1995: lost to Philip Walton, Murphy's English Open
1995: lost to Steve Elkington, US PGA Championship
1998: lost to David Carter, Murphy's Irish Open
2002: lost to Tiger Woods, Deutsche Bank – SAP Open TPC
    of Europe
2002: tied with Bernhard Langer, Volvo Masters Andalucia
2006: lost to Langer/Siem, World Cup of Golf, Barbados
    (with Marc Warren)

EUROPEAN ORDER OF MERIT VICTORIES (Harry Vardon Trophy)

1993, 1994, 1995, 1996, 1997, 1998, 1999, 2005

MISCELLANEOUS AWARDS

European Tour Golfer of the Year: 1995, 1996, 1997, 1999
European Tour Shot of the Year: 1996, 1997
Association of Golf Writers Trophy: 1996
Tooting Bec Cup (Awarded to the top British Player in that
    year's Open Championship): 2001, 2002, 2005

Braid Taylor Memorial: 2005
Elected Honorary Member of the European Tour: 1997

EUROPEAN TOUR RECORD

(To the end of the 2006 season)

European Tour events played	444
European Tour official wins	30
European Tour runner-up finishes	30
European Tour top-ten finishes	173 (European Tour record)
Years in top-ten of European Tour Order of Merit	13
European Tour Official Career Money	€21,338,983 (First)
European Tour holes in one	8 (European Tour record)
European Tour albatrosses	2

MOST OFFICIAL VICTORIES UP TO END OF 2006

1	Seve Ballesteros	50
2	Bernhard Langer	42
3T	Nick Faldo	30
3T	**Colin Montgomerie**	**30**
5	Ian Woosnam	29
6	Neil Coles	25
7	José Maria Olazábal	23
8T	Bernard Hunt	21
8T	Sam Torrance	21
8T	Ernie Els	21
11T	Mark James	18
11T	Sandy Lyle	18

MOST EUROPEAN TOUR AND INTERNATIONAL VICTORIES UP TO END OF 2006

1	Greg Norman	71
2	Seve Ballesteros	69
3	Arnold Palmer	68

4   Gary Player 58
5   Ernie Els 51
6   Mark McNulty 49
7   Bernhard Langer 47
8   Vijay Singh 41
9   Nick Faldo 37
10   Ian Woosnam 36
11   Colin Montgomerie 35

MOST TOUR VICTORIES IN A SEASON

Six in 1999 (Shared record)

Benson and Hedges International Open, the Oxfordshire: 273 (–15)

Volvo PGA Championship, Wentworth: 270 (–18)

Standard Life Loch Lomond Championship, Loch Lomond: 268 (–16)

Volvo Scandinavian Masters, Barsebäck: 268 (–20)

BMW International Open, Nord-Eichenried golf club, Munich: 268 (–20)

Cisco World Match Play, Wentworth: Defeated Mark O'Meara 3 and 2 in final

INDEX